# EARL FEE
# IS
# RUNNING

*Best Wishes!*

## AN AUTOBIOGRAPHY

*Earl*

## EARL W. FEE

Tellwell Talent
www.tellwell.ca

ISBN
978-0-2288-0602-8 (Paperback)
978-0-2288-0603-5 (eBook)

# Table of Contents

# ACKNOWLEDGEMENTS

The high quality front cover photo of me was taken by professional photographer/ friend Gary Gerovac of Mississauga Ontario. The excellent back cover photo of me  was taken by friend Bill McIllwaine. The great 800m photo of me at Gateshead Worlds was taken by friend Chuck Sochor. The great 800m photo of me  at Eugene Oregon was take by Gene Hart. The great 400m photo of me at York U  was taken by Doug Smith.

# PREFACE

IT ALL STARTED IN THE YEAR 1929 AT A LONELY FARM IN THE CANADIAN prairies, at my grandparent's white farm house near Elstow Saskatchewan. A short time later, I had my name, picking or supposedly pointing out "Earl" in a hat with other favourable alternatives.

I promise to make this memoir of my life interesting, and aspire to be concise and not use three sentences where a single word will suffice, but at the same time providing some useful facts and information about longevity and revealing my running training secrets. And it is possible there might be some humour and philosophy here and there.

There will be details in 20 chapters, up to mid 2018, prior to my participation in the World Masters Athletics Championships in Malaga Spain In September 2018. For example:

- My adventures at my grandparents farm in Saskatchewan up to age eight,
- Experiences in growing up in Ontario,
- My three years in England including a two year Earl of Athlone Fellowship,
- My sometimes rocky marriage,

- Some details of the working years,
- Life in the Ontario countryside during marriage,
- Thirty six years (1957 to 1994) as a pioneer in the Canadian nuclear power industry
- Designing nuclear power reactors, Designing two large homes,
- 56 world records in masters running and hurdling up to age 85 inclusive,
- Experiences competing in 16 World Masters Athletics (WMA) championships around the world, and two World Games and numerous North American (NCCWMA) Championships,
- Carrying the Canadian flag at the largest WMA Championships Games: in Miyazaki Japan in 1993,
- Articles about legendary athletes Ed Whitlock, Olga Kotelko, Jeanne Daprano, Payton Jordan Johnny Bower and some interesting characters,
- WMA Male Athlete of the World award in 2015,
- Two personal interviews,
- Earls quotations,
- Five of my books published up to age 85:— *How To Be Champion from 9 to 90—The Complete Guide to Running—100 Years Young the Natural Way—The Wonder of It All Poetry* (coloured + black and white version),
- **Four chapters describing my training methods and experiences at major meets,**
- Photos and some of my poetry to help illustrate my adventures and escapades,
- See also the Contents page.

With a memoir you get to talk about yourself, whereas for others it's much more enjoyable to hold the floor and talk about themselves. That reminds me: never ask a senior how they are, if you have something important or urgent to do that day. You will be inundated with their mental and physical problems and their operations. You will be thinking only of how to escape this flood of words gushing out like water from a burst dam. In my case fortunately, there were only three operations to brag or complain about, not counting dental. But the good news—is this memoir is about life, love, laughter, and spirit with some unavoidable pathos as in all lives. Most seniors will find as I have that the attributes of spirituality increases as you age. Not just the religious aspect but spirituality of gratitude, empathy, helping, loving, and appreciating others. Bill Cosby in jest said: "Ladies as they get older become very kind, cooperative and more helpful. But they are just trying to get into heaven." We give thanks at the beginning of meals, but should give thanks for everyday benefits and particularly gratitude for health and life each precious day. Too many things are taken for granted.

Writing an autobiography gives one a chance to get things in perspective— like one's philosophies and targets. Now let us begin with this exciting life story. Thank God for memory for we get to relive our happy memories. It is like having a second life.

# 1

# LIFE ON THE FARM
# IN SASKATCHEWAN

MARCH 22, 1929— IT WAS A HAPPY BIRTHDAY ON MY DEAR GRAND-
parents farm near Elstow, Saskatchewan. A few months later I survived from
a serious ailment, whooping cough and have been whooping it up ever since.
My earliest memory was when I was helpless in the crib so maybe just a few
months old, and one of one of my mother's sisters or Grandma Hampton
was leaning over me and making a big loving fuss over me. It was my first
distinct feeling of warm love.

Grandparents, Flossie and Tom Hampton on my mother's side— about
100 miles south of Saskatoon near Elstow —provided me with lots of excitement and adventures, and particularly around age five to eight when I had
developed more mobility and freedom to roam about. There was strangely
non-existent contact with the grandparents on my father's side. One brief
meeting when I was not yet in my teens with my other grandma, called
Ma, on my father's side. She seemed a cold heartless person. I do not recall
meeting the grandfather. However, my mother's side grandparents made
up for this deficiency many times over.

Grandad Tom Hampton was my hero, strong, muscular and kind. He had a poetic inclination side to him and entertained us all with a large repertoire of Robert Service poems —the alcohol, especially the apricot brandy a potent liquid— seemed to improve his memory and his gusto. I was impressed with his great memory. I also greatly admired and loved my kind Grandma Flossie, tall and straight as an arrow and never a bad word about anyone. In my youth I would sometimes go to Flossie at times for good advice. In the early 1900's my grandfather at just sixteen had built a house for his mother in Tichborne, Ontario, near Kingston. In his early 1900's, during the pioneer years 1892 to 1914, he rode the rails out West one winter in search of cheap farm land. In the 20th century Saskatchewan was the fastest growing province and many optimistic immigrants came from Europe in search of cheap land and new life.

On the railcar journey while he slept in a box car, grandad's winter jacket was stolen. In the bitter winter cold traversing each box car in the speeding and gyrating train— he checked each box car and the occupants until he eventually located the culprit and his precious jacket. To me, his favourite grandson, he was a true pioneer of the West. After examining and rejecting land near now Edmonton—prime land now that would have made him a multi millionaire decades later —he selected a quarter section, 160 acres, of government farm land near Elstow, Saskatchewan— for a small filing fee. But initially, it was a hard land, trees to be chopped, rock to be hauled, house and garage to be built, 50 degree below cold winters, unbelievable thunderstorms, blizzards and swarms of grasshoppers, drought, hail storms, etc. But there were golden days and golden wheat too. But by working together with neighbours, the help of the animals, and the whole family eventually it was a smooth running farm. Then later the addition of a tractor and later hired help at a dollar a day, particularly at harvest time— all this effort to produce those golden wheat sheaves. And eventually the farm grew to 640 acres — four quarter sections. In the good and bad years my grandparents raised three hard working daughters, my mother Lola, Aunt Della, Aunt Bertha, and also raised Aunt Alice. Aunt Alice was not a sibling, but a daughter of my Flossie's sister Grace. Notice the ample use of the letter 'a', all happy names. Aunt Alice was a merry soul and loved by all, but I heard Aunt Della had some reservations in accepting her as a real sister. My mother Lola Pearl and Alice—best friends and sisters — helped do manual labour with the horses and, other animals, the seeding, the harvest and the tractor, while Bertha and Della helped Flossie in the kitchen. I can see now where my good genes came from. Mother told of returning from Elstow on a horse after picking up some heavy metal parts for the tractor. The saddle bags with the heavy parts kept hitting the horse on each stride so the horse began to accelerate and didn't stop for the several excruciating miles to home. But Mamma, as we lovingly called her —held on for dear life. On the farm the horses became just like pets and all had affectionate names. It was a sad teary day indeed when they left the farm and allocated the horses and other animals to friendly neighbours.

My grandad had hired help that resided on the farm, as the farm continued to grow. One married helper, a giant of a man, had been beating his wife. My grandfather an advocate of the pugilistic arts taught the helper a lesson that ended the beatings. Grandma had a keen sense of prophecy and intuition. She could tell when company was about to visit and would start baking. One time grandad lost his wallet with considerable money inside. Grandma had a dream that he had lost it in the outhouse— sure enough there it was in the worst place possible. Grandad built a two story house and a grand red barn, consisting of huge wooden beams, the largest barn in this vast area, which stood the test of time many decades after his departure —in the end used for many retail outlets. But eventually, destroyed by fire. In those early1900 days a barn could be built for $200 and a house for $100, but a lot of money in those days.

Saskatchewan had rich soil for growing golden wheat— particularly the Marquis brand— after the sod and rocks and occasional trees were removed. It was a life not for the weak at heart. For the thousands and thousands doing this hard labour— there were rich rewards for those with patience. Grandma and Grandad and my mother and aunts had what it takes.

Now the West is just a fond memory. Although our family lived in a tiny distant town Vonda, there were frequent visits to the farm. I was sorry to leave these adventures and the farm behind where I was born. I was told I picked my name Earl from a hat, so can't complain of my name. It was a good choice since my mother's middle name was Pearl. The farm was an exciting time for me for a few years after about age five when I had developed my roaming/active legs and when I had an active quest and a thirst for adventure. At about age five and my brother Maurice at age seven, but not as adventurous as me, managed somehow to get into an empty tar barrel one sunny afternoon— an episode that produced considerable parental chagrin and scrubbing by mother. Another escapade resulted when I turned the crank on the butter barrel, unfortunately with a loose lid, spilling the creamy contents on the kitchen floor. The only thing that saved me was my loving forgiving grandparents. Then there was chasing the roosters—riding the tractor in circles —stooking sheaves of wheat for one cent per stook— killing gophers for one cent per tail—trying to kill a rooster with an axe but missing and cutting of it's beak. A nickel was a fortune in those days. At Christmas a rare orange, a silver whistle and maybe a nickel was heavenly. I recall the travel in frigid winter at 40 below in a horse drawn caboose on sleds—inside the five of us me and Maurice, Mama and Daddy, and baby Wellwood, with hot rocks at our feet and the two horses plunging through the snow up to their bellies. Eventually, the snow was too deep and the horses refused to move. One sunny afternoon I went with Grandad in his car to a bootlegger. The potent smell could be detected from the tiny building in the distance nearly a mile away on the flat prairie. At Exhibition time in Saskatoon the fireworks could be seen from the farm nearly 100 miles away on this pancake land.

I recall the excitement at harvest time. I loved to watch and hear the roar and clatter of the monster threshing machine and the hustle and bustle of the many sweating workers —the roaring steam engine threshing with its black smoke reaching for the sky. In fact as far as the eye could see there were tiny black smoke trails from other of these busy monsters. This activity went on 12 hours a day for weeks on end. Needless to say this activity produced tremendous appetites. At meal time the large kitchen table would be groaning with mounds of food: vegetables from the garden, dozens of eggs, gallons of coffee, fresh meat, fresh baked bread and many pies. Watching all this hard work gave my brother Maurice and I quite an appetite as well—we could easily devour a pie between us— trying to keep up with these hungry men.

At a party at Aunt Della's in Elstow there was unfortunately further excitement at about age six. I learned an important lesson that stuck with me ever since when I proudly uttered a swear word in front of a large family gathering —the immediate unexpected result was a washing of my mouth with soap by mother. This cured me of verbal swearing but nonverbal remained—besides it is a good way to let off steam and universally practised. But I ask you where would I have learned these words except from an adult, most likely even a relative? But alas, I was too young to defend myself, and it was too difficult to even speak at the time without bubbles. In later years, my brothers and I would learn more lessons from my mother's broom handle—always handy. However I can't recall her actually using it as correction tool.

At my surprise 75th Birthday party my Aunt Della sent a message from Edmonton Alberta. She said: "Earl as a young tot used to chase the roosters on our farm in Saskatchewan." My friends presented me with a funny farmland rooster doll which I still cherish as a reminder—they said this was the beginning of my running career. Maybe so.

Our home was in a small town, Vonda, about 20 miles from my grandparents farm. My mother ran the switchboard at the telephone office for the area, from our home. There was no refrigerator in those days, instead there was a pit below the kitchen floor to keep things cool, a home for lizards I suspect. In later years I recall a boisterous party at the house. One of my uncles, maybe Uncle Wellwood or Uncle Kenny, was carrying two large jugs of home brew from a pole over the shoulders. As luck would have it, with all the frivolity, the two jugs collided and smashed, considerably dampening the party. I recall one dark night near our local curling rink. There was a huge fight between my father and another male—no doubt some controversy about a curling game. My father was a good curler and had won a lot of silverware. One day he went to Saskatoon and had all his teeth out in a single operation. My Grandad Tom had false teeth too. My brother Wellwood was happy to have all his teeth removed. My mother had beautiful teeth, and not a cavity, At one point she was advised to have them all removed. Fortunately this bad custom is now In the distant past. no more.

I had some narrow escapes when young. One time my sled and I wound up under the feet of two huge horses— they seemed to know I was there. Another time I fell through a huge pile of decaying hay to the bottom, nearly choking, but survived by holding my breath and crawling out from the bottom. Brother Maurice and I one weekend, wandered off far away from our home in Vonda to a distant lake where we did some rafting although swimmers we were not —getting lost for most of the day —rescued by a farming family —enjoying a memorable meal of bacon and beans —and returned home exhausted with withered flowers to distressed parents. My parents started me at school one year late for some reason—must have enjoyed my company while father was working.

There is a belief the harsh weather in Saskatchewan, particularly the winters is good for the character. By a strange coincidence, the legendary Olga Kotelko, was raised in a farm near tiny Vonda with 14 siblings. For those not familiar with Olga she was famous and loved for all her many world records in track and field while in her 90's, but passing away in 2014 at age 95. See Chapter 16 for details about my friend Olga.

When my family left Vonda, Saskatchewan, with its population of about 200 in 1937, with prospects of a better life in Gravenhurst, Ontario, in the Muskoka's, but not a prosperous one as hoped— I was age eight. At the railway station my grandparents were standing on the platform with our dog Brownie. There was not a dry eye, even Brownie was crying. I learned even dogs have feelings.

Sixteen years later, after University I returned to the West In my new Pontiac car—driving my father and Uncle Wellwood. The car felt very much like a travelling bar with me the sober driver— scotch and beer always available... When we arrived at Saskatchewan my father, in between beers and the scotch, started raving about the beautiful scenery; no doubt since he was born on the prairies near Pincher Creek Alberta. We were surrounded by the endless golden wheat fields gleaming in the sun dwarfed by the infinite blue sky. Uncle Wellwood had a right wooden leg which started with gangrene in his big toe. When we came to the winding roads in the Rockies— in those days missing many guard rails, he had the bright idea to drive my car. I reluctantly agreed as he was used to having his own way. He drove with his right leg spread wide to the right in front of me. To make matters worse and add to my anxiety at one point he said, "Pass me another beer I am feeling sleepy." I was paying a third for the daily drinks but not drinking. One day, on the way back to Detroit and Toronto, I decided otherwise and ended up going for a swim in the pool in the nude at our motel. My dear father put a hole in his mattress from smoking, but my companions turned it upside down before leaving. But we survived the whole trip with me doing 99 percent of the driving. My father said I was the best driver he knew. In those days I loved to drive fast and at one point even thought of entering a competitive drive across Canada contest.

See below my poem about my experiences on the farm as a young tot.

# Childhood Memories of the West

Pigs as big as horses,
Horses as huge as elephants,
A bull as big as a hippo,
A rooster as ferocious as a lion;
All these caused me fear when I came near,
As I recollect on my days as a tot
Down on the farm near Saskatoon Saskatchewan.

Later as a braver tot chasing my adversary the rooster,
Getting into the tar barrel with brother Maurice,
Gleefully catching gophers at one cent per tail,
Wearily stacking wheat at one cent per stook,
Turning upside down the butter churn and spilling all,
I found adventure and life was never drear
Down on the farm near Saskatoon Saskatchewan.

The prairies like a tamed sleeping giant
With golden silken hair that flows forever in the summer sun,
Underneath a sky unending,
And land so flat the fireworks at the fair a hundred miles away
could be seen,
With only a few forlorn farms or barns dotting the horizon.
It's all with me still— when life was serene and dear
Down on the farm near Saskatoon Saskatchewan.

The monster threshing machines were seen and heard miles away,
Spewing and chugging from dawn till early night.
Ah! those threshing meals—Grandma would cook all day—
The table creaking with mountains of meats, pies and other treats;
After watching all that work even Maurice and I could demolish a pie.
Grandma always sensed when company was coming,
then she would cook some more.
Then at night Grandad would recite poems like Sam McGee...
It wasn't all work you see—

Down on the farm near Saskatoon Saskatchewan.
    The winters sometimes fifty below;
    Colder than the feel of flesh stuck on chilled steel;
    The horses with bells, plunging through snow drifts up to their knees,
    Pulling the covered caboose with glowing iron stove,
    Rugs, hot rocks, Mama, Daddy and brothers all snug inside;
    These I warmly recall of childhood
    Down on the farm near Saskatoon Saskatchewan.

    Soon I knew the horses were not to be feared but loved;
    Grandad boasted of the finest work horses in the world;
    But Goldy, Sandy, Fany, Roxy and many others
    Were more, much more than beasts of burden;
    When the tractors replaced them years later it was the end of an era,
    And these faithful friends were sadly missed
    Down on the farm near Saskatoon Saskatchewan.

    The pain we caused our parents dear
    When Maurice and I wandered afar to distant lake,
    Pushing a raft like Huckleberry Finn,
    But since prairie born we could not swim,
    Then straggling home at dark with withered flowers to make amends,
    On one of those happy-sad days
    In Vonda the tiny town near Saskatoon Saskatchewan.

    Those prairie days were too precious to last;
    I learned at eight nothing lasts forever.
    When we left behind Grandma, Grandad and loving pet Brownie
    All down-cast at the Railway Station platform,
    Not an eye was dry and I saw for the first time dogs can cry
    And have a broken heart too—all this I knew
    On moving East, leaving all we loved—behind—in Saskatchewan.

# 2

# YOUNGER YEARS

## 𝔉earless Youth

When life was a blast —
When I was fearless, foolish and fast—
It's all in my youthful past:
Seemingly past senseless acts now,
But joyful, heart-pumping then—
Youthful foibles way back when.

In younger years:
A pugilistic upstart—
But learning soon this not too smart.
Clashing in combat with long poles near Christie Pits,
In Toronto the Good,
Giving our parents fits.

Defying gravity:
Pushing the limits of stupidity
Walking on slim high-in- the sky beams—
Oblivious to death it seems—.
Then leaping across yawning gaps

Between buildings high as a gasp.
Now, looking back it's hard to grasp
The thrill of surviving on the edge.
Later racing in cars trying to be first not last.
When I was still fearless foolish and fast.
One frigid winter day on Eagle Lake —
Driving my relative -loaded car on ice,
Crashing through—but thank you Lord— near shore!
Learning: on ice never throw the dice,.
And learning discretion is the better part of valour.

When life was a blast —
When I was fearless, foolish and fast—
It's all in my youthful past.
Eventually, reason prevailed somehow,
Seemingly past senseless acts now,
But joyful, heart-pumping then—
Youthful foibles way back when.

**AT AGE EIGHT** WE LEFT THE WEST IN 1937—AT THE RAILWAYS STATION leaving my grandparents and dog Brownie—there wasn't a dry eye including Brownie. My parents were lured by an offer from Uncle Jack for my mother and father to work in Gravenhurst, Ontario—my father at Uncle Jack's Browns Beverages Co—and my mother to help part time at Aunt Grace's and Uncle Jack's home. We lived in the factory a floor above where they produced the bottled beverages: orange, cola, root beer, etc. During the day except weekends the noise from the bottles clashing and clanging on the conveyor belts was near deafening. This was our new life—maybe even a step backwards. Other close relatives had tried it for a short time and moved back West. It was poverty time due to the meager wages. Uncle Jack reminded me of Scrooge and not a likeable type. I suspect that Grace and Jack were using my parents as cheap labour. To make ends meet, Mama baked donuts which Brother Maurice and I had to sell by going door to door. I hated this task, but it was no doubt good for character building.

During our stay in Gravenhurst my relatives thought It a great idea if I would be the eyes on fishing expeditions for my blind cousin Gordon Offord, an offspring of Aunt Grace long before she married Jack, Gordon was blind since youth due to a toboggan/tree accident. Gordon was clever for a blind man, able to dance, play cards, read, and was a ham operator —one time saving three lost females in a storm on Lake Huron directing them to a safe port. On fishing outings on nearby Lake Muskoka, I was to observe landmarks and direct Gordon to desired destinations, evidently, he had a map in his head. On our first and only outing we got hopelessly lost— fortunately ending this nonsense and I was fired from this non-paying job. Not sure why Maurice was not selected for this glorious opportunity.

My parents couldn't stand living in the bottle clanging factory so after a couple of years moved to a one-story house near the railway tracks—more poverty. One advantage was Brother Maurice and I could gather the spilt coal on the railway tracks to heat the house in the winter. Public school was strict; punishing with a leather strap for misbehaviors was frequent... One occasion nearly all students got the strap after a ferocious snow ball fight broke out at a recess when everyone took sides. But there was free milk every morning; I have never tasted such creamy delicious milk. And I have a good memory of falling in love for the first time with a pretty girl about nine or ten years old. Do you remember at Valentines day getting many valentines— as I do?

After three years in Gravenhurst we moved to Toronto after my father had secured a job at a 7Up beverage company delivering the pop to various stores and restaurants. We entered this huge city at black night and I recall being overwhelmed and enthralled with the many flashing neon lights. On my father's delivery route, while a young teenager—I would sometimes go with him and carry the empty and full cases. This built some muscle.

To earn extra money— spare rooms in our three story house on Christie Street near Christie Pits were rented to roomers—for example to three sisters for a couple of years. Many years later one of the sisters met me and said, "Earl you ran everywhere in those days." I recall a party at a relative of the three sisters. It went on and on until about four in the morning, mainly dancing, until the host asked sarcastically if we were staying for breakfast. Also, I would cycle all over Toronto. One day while cycling miles from home with a friend, our dog continued to follow. So, we put it in a back yard with a fence. Fortunately, but as expected the dog found his way home a few hours later. Amazing, now that I think of it.

I loved to practice the hurdle training on my single hurdle in my back yard. My teachers were impressed with my prowess on the hurdles and one day I was excused from class to show two teachers my technique. But at the first meet I feel at the first hurdle. Fifty years later I would break some world records in the hurdles. So never give up. During the many years on Christie Street— mother did house cleaning and sewing. But for many years my brothers and I had to wear clothes supplied by the City to assist low income families. This was quite embarrassing since other children knew we were wearing so called "poggy" clothes. But I had toughened up and believed in a stoic attitude —no crying in any situation.

I had a heavy punching bag in the basement and boxing gloves. One time my sparring partner, father, ended up with cracked ribs unfortunately. On another occasion I accidentally knocked out a friend who asked to spar with me. Then there was the persistent boy who was overly eager to fight someone, me or one of my two friends at Christie Pits. I agreed. After a big crowd had gathered and my two black eyes, and after what seemed like an hour or more— I became enraged when "persistent boy" tore my shirt and I somehow landed a knockout punch. Fortunately, I soon came to realize that mental development was far superior to physical activities such as boxing and fighting others with long wooden poles.

At Essex Public School I got involved with what we called the "backward class," slow learners I suppose. I had a game with them at many recesses where a dozen or more males in this class would chase me, but if any caught up to me I would dispatch him with a shove or a punch and takeoff again. So it would appear I had above average speed of foot. It wasn't too ferocious as no teacher ever intervened to stop these antics.

At Christie Pits, the rectangular bowl with steep grassy walls, I had many adventures. One time when not yet a teen, a gang of older boys grabbed me and suspended me upside down over an open manhole and threatened to drop me in. But I did encounter disaster one day: We used to play like Tarzan swinging high from long ropes tied to tall trees half way down the steep slope. But I Tarzan, losing his grip ended up in the hospital with a broken arm and a sprained back; here I was strapped to the bed to prevent turning in my sleep. After a week in the hospital I didn't want to leave the pretty pampering nurses.

One of my female Public School teachers convinced me and others in her class that there was a God. I am forever grateful for that. I had to make a decision when leaving public school as to what to specialize in at high school. A public school teacher recommended I become a draftsman rather than take a matriculation course leading to university, She had noticed that I had a good talent for drawing —Maurice was the artistic one and we used to sit together and draw for hours, so I took her advice until after four years at Central Technical School I switched from "machine shop and drafting" to matriculation on advice of a very clever and kind teacher, Professor John Dodd who befriended me for many years. He convinced me to take his one year of French immersion where he would cover the required four years of French taken by the matriculation class. This would allow me to take my final year in the matric class and go on to university. I managed to excel in my final year and was selected to give the valedictory address. John Dodd coached me in my committed-to- memory speech which included some humour. He told me: at his university graduation he gave the valedictory address in poetry format.

In a lifetime if we are fortunate, there will be some people who see some-thing likeable or see a person with special future qualities who befriends and helps you on to a better outcome. There were no others more helpful than Professor John Dodd and my parents— I miss them all. I also had some help also on my future career when I went to England on a fellowship as explained later.

I had many part time jobs before starting University: initially selling newspapers— then delivering fliers— delivering groceries on my bike to pretty ladies— multi tasks at a local bakery— then when older unloading freight trains (coffins,, boxes of chains, cigarettes (who stole those cigs? not me a non-smoker)—later doing mostly quality control office work at the Hepburn Co (I had some narrow escapes there in the shops— one day while drilling a huge casting the drill stuck and the casting swung round just barely missing my stomach. Then later, the head of a drill flew off narrowly missing my head. At age 15 or 16 one summer during the Second world War I did some quality control work at a munitions factory in Mimico manufacturing Bren machine guns At this factory one day while I was doing an experiment an Army General came by and said, "It helps if you know the answer." See my poem at the end of this chapter abut my young working years.

Finally, after starting at Central Technical School in the machine shop and drafting course I secured a part time drafting job at the Ideal Stoker Company on Wellington Street Toronto after miles of walking factory to factory with drawing samples. There was so much walking looking for drafting employment that, I wore out a pair of pants in the crotch. I did drawings in ink of all the Ideal Stoker machines while working in dingy dark conditions in their factory at 50 cents an hour. The owner, Mr. Shaw, liked me so I asked for and got a dollar an hour with a move to the front office. I would work there after class and on weekends and walk home in over an hour memorizing my French. This walking was also helping my running at high school. At Ideal Stoker at age 16 Mr. Shaw asked me to measure and make drawings of a competitor's machine. The existing Ideal machine was buried under the coal —very inconvenient for maintenance, but the competitor's machine was conveniently outside the coal bin. There was a court case accusing Ideal Stoker of copying the competitor's machine. I was worried sick that I might be involved and accused. But no— the case was thrown out. When I graduated Mr. Shaw wanted me to join his company but I had bigger ambitions like accepting a two year Earl of Athlone Fellowship to England with all expenses paid. These part time jobs particularly the latter allowed me to pay for my own clothes and expensive dental operations, two impacted wisdom teeth extractions and many gold fillings which have lasted for over 70 years—and also to finance my tuition with the help of five monetary scholarships mostly which I did not apply for.

The Second World War—Maurice and I were too young for military service being 17 and 15 respectively, and at high school one year before the end of the war. Although thousands of miles away from the war, there were repercussions in our neighbourhood, the rationing and the following: For example, at Essex Public School we made model aircraft for military identification training. And we had a pretty young girl about 18 years rooming with us. Her young husband was in a local hospital badly scarred and disfigured with burns to the face and body. Then one sad afternoon some good close friends came to our house to announce their son who we knew well had been killed in action. I knew him well. There was a terrible lot of crying by my mother and our friends. The war had come to us. Also, at age 16 near end of the war I had a summer job at a munitions factory in Mimico manufacturing Bren guns. The job I had involved quality control, to ensure accurate machining of parts for the Bren gun, hence a fairly responsible position. When this terrible war ended I recall a huge celebration on the main street in Toronto, Yonge street. There were thousands filling the street walking, smiling,. yelling, waving flags and embracing each other. I recall kissing many pretty girls that day; they were all quite condescending.

At Central Tech it wasn't all study. One year I was selected by a school vote to attend a week long travelling tour of mines and landmarks in northern Ontario—one or two male students selected from each high school in Toronto. It was sponsored by the Timothy Eaton Co. now defunct. I became friends to Ian McDonald, a genius type and fellow athlete later on our U of Toronto track team, who later became the head of York University in Toronto with its more than 20,000 students. The T. Eaton personnel in charge of the trip took a liking to me and my appearance. As a consequence, I was selected to be the T. Eaton representative at my high school, a one-year term. It was considered an honor since, for example, we could arrange dances with T. Eaton equipment. The T. Eaton Company was good to me— I could run a bill from purchase of goods during the school term and not pay until the summer when I started to work more frequently. Also for a year I was selected as the top Eaton high school executive over about 100 or more other junior executives. This lasted until they found I had a chip in my front tooth; therefore not suitable for advertising photos and modeling. In any case I was more interested in my running.

With running training only during recess, I could run a five-minute mile without any warmup. I would also participate in an International relay race where teams competed against each other and each team member running 5K. I was able to run a respectable 5K based mainly on 400m training, and a lot of walking and cycling. On our annual field day at Central Tech I would do all track and field events including an optional relay, except the pole vault and would normally finish 2nd overall. On the field days if I had dropped the relay for another event the outcome might have been different. During my final year at Central Tech our 4x400m relay team tied the Canadian University indoor record at the indoor Copps Stadium in Hamilton. On the wooden 150-yard track I led off since I was considered to have a fast start. Our school provided us with outdoor spikes with spikes about 3/4-inch-long, whereas indoor spikes nowadays are 5 to 6mm or less than ¼ inch in length. This did not help the fast running at all. During my final year at high school at age 18 at a meet of all high schools in Ontario I was able to come 2nd in a time of about 52 seconds on the cinder track at Varsity Stadium—and our 4x400m relay team finished first. I stopped midway in the 5K final race —which I had qualified for with little if any training —to save energy for the 400m and the 4x400m relay. (My son was unfairly kicked off his high school track team for following a similar tactic following my advice.)

During the University summers I trained with the Red Devils Track Club coached by Lloyd Percival —considered one of the best if not the best track and field coach in Canada at the time. One summer I trained hard practically every day with Murray Gazuik, a member of our U of Toronto 4x400m relay team and the Red Devils. In September after that hard summer I was drained of energy and couldn't compete, but recovered in about two months. Lloyd wrote a pamphlet on hockey training and the Russian hockey team used this for their training, but this was in the 1940's. One day after training hard the day before, I told Lloyd I am too sore even to walk, but he said," "But you are not too sore to run." He used to say, "The mind is the weak link, you can always do more than you think you can." I firmly believe this—I call it the "chicken mind" in my running book: *The Complete Guide to Running.* Lloyd had a terrible disaster one day at Varsity Stadium when I was there training. A young boy had just finished a long training run, he came up to Lloyd still breathing hard. Lloyd had a starting pistol in his hand from just starting some sprinters. The gun went off right in front of the boy's chest—the unbelievable happened — his heart stopped and he died on the spot. But, his parents forgave Lloyd and the other son continued to train with Lloyd. It was the end of the good old days.

Lloyd Percival spent most of his time with elite athletes, for example two Olympic type athletes—a male shot putter and a female hurdler. But one day he saw me long jumping and remarked of the exceptional spring in my legs end suggested maybe I was concentrating on the wrong events, e.g., 400m and 800m. Another good coach in Toronto at the time was Fred Foote who coached the East Your Track club. Their two best athletes were Bill Crothers and Bruce Kidd. The tall Bill Crothers who came second in the 800m in 1:45.6 to Peter Snell of New Zealand in 1:45.1 at the 1964 Japan

Olympics out of 47 initial competitors. Bruce Kidd, short light and fast, was a world class distance runner. Crothers, a pharmacist, claimed that Lloyd Percival was giving some of his athlete illegal drugs, but it was never proven. Bruce Kidd spent most of his running days as a U of Toronto student and grad and later as a popular professor. Fred Foote had Kidd's arms moving as a "wheel: in an unorthodox relaxed circular motion rather than the usual horizontal piston type of movement. But his impressive international career ended due to too many cortisone shots in his ankle which as the exaggerated story goes: it turned to "mush".

After university I didn't run for 33 years due to a testicle hydrocele problem, but believed in some exercise every day, tennis, water skiing, snow skiing, etc. and 50 pushes most days. Then after 33 years my body and muscles remembered and a year later with the North York Track Club under coach David Welch, an ex- marathoner, I was able to tie a world indoor record in the 400m in 56.7 seconds for my age group 55 -59. I thought this is a good hobby and later realized it was a most healthy one. A year later my body was noticeably more fit and muscular and also younger looking.

I started at U of Toronto at age 19. My letter of acceptance went astray somehow and I found out by making a query— nearly too late— that I had been accepted. My parents gave me $500 for the 1st installment fees—a lot of money in 1948 based on my parent's financial situation. After that I paid my own way working and assisted by five monetary scholarships most of which I didn't apply for. I even had excess money to lend my young brother Wellwood for a used car. He never paid me back —I had to collect or try to collect from the young man he later sold the car to. When Wellwood sold the car it wouldn't back up so it made parking difficult if not impossible.

I was the middle son, Wellwood five years younger and Maurice two years older than me. Our parents could have described us as hard (Wellwood), medium (Earl), and soft (Maurice), Wellwood didn't like his name so went by his middle name Allan—Maurice wanted his pronounced like Maureece, not like Morris. Incidentally, my cousin named Beryl in grade 1 told the teacher: "Call me Beverly.) I had more in common with Maurice the dancer/artist than Wellwood, the pool shark gambler type. But I loved them both. Maurice took an arts course for four years at Central Tech and later taught dancing at Fred Astaire's and Arthur Murrays In Toronto. New York and San Francisco —while Wellwood lasted at Central Tech but one year unfortunately with a poor attitude. Now I regret when I was young and foolish when I would sometimes take advantage of my age with young Wellwood. But my conscience is clear for he did get even one time when he matured.

At our home on busy Bloor Street near Bathurst above a store. I would usually be doing my university studies and homework. When there were family chores I was exempt. "Earl is studying," my dear mother would say. So I was not popular with my brothers. I took my time at university seriously, but many of my classmates were there just to pass and play, for example, putting a Volkswagen on top of a U of T building, and other antics, etc. And many of my class would frequently meet after class at the "KCR." It took me years to learn this was a nearby pub, the King Cole Room.

When I was about 21, Wellwood being under restricted age 19 asked me to buy a bottle of wine for him at the local Liquor store. They refused to sell it to me since I had not brought my identification. In desperation, he returned to the store and was able to buy it although he was just 17 at the time, but looking much older. When we had our tonsils removed many years before by a Dr. Fee the nurses thought we were twins. Wellwood was involved in the Accident of the Month in Toronto when about age 20. While taking pills for an ulcer and too much alcohol (a bad combination) he rear ended a parked car and was thrown into the backseat leaving behind his shoes in the driving position. His ballooned face required hundreds of stiches and one eye looked lower than the other. But he took it bravely and with optimism, and amazingly the scars and stiches rarely showed.

Wellwood was clever besides being a good travelling salesman: He married an attractive classy lady Betti and they had two sons Rod and Tod. I had several happy trips out West to visit Wellwood and Betti and several times after Wellwood died— with Curtis, Tyler and Melanie during the Calgary Stampede. Wellwood could duplicate a signature by starting at the end rather the beginning. At big parties in Calgary in black face he would dress with black face as and sing "Mammy" and other songs exactly like Al Jolson the black singer. But Wellwood passed away at the early age of 44 from over-drinking, poor diet and smoking. For example, on many mornings he would just have a beer for breakfast, then a further drink with customers.

Maurice in his early 20's revealed he was a homosexual, but our family accepted it in a loving way and welcomed his male friends that we knew.

He became an accomplished artist painting over 200 portraits, mainly portraits of women —in an impressionist Picasso-like style. His colourful acrylic paintings. were his joy and further livelihood for many decades. He told me he could produce a large painting in a couple of hours. When young Maurice and I would sit and sketch together for hours on end —there is nothing like practice— I became quite proficient like Maurice and this facility has stayed with me. He also loved to write and while traveling abroad or in Canada he would always have a notebook handy to record in capital letters his experiences. I am the proud owner of over 120 of these acrylic paintings since his early departure at age 64.

Maurice was also a dance instructor at Fred Astaire and Arthur Murry's studies in Toronto, New York and San Francisco—looking graceful and fluid at six foot three. He hated the dance instruction since it involved convincing customers with "two left feet," that they had talent and should continue with more and more lessons. He had a way of life many would ascribe to and love: He worked for half a year and for the other half travelled the world; to Europe, Asia, e.g., Greece, Egypt, Maui. And all the while making friends and writing of his adventures. But I'm sad to say and reveal at age 64 he died from HIV in 1992. At this time there was no cure for HIV. No one would have suspected from his behavior and mannerisms that he was homosexual. His last short weeks were spent at Casey House in Toronto, a hospice for the hopeless HIV victims. In view of his wasting away at rapid rate he wanted no one to visit except me, his sole remaining relative. Diane of England visited there to provide cheer to these terminal patients. In the 1990's only one patient ever survived a visit there. The pills for HIV in those days were experimental and extremely expensive. Now similar cases to my brother would survive due to the advanced technology. This is one big advantage of living longer —In the interim new cures may or will be found.

A couple of months before he passed away — actually the day I retired from 34 years at the Atomic Energy Canada —he had strength enough to visit his lawyer and the hospital with my assistance, He was so frail and week his pants fell down during the hospital visit. At the hospital HIV section, I could see many similar cases on the verge of extinction. The Doctor kindly offered my brother a book," Living With Death." Maurice said in his usual authoritative confident way, "I don't need it, I already know about living with death." Maurice, an atheist, is buried at Mount Pleasant Cemetery with my mother and father —this cemetery has many famous interred people and the subject of a long poem of mine. See at the end of this chapter a poem about Maurice—an amazing true happening months before his passing. Another poem titled, "No More, No More" about his courageous last hours is too sad to include. (But I now *my* longevity methods are working. In March 2018 I achieved an age grading of 107.5% for an indoor 400m race where 100% is equivalent to the open world record, See Chapter 19, Interviews, for details.)

My two brothers and father, it's sad to say, all departed at an early age due to neglect of their bodies, i.e., unhealthy lifestyles—Wellwood at 44, Maurice at 64 and father at 69. My simple but undisputable theory is that the more unhealthy indiscretions the shorter the life and it follows that the more healthy habits the longer the life. See my book. *"One Hundred Years the Natural Way."* for other valuable information on anti-aging. Unfortunately, most people don't care, they love their bad habits— in other words working at dying rather than working at living, as Jack Lalanne would say.

At Toronto University I developed some good study habits of consistency and diligence—habits that would enable me to win five scholarships and two fellowships and that would stand me in good stead 33 years later in my masters running career. I was determined not to let my parents down after giving me their last penny to get me started at University. I learned from a brilliant older student that it was important to review the lectures the same day and on the weekend. I was not looking merely to pass as a large fraction in my class of about 75 in mechanical engineering. Now 65 years later (1953 to 2018) since graduation less than 12 of all 1953 engineering grads ( electrical, mechanical, civil, mining, physics etc) are accounted for; a few others may be around but our 1953 grad executive have lost touch. With good study habits and dedication I was able to win some monetary scholarships and also find time to train with the university track team. (I recall the great satisfaction from reading in a newspaper one day on a bus of winning my first scholarship I was even tempted to show this information to the stranger beside me.)

While at Toronto University we trained on the indoor 150m track at Hart House in the winter and in other seasons on the cinder track at Varsity stadium. Looking back with my present running knowledge today I am amazed how any good results were achieved in spite of grossly inadequate coaching. I recall the training for the 400 indoor as follows: Without any warmup and no stretching, we were told to run 400m as fast as we were capable several times with short rest. Then there was no cooldown. One of the Brown brothers coached us, both brothers had competed in the Commonwealth Games in track and field events. However, the unscientific methods did produce results quickly and I was capable of 51 seconds in the indoor 400m. The fact that it was more difficult to get injured when young certainly helped. The 400m training involved no weight training or sprint training like nowadays, although in the outdoor I could run under 24 seconds for the 200m. In those days, I would tense up my neck when sprinting the 200m: but no one pointed out this bad habit. I learned much later that relaxation is key to speed. The 800m training involved negligible aerobic training in spite of the fact that the 800m is about 50% aerobic. Doing repeat 400s at 60 seconds was done easily and with fluidity. Consequently, I was usually way out in front at 400m of the 800, but usually faded near the end, finishing in about 2min 6 or 7 sec. One day while still at university I returned home after winning an indoor 600m race (probably my best event) at the Armories on University Ave. in Toronto. I was bragging a little bit too much to my parents. They reprimanded me. It was good lesson for future years. I was fortunate to have good parents and hence a good upbringing. I realize now: "There is no greatness without humility."

My final exams in my last year at university were a nightmare. There were 13 exams in just over two weeks. I was well prepared but my eyes became extremely tired and painful from constant overuse. I started to wear glasses for the first time. Perhaps the prescription was wrong. One day I tried No Nod pills. They worked for one exam but for the next exam I was completely drained of energy. Then during these exams, I missed one exam thinking all were in the afternoon— but the one I missed was in the morning. Fortunately, the professors knew I was honest and could have asked others what was in the exam and I was able to take the exam in the afternoon. Consequently, I tried to be not too perfect. Somehow, I survived the ordeal of these final exams with good results (usually I stood second out of about 100 in the class but this last his year I stood third —when I graduated in 1953 I was awarded an Earl of Athlone Fellowship for two years study in England with all expenses paid. I thought this is too good to refuse. It was an attempt by the English to increase trade between England and Canada. In 1953 there were about eight of us— from major university's in Canada. The trip to England was by ship since air travel was uncommon at the time. The ship was one of the Princess line, but this one was aptly called the Drunken Princess because of its excessive role. This bothered many of my mates but not me They were not happy to hear my story of travelling across Lake Ontario in a passenger ship from Toronto harbour when a nasty storm came up and most passengers and everyone in my family were seasick except me and my grandfather. I was surprised and dismayed to see many of my mates looking down on the waiters and waitresses and acting superior. But the trip was a great adventure for a young man who had never travelled except across Canada twice.

The spectacular coronation of Queen Elizabeth at age 25 in1953 couldn't have been a better time to be in England. For the coronation, London was bedecked in decorations especially for the route of the gilded 200-year-old carriage pulled by eight white horses with its 20 walking grooms, footmen and yeomen carrying the Queen. (The Queen 50 years later used the same carriage at her Golden Jubilee.) Following the coronation carriage was a massive parade seeming to represent every institution in England imaginable. And of course, surrounded by millions of cheering British. After her coronation the new Queen in her ornate gold thread stitched white gown, with crown on head, orb in one hand and sceptre in the other was followed by six maidens carrying her trailing gown. Winston Churchill said Elizabeth is loved because she is the Queen but also because of herself.

To add to the celebration of coronation day, June 2, 1953 it was announced: Edmund Hillary and his Sherpa Tensing Norgay had reached the summit of Everest, the highest peak in the world —the first to do this feat. Hillary was promptly knighted Sir Edmund Hillary for this difficult accomplishment. These two events added greatly to my excitement in arriving in England in 1953.

The Earl of Athlone fellowship organizers had booked me initially for some initial training at the huge English Electric Co. in Rugby Warwickshire England. I had asked before accepting the fellowship to be booked at Birmingham University in the Thermodynamics Department for the two years. Now on arrival in England I was told that there were other Athlone fellows already there and this was not possible. I learned there were some other Athlone fellows treated similarly—the organizers reneging on earlier promises. I could have insisted based on our earlier discussions, but I decided not to—I feared my tired painful eyes as in my last year at U of Toronto might return. What greatly affected my decision was an opportunity to study nuclear power generation at the famous Harwell Research Facility near Oxford. In 1953 nuclear power generation was in a pioneering stage. The chief engineer at English Electric in Rugby, also a tall Canadian, had befriended me and offered me this great opportunity at Harwell. I trained with an English Electric team of three senior English Electric engineers for two exciting years—no work just studying nuclear power, mainly secret papers, to my heart's content. But no secret papers to be taken outside— so there was a daily search at the exit gate. One day I did take a technical paper home for the night and nearly got caught at the gate. During this time English Electric, Westinghouse and General Electric facilities in England were in competition to design the first gas cooled nuclear reactor plant to produce electricity. English Electric didn't win this competition with their design but received orders later to build their design.

Before leaving for Harwell I spent a few months gaining training through the various English Electric departments at Rugby. A Mr. Lacy in the personnel department was in charge of new trainees. I made the mistake of calling him by this first name as he was not much older than me. But I was firmly reminded that he was Mr. Lacy— this was not typical of most English customs. One day he asked me if a new trainee with name "Shitu" would be harassed by the other trainees. I observed when workers at the plant were rewarded with a bonus for completing more units in day (e.g., inserting blades into a turbine rotor)— they would work rapidly cutting corners and fool the inspector, making the product less safe.

I stayed at a rooming house with several other males where all meals were provided— and promptly gained about 15 pounds in a month, from the stoggy food, big meals and plenty of custard. The entertainment was mainly attending the pubs. But prior to arriving in England I had been a non- drinker except at Christmas. I soon met Yvonne a beautiful vivacious girl looking about 18 but I learned later was just 16. She was a nude model for art students in her spare time at Coventry, a nearby city. Her parents liked and trusted me, and I was impressed by them, so Yvonne and I had some memorable overnight trips to London. One show I recall was Mantavani and his violin orchestra and a theatre show, The Red Wagon. One time, on leaving at the London train station she insisted to stay longer, but I had promised her parents. It was tempting as London is an exciting city. She was eager for us to be engaged, but I felt she was not trustworthy and my mother was against a marriage, no doubt fearing I would be lost to another world. Besides marriage would have been a step too big for me at this age 24. One time in London I purposely had lodgings nearby to her hotel,—and when I came to pick her up in the lobby in the morning the hotel personnel thought she was a prostitute and accused me of being a customer. Naturally I gave the manager a piece of my mind. I felt sorry for Yvonne. I kept in touch for three years after I returned to Canada by mail. Later I found I had a delayed reaction thinking I should have gone ahead with her. I still think fondly of her. I did see her briefly in Rugby England again a few years after I returned to Canada. She was married and I could tell from her grumbling husband that they were not a happy couple. We had a drink of scotch and just a short chat.

To get selected for training in nuclear power at the Harwell Research Establishment, near Oxford, it was the usual custom to answer some tricky technical questions which I was able to do. Our small team of engineers and draftsmen were stationed in some huts. In the winter there was heating only from some hot pipes near the ceiling. Normally on a cold day we would sit with our feet covered with cloth in a box. One day, it was particularly cold so me and my three senior engineers decided to get closer to the hot pipes putting our chairs on our desks and sitting up there. As luck would have it this day Sir John Cockcroft, a high official of the government, came through on tour. He understood the embarrassing situation perfectly and passed through without comment. At Harwell there was a large room where about 25 ladies worked on numerical calculations. In those early days there were no computers so the machines they each used required some very frequent cranking before inserting the numbers. This room sounded like a thousand giant bees humming loudly. What working conditions! Such was the technology in those early days.

At Harwell I had some lodgings in beautiful nearby Oxford. One morning I was cooking some sausages on an electric hot plate. Meanwhile, I went up to the bathroom. When I came down to my room an announcer on the radio was doing a commercial on sausages. He was saying in a loud excited way, "Just Look at those assuages, Just look at those sausages." But meanwhile, my sausages were burning with a lot of smoke. It was as if he was warning me. It was the weirdest coincidence.

Also about this time in 1954 a historic event occurred in England: "**Roger Bannister Breaks the Four Minute Mile.** " His momentous world record: breaking the four-minute mile barrier occurred on May 6, 1954, on a blustery wet day.at Iffley Road track, Oxford, close to my future lodgings in Oxford. *So I divert from my personal story to discuss briefly this great feat of Bannister a fellow runner:*

In 1952 at the Helsinki Olympics Bannister had finished 4th in the 1500m, citing the many heats as his downfall. Bannister had nearly given up running a year before his mile record— citing his studies as more important. But he firmly believed the four-minute mile was achievable. Two others: Anderrson and Hagg of Sweden had raced on separate occasions on the verge of under 4 minutes for the mile, just a bit more than a second away— the tempting record of Hagg at 4:01.2 had remained for 10 years.

Bannister's mile record transpired at an Iffley Road track competition attended by a huge crowd in anticipation of a new world mile record. It was a big decision to go ahead with the attempt in view of the excess wind and the driving rain— also a coolish day based on the overcoats worn by the officials. But the weather subsided and the attempt was on. Bannister had two pacers Chris Brasher an Olympic steeplechaser—and Christopher Chataway a world record holder in the 5000m. Four others in the race quickly faded. Brasher led for the first half, Bannister following in 57.5 seconds for the 1st quarter and 1:58 for the half, Chataway then took the lead…running 3:00. 7 for the 3rd quarter, where Bannister took over and passed Chataway with 300 yards to go. With huge strides and somewhat exaggerated shoulder movements and flying blond hair—he powered his way towards the tape… with his customary pronounced burst of speed in the last straightaway in a final time of 3:59.4…falling totally spent and exhausted into ecstatic amazed arms.

His training, at lunch, skipping a class had consisted of 10 quarter miles at 60 seconds each with a two-minute rest, no warmup and no cooldown on the cinder track. Over a six month period his times reduced to 58 seconds. And Just 28 miles per week of running training in the six months prior to his record..

His next test would be at the Commonwealth Games in Vancouver in August of the same year 1954. Landy of Australia was his main competition having lowered the mile record to 3:58 in the previous June 1954--- but Bannister was known for his blazing finish. On the night before Bannister was nursing a cut on his foot from broken glass on the field, and Landy was bothered by a cold. In this famous race witnessed by 35,000 at the new stadium there were seven competitors. Landy with his quick shorter stride, compared to Bannister, had a big lead after the half mile with Bannister back about 15 metres Gradually Bannister reduced the gap… and in the last straightway while Landy looked back over his left shoulder Banister with by his long strides devouring the cinder track flew by on Landy's right. Landy was spent from his earlier lead in the 2nd half. In December 1954, Bannister retired from running to concentrate on his impressive neurologist there career. In spite of his fame and knighthood in 1975 Sir Roger Bannister, was a quiet, modest gentleman, and also a noted neurologist. He passed away peacefully in Oxford in March 2018 at age 88, born in 1929 as myself.

It is notable that in the Commonwealth Games in 1954 Rich Ferguson from my past track Club, the Red Devils in Toronto, under coach Lloyd Percival— came a very respectable third in 4:04.6 in the above is legendary race. His previous best time was 4:13.

**Now back to Earl Fee.** My two years scheduled stay of two years in England turned into three when I decided to stay an extra year working at the English Electric nuclear design department in Coventry to gain invaluable experience for a decent salary. The Athlone organizers did not object to the insistence of a stayover no doubt in view of their reneging on my promised university attendance. And they paid for my return travel home by ship with other Athlone returnees. The experience at Coventry was invaluable but involved working long hours—since there was much design work to be done before the decision for the best and first nuclear plant design in England was decided. I concluded that the extra hours didn't help the schedule at all as the engineers just worked noticeably slower all day

**The following are just a few of my outstanding adventures during my three year stay in England:**

It was an exciting three years —looking back it was the best three years of my life involving some of the following highlights: The first year took some getting used to; the fog and smog and infrequent sun: for example, the fog and smog so thick someone had to walk in front of the bus to avoid a collision — dampened my spirits. (Bad weather has toughened the English giving them the necessary fortitude during the past war.) But then after a few months, friends were made and we all suffered and complained together— the sun seemed to shine more frequently— the green countryside was a treat with its stately castles and magnificent cathedrals, such as the York Minster, that I marvelled at— and then of course the multitude of intimate pubs with quaint names were an enjoyable habit. practised by all. In each and every English pub, everywhere you go, you felt immediately at home and of course thirsty, with their quant names—for example: Half Way House, First and Last, Hop Inn, Dew Drop Inn, Hole in the Wall, Happy Man, Three.Horseshoes, Odd Fellows, Cock Coach, Horses Fox and Hounds, and Nutshell (claimed to be the smallest in the world). And a noisy crowd always added to the flavor of the event, and the poignant smell was inviting leading to increased thirst..

Then there were many opportunities, without trying, to meet numerous pretty English girls with their musical accents, — ah youth how I miss you. One pretty English girl confided to me on our first date that she was in the family way and had to get married. I met Canadian travellers and other nationalities especially the frequent Aussie travellers too. In two of my hosteling holidays in Europe the Canadian badge went a long way to easily to hitch a ride while back packing. Canadians were much better accepted than Americans. After touring the Alps in Switzerland and Austria, Paris, and Germany with their many castles and vineyards with a male South African friend— I met Marie, a Dutch girl, and visited her home in Amsterdam. However, after corresponding from England for some months I had a letter from her mother suggesting I break off this friendship. Reluctantly, I did.

A highlight of my time in England was meeting Yvonne Pallet, a vivacious 17 year old blond mentioned above. I still think fondly of her and her parents.

One adventure while in England was a counter clockwise ride around the perimeter of Ireland with its emerald green fields— on the back of a motorcycle driven by Andre, my South African friend. Some of the highlights I recall were: Belfast, home of Titanic shipbuilders, the Giants Causeway on the north coast (many thousands of polygonal rock columns formed by ancient volcanos), Cliffs of Moher (on the West coast from 120m to 214m high),

Ring of Kerry (south coast with glacial lakes and mountains),more 200m high cliffs, many national parks, many ruined castles, everywhere villages, friendly pubs, and the unforgettable rolling green hills and amiable garrulous people. Finally, ending up in Dublin in a roaring pub. Another adventure,

Renting a tiny car and travelling southern England and Wales with four of my Athlone buddies for four days : Each day we took turns in selecting a new route. I was nervous and guilty when I returned the tiny car as with the weight of four big Canadians the springs at the back were broken and the car was dragging on the ground.

Apart from my rooming house in Rugby and Coventry I loved my room in Oxford with its river nearby, and many traditions: Highlights of my stay in Oxford were: the Oxford University, the stately old buildings, and meeting a Rhodes scholar from Canada. I also had a room in a bungalow in beautiful Wilmington, a small town close to Oxford and Harwell; this house was heated by a lone fireplace. A bath was allowed once a week by pumping water from the kitchen. My landlady was a sexy attractive lady looking for a husband— on weekends she would parade around town dressed flamboyantly to lure on some males. So, I stayed well clear. My landlady in Coventry was the opposite, an 80-year-old; I came home one day and saw she had rearranged all the very heavy large furniture in my room all by herself.

In England the Lakes District is a major attraction, a must see, which I visited one weekend with my Harwell compatriots. On the west coast it occupies about 30 miles by 30 miles in area with several mountains over 3000 ft. (the largest in England is here at 3200 feet) —and hundreds of small mountains or peaks called fells and small blue lakes, all ideal for ambitious walkers. And of course, many pubs to go with it for the countless thirsty walkers.

The frequent trips to London with it's many attractions, the theatres, cathedrals and museums, the Thames River, and the friendly people were exciting and unforgettable.

There were some mishaps too. For example, on return to England on a ship from Norway after another trip to Europe— I met an amiable couple of gents about my age on the ship. We enjoyed a fine buffet together and they invited me to visit them for a short visit in a city in southern England. At night in their city I was invited to stay overnight with one of them. Before the other departed they got to arguing with each other about something.

At bedtime I was surprised and shocked to learn I was to sleep in the same small bed as my host. Now I understood about the arguing. At the first opportunity in the dark I gathered my clothes and made a rapid exit without explanation to find the first train leaving in my home direction.

I was well treated by the English government so am very grateful for their kind generosity. And also thankful for the two free operations—an operation on a testicle and two impacted wisdom tooth extraction, both on the operating table. But as luck would have it operated on by trainee surgeons both times. During my stay to fix a testicle hydrocele (fluid on the testicle) a pretty young nurse came one day to give me a long needle in my rear end (gluteus muscle); as she inserted the six inch (it seemed) long needle, I flinched and bent the needle 90 degrees. The nurse went down the hall displaying the needle on high and saying. "Look how tough are these Canadians. After my testicle operation I noticed a fellow patient, I had met previously. near me in our general ward was missing. I was told, "He didn't make it." After my operation on the operating table for two impacted wisdom teeth I asked a nurse to find my glasses She searched in my adjacent cabinet and everywhere. Finally, she says, "Oh, you have them on your nose."

Overall, I was very grateful to the English and England for my treatment and the hospitality. It was "grand" as they say in England. Even now England seems like my second home. I sailed back with other Athlone fellows, bringing back many fond memories', on docking at Montreal I experienced a huge feeling of pride to be a Canadian. I soon noticed the Canadian homes were too warm as I had become accustomed to unheated English rooms. And in my three year say in England I had picked up an English accent but no English wife, and reluctantly leaving behind many friends.

Gone are the younger days such as: the old washing machine, the clothes line dryer, the horse drawn caboose in the frigid winter, the coal man, the milk man, the sheeny ( junk dealer) man, and the slide rule at university, to mention a few oldies. But the fond memories linger on.

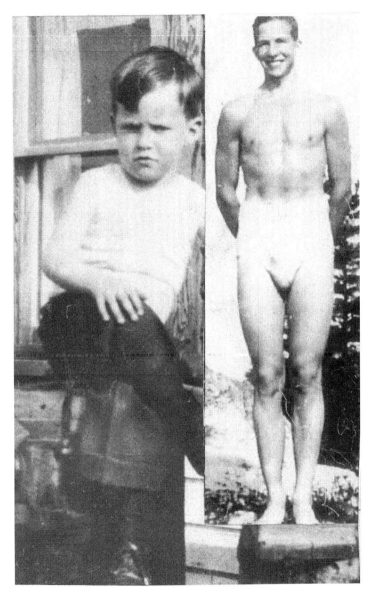

*Youthful bliss and Tarzan*

*High School and University grad*

*Melanie, Curtis, Me and Tyler*

*Mother at age 69*

# **W**ork, Work As a Young Boy

On Grandad's farm as a tiny tot
I first earned pennies and cherished my lot:
Catching gophers at one cent per tail,
And piling sheaves of wheat one cent per bail.

Work, work, work started for me at eight,
A task my brother and I did hate;
Selling mother's donuts door to door;
Days of poverty to deplore.

Shovelling snow when blizzards blow,
When it piled high it was time to go,
But if the reward was too slim—
We shovelled it back ag'in with vim.

Selling papers was not much joy:
I lacked the drive as a shy young boy.
Dropping flyers for a buck or two;
Forgive me Lord I did dump a few.

Delivering groceries on my bike
To sexy ladies, but alas still a tyke.
Then rats I had to drown at night;
The welcome pay didn't make it right.

At Barker's bakery sorting garbage,
Then on to baking at meagre wage.
I remember still the sad day we
Left out the sugar in tons of cookie.

Then when older at CN freight shed
Loading dynamite, and coffins with dread,
Barrels of chains, tons of coffee and tea.
A mystery who stole those "cigs"—not me.

During the Second World War I toiled
In munitions where my mind got soiled.
On day a General came up to me,
"It helps to know the answer," said he.

As a draftsman at Ideal Stoker,
At sixteen, I only once did err.
Fifty cents an hour for many a design,
But let's face it, I was no Einstein.

Hard to say how these jobs shaped a boy;
Difficult to say they were a joy.
The pennies earned were spent quite soon,
But the memories remain for many a moon.

# Bird in the House

*-Based on a true incident in Rosedale, Yonge Street,*
*Toronto in April 1991. Truth is stranger than fiction.*

"A wild bird inside a house portends death," so they say;
When first I heard this superstition so sad,
My mind raced back to decades ago
To the crowded Greek restaurant in Rosedale, Toronto,
Where the tiny bird darted in from the hot summer street
Into the cool semi gloom—
Smashing itself on the wall above—
And falling limply on my ailing brother's empty plate.
At sixty-four many other unaccountable events had happened
To him a poetic wander of the globe
Now life was but an aimless journey of pain unending
Had he known this he would have rejoiced, perhaps,
Since death was his daily wish—
And death was his constant companion
Riding on his shoulder.
This hapless foul incident marked the last meal with dear brother Maurice;
Sadly, I sensed he had lost taste for food and life.
A few months later the superstition rang true!
Strange how the bird knew its destination in its final flight;
Picking my brother out in the over-crowded restaurant,
Strange that it knew the superstition too.

# *3*

# COTTAGE LIFE

MY GRANDPARENTS ON MY MOTHER'S SIDE LEASED SOME CROWN land on the shores of Eagle Lake 40 miles north of Kingston, after they sold their large farm out West and moved East. It was a district of small lakes in eastern Ontario. Sharbot Lake, a larger one, is 15 km to the north next to a beautiful provincial park.

Our family had many vacations to my grandparent's cottage on Eagle Lake near the small village of Tichborne; the cottage was named Shangri-La by Brother Maurice. It was indeed a Shangri-La paradise. I recall the lake like glass in the misty morning to relive all stress, and the soul stirring cry of a lonely loon —my vote for the national bird next to the eagle. I suppose Eagle Lake had eagles at one time. In my late teens and early 20's I would swim in the cool water as fast as Tarzan of the apes in the bay in front of the cottage. And on many occasions I rowed most of the family on a sightseeing two or three hour tour around the lake.

Prior to Shangri-La my grandparents had a rented cottage on Eagle lake. One day on driving to this rented cottage on a small country road through some dense woods my passenger and I we were nearly hit by a freight train as we crossed some train tracks in heavily wooded area. The train was not using it's whistle on small country roads. It left us shaking

A funny thing happened one sunny afternoon at Shangri-La. My Uncle Wellwood, big bold and brusque was visiting from Detroit and questioning a senior neighbour, actually deaf as it turned out. "How long have you have you lived in this area? Receiving no answer my uncle continued to press the question louder and louder each time. I thought soon they will hear him across the lake. Finally, after the third or fourth query he gave up in exasperation. And even louder than before shouted, "It doesn't matter a God damn anyway."

One dark summer night when my grandfather and father had run out of liquid refreshments—I was enlisted by the females to accompany these thirsty men but unsteady men in their quest for replacements. I was to be the engine for the rowboat,but mainly lifeguard in case of a calamity. Fortunately no problems.

About 300 meters away from Shangri-La there was another cottage —the story goes that a young man was murdered in the boathouse and the perpetrator was never found.

The fishing was good at Eagle Lake—as a teenager I caught a large bass weighing a few pounds and also caught on my line a huge turtle at least two feet in diameter. It provided several varieties of meat for a couple of weeks. I would have let it go but my grandfather had other culinary ideas. We towed it back to the cottage. Later, it was hanging on the clothes line supposedly to cure the different kinds of meat in the shell. One night while fishing with my grandfather and me in one boat— next to a boat with Maurice and my grandmother— we fished for the horny but tasty catfish. Oddly my grandfather and I pulled in one catfish after another but in the boat next to us they caught none. I loved grandma's catfish soup with potatoes, onions, milk and spices.

Years later, when my grandparents left Shangri-La and moved to another lakeside cottage by highway 38, my grandfather and friends and relatives would install a long net across a narrow channel in the lake overnight and catch a prohibitive multitude of fish.

Melanie, Curtis and Tyler will remember the cottage by the highway, first Melanie and then five and six years and later Curtis and Tyler respectively. My mother, as a doting grandmother was overjoyed with Melanie and loved to see her at the cottage. I recall this cottage was old and smelled very musty —causing my allergies to act up. But still it was always an enjoyable and memorable experience.

One sunny late winter day when the lake was frozen thick with ice, disaster nearly occurred. Vehicles were driving on the ice —and after seeing a pickup truck takeoff on a path on the lake —I had the bright idea to take some trusting passengers for a ride on the lake in my nearly new Pontiac on the same path as the truck. There was Grandmother Flossie and Aunt Elsie in the back seat and a passenger beside me. But after following the beaten path on the lake my car broke through the ice… fortunately just a short distance from shore, hence only the front edge of my car was submerged. I think of this as one of the luckiest days of my life as it could have happened in deep water.

While visiting this cottage my grandmother and Aunt Elsie one day offered me for $10 only, a beautiful patch work quilt that they had been labouring over for many hours. I was in my early 20's and thought what do I need a quilt for? In later years, I realized this was a big mistake not realizing at the time this would be a cherished keepsake item reminding me of my dear loving relatives. I believe the quilt went to my mother.

One early summer day, Grandad at age 86, was making concrete steps on a slope leading into the cottage by the highway… when he slipped and fell knocking his head. Groggy and in pain he had to continue as the concrete in the mixer was hardening quickly. This fall caused some amnesia and shortly after Alzheimer's. He was bed ridden in a hospital bed at the ecotage for just a week. It looked like the end of the road was imminent. Grandma suggested I, his favourite grandson, should have a last drink with him. See my poem below. In the hospital he could not recognize me and others and passed away after a short stay. He was my hero —I still admire his toughness, his poetic talent and his kindness. (Unfortunately the antique six gun revolver which he gave me was stolen when I was away in England.) But I have something more valuable—I am happy to have the genes of my mother and grandfather Tom.

Jack Stanquits, the husband of my Aunt Bertha, was very proud of the boat he gifted to my grandparents for their use at the cottage by the highway. The boat It was unusual to put it mildly: the size of a rowboat with a roof that made it dangerously unbalanced and hence very tippy, painted in several loud colours and with lights and reflectors on both sides. Unfortunately it never got used and was later filled with earth and graced the garden as a flower bed. Se more on Uncle Jack in Chapter 16.

My dear Grandmother Flossie died a decade later in Detroit at age 94 from Pernicious Anemia about the same final age as her daughters Aunt Della, Aunt Bertha and Aunt Alice. She always walked tall and straight and was a perfect example of a caring person, loving and helping all around her—and never a bad word to say about anyone.. I was the executor of her remaining estate and for my efforts awarded myself a $1 fee.

My dear mother, Mama, the other sister, passed away at age 69 from angina of the heart in spite of a healthy life— many years before my grandmother died. Mama at age 69 looked about 30 years younger and had male Italian dancing friends in their early forties. My mother was told her teeth were infected and had to be all extracted. She rejected the advice. She had perfect teeth with not a single cavity. My father was also a loving caring person, in spite of his heavy drinking and smoking faults. Every day he had to make a trip to the famous Brunswick House-on Bloor Street to drink beer with his male friends. He was working but meanwhile my dear mother had to clean houses and take in sewing to make ends meet. The heavy drinking and smoking had him in their evil grasp—he was in the hospital with a broken hip when he passed away from pneumonia, as often happens, at age 69— just a year after my mother, as also often happens in married couples. My father, Daddy, had a serios operation in Toronto where they removed about 2/3 of his stomach. In his will he left all his savings, about 1500 dollars, to my daughter Melanie. Mama was overjoyed with young Melanie so his bequest to Melanie helped to relieve my father's conscience somewhat as he felt guilty about his sometimes abuse to Mamma. With interest over a decade the 1500 dollars doubled and more than paid for Melanie's first year at York University.

My dear mother in her will left a cottage property on Eagle Lake near Shangri-La to me and my two brothers Wellwood and Maurice. Maurice although never rich in money but always rich in generosity— sold his share of the property to me very cheaply. I arranged for sale of the property as it was not practical to have a cottage near Kingston and so far from Toronto, which required a boat house near the highway and a power boat to get to the cottage. I distributed a third share to Wellwood's boys, Rod and Tod, as Wellwood had passed away at an early age of 44 due to too much drinking, smoking and poor diet. The day I retired from AECL, Maurice passed away from HIV at age 62 in 1992. Princess Diane had visited him and other HIV patients at Casey House in Toronto. Now in 2018 reasonable priced drugs for HIV save lives. or prolong life. This ended the happy Eagle Lake adventures and the large celebrations, but the happy memories remain. Now in addition to my three children and four grandchildren I am happy to have one close relative, a lovely cousin Donna Mae Lewis,her husband Gary and son Ryan in Edmonton.

I was thinking recently: If I have a new friend I am tempted to say, "Are you sure you want to be my friend,? as my friends and relatives all end up dying on me?" Actually, I keep making new friends. It's a blessing. Another thing to be grateful for.

# 4

# EXTRA CURRICULAR ACTIVITIES BEFORE MARRIAGE

ON RETURN TO CANADA FROM MY TWO YEAR ATHLONE FELLOWSHIP AT the Harwell Research Center near Oxford, and one year employment in the English Electric nuclear department— I had offers of employment with the General Electric Company in Peterborough Ontario and the Atomic Energy of Canada in Deep River in northern Ontario. But I decided to take the Atomic Energy Canada Limited (AECL) offer as there was the more promise of long term work in my chosen field nuclear power.

Deep River was a small isolated town, way north of Ottawa with few amenities, and the home of the AECL research establishment with its research reactors. As you could imagine the liquor store was very popular. But also very cold in the winter, e.g., cars would not start in the sometimes minus 40 degrees Celsius winter mornings— and lots of black flies in the summer. However, the Ottawa River was nearby and everyone was friendly and knew each other. There were two residences for single AECL employees, male and female. As luck would have it I was placed in the female wing as the male wing was filled.

I spent a lot of time with an English couple who had arrived recently from England, John and Kate. We were a happy threesome: it is not often in life you meet people who are a perfect fit in personality. John was an engineer and one day I recall he had a terrible worry that he had left something out of a design he had worked on just before leaving for Canada. I have had a similar experience remembering even months later of some possible serious omission. It is like after leaving your home you remember you have forgotten something —then with concentration it comes to you. The mind is a miracle.

There were a lot of single males and females in residence at Deep River at this time—so we had many parties, sing songs, debates, etc. And I played the guitar and sang badly I believe. When I first arrived non of the abundant ladies interested me —but strangely after a year in this isolation all were looking good. One good friend was Nanci, a pretty vivacious young lady— the nutritionist at our cafeteria who I dated several times even after she moved to Montreal.

On one occasion on way back from Toronto to Deep River I had two female passengers who both had some interest in me—an argument soon started about who was to sit next to me in the front seat. My negotiating skills didn't help as I was a poor negotiator. Ah! the good old days when the beauties were most prevalent— but now at 88 it is: "Were have all the good girls gone?...long time ago. When will they return?"

During the winter in the bitter north there where a few driving mishaps: On our way to Toronto with the car loaded with shopper hungry females —on a steep downhill with a big drop off one side a huge truck right in front of our startled eyes made a 360 degree turn on the slippery road. On a bitter cold late winter night, after dropping off my date many miles outside Deep River my car became stuck in the unploughed road—but a good Samaritan offered to push me out with his car— but unfortunately our bumpers became hopelessly locked together for over an hour. Later, on returning on another bitter cold night from a date with the same lady, this time in a snowstorm— I made a wrong turn on a curved road and ended up stuck in deep snow overnight: I was afraid to run the engine to keep warm since the tail pipe might be plugged. Then on a return to Deep River from Toronto one winter day I ended up in the ditch again, but this time the very first vehicle to pass shortly after was a tow truck. Just remember, good and bad luck in the long term should normally balance out, but if you are a runner good luck is more frequent the harder and more consistent you train.

After a year at Deep River, I hated to leave all my many friends. And I still cherish the engraved mug they gave me with 40 engraved names— when they sent me on my way to new adventures in Toronto.

While working at Power Projects Atomic Energy Canada Ltd (AECL) at the Ontario Hydro Manby Center near KIpling and Queensway in west Toronto— I lived in an apartment on George Street near Varsity Stadium. My family were also living and working in the area. These were days mostly filled with work it seems and no running. Since my operation in England, during my Athlone Fellowship tenure, for a testicle hydrocele (fluid on the testicle) — from one too many accidental kicks in the scrotum— I stopped running for about 30 years fearing the problem would reoccur. But I believed in some exercise every day. This usually involved slalom water skiing or snow skiing, tennis, swimming in the summer, dancing, lots of walking and 50 pushups daily. Somehow, I had a good amount of muscle—a Tarzan look. In those days There was no concentration on a healthy diet, never discussed in my family—the importance of a healthy diet came when I started back running. I recall at about age 55 before I started running again —having a V02max test on a treadmill and the result was: I was among the top 2% males in fitness in Canada.

I had an engineer friend Bill Casey, slim and slightly weird, who worked at Power Projects as well and who lived near my apartment. But my mother liked him so that tells you about something about his character. In the summers there would be many trips with him, Ernie Mills, and others to Muskoka a great tourist area in between Sudbury up north and Toronto with its many lakes and resorts. There were many trips with "Casey", as he was called, to Lake Rosseau in the summer for water skiing. Windermere Lodge where we lodged was very high on a hill and over looked the glistening lake providing a superb view. The balcony looming high over the peaceful lake at sunset was the idyllic place for a gin and tonic or two after a hard day of exhilarating slalom skiing. One day Casey towed me on one ski about 10 miles to Bala. On other unforgettable day I towed his boat behind my car up the winding hill to the lodge only to realize too late that there was no parking, and the gravel road had been recently tarred. I had to back the boat and trailer *backwards* down this winding recently tarred- steep road— and

I was not used to towing or parking boat trailers. I nearly aged a year in 20 excruciating minutes.

Usually, it would be a competition to see who would return to Toronto the quickest from Windermere Lodge or Cleveland's House. Casey had some racing blood in him as he used to compete in motor cycle races. And I had a likeness to fast driving in those young and foolish days and also a likeness for fast women (just jesting), but these were the days of new cars and tailor-made suits, abundant females if one desired, and consequently saving little money.

On a fast- competitive return to Toronto a highway policeman stopped me one late afternoon and claimed I had "forced him off the road." I could not recall doing this— but I was most likely way over the speed limit—so he stopped about 10 cars behind and questioned every driver. Finally leaving me to last he said, "You were the one." and handed me a speeding ticket. While he was doing his questioning behind me I had thrown some unopened beers in the woods as he might not understand that I had not been drinking. but the car behind reported this — the policeman said, "Go and get those beers and put them in your trunk."

Casey was a man of some bizarre experiences such as: One dark night on Lake Rosseau while travelling in his boat he went over the Cleveland House ski jump which was about six- foot- high on the high end. But he and his boat survived the shock. At a pub near beautiful Lake Rosseau he got in a fight with a man with a hook on one arm. He lived in a big house by himself after his dear brother died. In the winter he closed off all rooms except two. The gas company couldn't figure out why his heating bill was so low. On one occasion Casey and I left Windermere House in his boat to go to Bala for alcoholic supplies and on the way back we encountered some young lively Bikini ladies in a house boat. We were invited aboard with our supplies. After a few hours we had to return to Bala to replace the supplies, but with no tempting stops on the way back. There was dancing at Bala and even Louie Armstrong singing on one occasion.

In 1962 I joined the Timothy Eaton Memorial Church Trident Club; it consisted of about 750 young single people above age 30, and mostly women. However, there was only two which really caught my eye. A year later I became president of the club which held many charity functions and weekly dances. I became best friends with Ernie Mills a short man with a good sense of humour and a big heart. Ernie was president of the club the year before me. Ernie was a true friend who would come quickly to the rescue in time of need. In the winter Ernie and I and other friends would ski on weekends at Collingwood getting up at five in the morning. And one week in January the coldest time of year we would ski at Mount Tremblant in Quebec or even go up for the weekend and drive home late at night after a long day of skiing. The late Anne Primeau, also an AECL librarian employee whose father, Joe Primeau, was one of the Maple Leaf best players— was one of our female skiing companions, and a close friend. Her mother did not approve of me as I was not a catholic. Anne was the only person I have ever met who had two different coloured eyes. I sadly regret not reconnecting with her. I had her phone number for many years after I divorced. Then one sad day I leaned she had died from a stroke. Opportunity is fleeting, waiting for no man.

In the 1960's I enjoyed a week long ski holiday to Aspen Austria and Ste. Moritz Switzerland in a glorious month of March –the best time to enjoy the long runs in deep snow from the top of a mountain through small villages, loving the sights, the warming sun, the fresh air, comradery and the warm gluwine after skiing all day—it was all hard to beat. The skis I brought from home were too stiff for powdered snow, but more suitable for packed trails. Hence, the deep snow I found quite tiring.

Also, in the 1960's I had the good fortune to meet Shirley Gleason, a beautiful blond with a great personality from a good family. We became engaged, but somehow my heart wasn't into marriage although I was about 35. I think my son Tyler is having the same doubts about marriage even in his early forties. Shirley and I split up when she told me she planned to open a domestic placement company. It would have been in competition with my mother's domestic agency. So I took this as a slight on my mother and took perhaps the wrong slant on things. Shirley would have made the perfect wife.She took the break up very hard. One day while driving down Yonge Street I saw Shirley and her mother walking. I could see even from a quick glance and faraway that Shirley looked sad and forlorn. So, I am left with a guilty conscience. I gave her the engagement ring. I have a great marble chess set from her as a reminder as well. For a while I had many dates with Margaret Hargraves, separated from her husband. Margaret was a tall beautiful English lady, and a singer. One day I asked my Grandmother,"

I want to buy a new car and I want to take my friend Margaret to New York for a few days, which one do you think I should do." She said, "Do both." And we had a great time in my new car in New York City. I was on cloud nine. And Margaret, happy with her voluminous shopping items— sang all the way home. Then along came Kathi. She had a lot of good features: good with money, sexy, attractive, good sense of humor, a musician, and a legal secretary. After we married and then divorced I found a lot of these attributes worked against me. I thought it best to be friends as it makes life a lot simpler for family get togethers. I speak of Kathi and our exciting life in the country in Chapter 5.

## CANOEING

While in Deep River I made an eventful three-day canoe trip on a local river with three friends in two canoes. Due mainly to the frequent rapids there were a few mishaps and mistakes: Firstly, bringing too many heavy canned goods and beers. While astraddle of my canoe at the rear—I thought this would be a good way to deal with rapids pushing them away with my feet—but quickly ended up thrown out, and my partner paddling madly away up front not missing me. Then later our canoe tipped resulting in sleeping in wet sleeping bags. Later, getting lost on a trail while portaging with a 60-pound canoe and a backpack on my shoulders. Then my camera was dropped in the water.

One summer but very windy day, I took a male friend for a short trip in my Peterborough canoe in the nearby Ottawa River. The river was rougher than anticipated and we tipped. Sailboats flying by tried to throw us rope without success. We eventually pushed the canoe to shore, We were not wearing lifejackets. A big crowd had gathered onshore and were worried about our safety. They asked us, looking like two drowned rats, "How many of you were there. " A safe good question actually.

Over 30 years ago a young male friend talked me into a ride in my canoe in the nearby Credit River at Erindale Park. It was spring when the rains bring a huge increase in flow in the Credit and other rivers. We ended in a section with many rapids. The swift currents and a collision with some racks broke open the front of the canoe. But strangely the water didn't enter—with the canoe moving swiftly onwards.

This second bad experience of canoeing in bad weather taught me a tough lesson. Canoe only in favourable weather.My red canoe still hangs in my garage appreciating in value each year, but languishing there eager to conquer the waters but the captain is not adventurous.

# TOASTMASTERS

For about eight years I was an active member of the Toastmasters International club— with over 360,000 members worldwide, 16,000 clubs in over 140 countries. And all of us desiring to be better communicators and proficient at public speaking. At the highest level of Toastmasters contests, the contestants sometimes rehearsed their speech hundreds of times and without reference to notes. At the beginning my only experience was giving the valedictory address at Central Tech High School where my coach/ teacher/friend professor John Dodd had prepared me well and I performed by memory. Professor John Dodd told me he gave the valedictory address at his university and it was all in rhyming poetry.

In our local toastmaster's club, I progressed about as far as possible except for the last step: to form my own Toastmasters club. I could speak in front of large crowds as long as I was well prepared—having done my homework. Some short words on small cards would sometimes be used to help to recall the facts and their order.

I gave so many speeches at the Toastmasters that they filled two medium sized suitcases. I also gave speeches to young athletes at their awards banquets, and anti-aging speeches at Rotary Clubs and retirement homes. On one occasion I was even asked to give a Sunday sermon. I had to decline. After giving an inspirational speech to some public-school children, I me was asked a question by a cute long-haired student. I said, "What is your quotation my little lady." The problem was it was male student. I did him a favour as I learned —he had a haircut the next day.

At my work place, Atomic Energy Company Ltd, for many years I was in demand to give humorous (at least I thought so) roasting speeches to suspecting retirees, after gathering stories about their bad habits, foibles and mistakes from friends, co-workers and relatives. But I have found sometimes a long search was required to find the appropriate discrete joke or twist of words. After roasting a good friend of mine in a speech his wife asked me, "Are those tales really true?" No, but without the exaggeration there would be no humour.

I have passed on my running training knowledge and experiences to running groups, for example —a two hour presentation with slides on various training aspects to the Longboat Track club in Toronto —a speech at their yearly banquet of the huge track and field club in Albany New York and a symposium to their master athletes —and a demonstration on the various plyometrics drills and sprint drills for runners in Mississauga. At this demonstration my sprinter friend Agnes Kuczalska demonstrated all the movements with her admirable flexibility and superb form. She is in two action photos in my book, "*The Complete Guide to Running.*" Agnes is a great example of a positive person—always bubbling over with enthusiasm and energy. I suspect she is on this type of diet. Agnes is married to a friend and best master male sprinter in Canada, Kerry Smith.

Based on my speaking experience. I was even asked by a friend to be the main entertainment at his wedding. He supplied the unusual happenings that he and his future wife had experienced. All I had to do was add the humour. See the speech below.

## Milad and Agnes Wedding Banquet Speech

Honourable guests, Agnes and Milad, it is a great pleasure and an honour on this auspicious occasion to have been asked to say a few words. According to Winston Churchill there are only two things more difficult than making an after-dinner speech— (1) climbing a wall leaning away from you, or (2) kissing tall girl leaning away from you. And there is but one pleasure in life equal to that of being called on to make an after-dinner speech and that is being called on **not** to make one.

When I undertook this assignment, Milad said he would supply all the funny material— so I was bombarded by tons of material: Murphy's Laws, Newfie Jokes, quotations, etc. Also, my instructions were simple, (1) religious jokes only, (e.g., Moses had a hernia in carrying the 10 Stone Commandments down from the mountain —might have passed Milad censorship), (2) if sex is mentioned be discreet, (3) no mother- in- law jokes since the mother in law will be present. This gives limited leeway. So, it was necessary to consult the experts like Stephen Leacock who says: go down to the cellar and mix up half a gallon of myosis with a pint of hyperbole, and a half a pint of paresis. Not easy to find these items. But I was saved since all I had to do was mix in the funny experiences that Milad had in the past around his unusual house and his experiences with his lawyer. But here again the lawyer would be present. So, I had to omit any lawyer jokes. Fortunately for Agnes I had little humorous material about her. Or maybe she just has been lucky.

It has occurred to me now. Perhaps Milad didn't know that when people retire or leave the company I roast them. But in any case, it is too late now.

Humour is the kindly contemplation of the incongruities of life. In other words, the misfortune of others provides the best humour. As you will see Milad recently has suffered the slings and arrows and cudgels of outrageous misfortune, but he always comes up smiling and wiser in the end. And he is above all a good sport.

They say the only statement worth making is an overstatement. A half truth, like a half brick carries further than a whole brick. So, there is some hyperbole mixed into my talk. Actually, there is nothing more hilarious than the misfortunes of others. In this way Milad has given me and others many enjoyable side splitting hours. For example, when Milad purchased his present beautiful county property by the Niagara escarpment where he would build his dream house. He had taken all kinds of courses since graduation on engineering subjects—but none on structural integrity, drainage, sewage, and animal (coon) husbandry. Such courses would have served him well in his present situation. I should explain prior to building his dream on this property he temporarily resides in smaller house at he bottoms of a hill with the escarpment at his back. The temporary house is somehow become detached into three parts. Also, a swimming pool has started in his basement due to his downhill location. A coon family has found they like his fireplace and chimney for a home. And to make things worse the septic bed had backed up.

When he had septic tank overflow problems, no plumber would take on the job— they turned up their nose at it. Now Milad has learned 10 important lessons the hard way, and in desperation Milad pitched in himself. He was up to his ears in it if you get the drift. Finally, after long search he found a plumber in Toronto. Once again, he came up smiling through the thick and the thin. When Milad got the bill, he said this is more than I pay my lawyer. "It's more than I used to make as a lawyer too," said the plumber.

All these misadventures have resulted in Milad learning the following lessons on life survival.

1. Never buy a crooked house from a straight real estate agent
2. Never buy a straight house form a crooked real estate agent
3. Confucius say, "Man who sells house at bottom of hill, not on level."
4. Water runs downhill an sometimes into a basement.
5. Don't be blinded by beauty of surroundings or the real estate agent.
6. Expectations exceed realization.
7. Coons are friendly as long as they get your food and your warm fireplace.
8. Murphy's Laws are not funny
9. By all means buy a house —if you get good one you become happy, if you geta bad on you become a philosopher. As a result Milad has become not only a philosopher but also an expert on sewage control, a naturalist and an expert plumber.
10. When drawing up a budget lay aside one third for calamities.


But Mel's troubles were not over. Mel's lawyer told him, on his behalf he had worked out a great deal with his ex wife, taking a lot of patience and hours and also some of Milad's money. He boasted about achieving a settlement fair to both sides. Mel said, "Fair to both sides? What the "blank blank blank" do I need a lawyer for —a fair deal I could have done myself without the legal fees. I apologize since I suspect there are some lawyers present. There is a lot of hyperbole in my speech.

Milad recognized a man must pay the fiddler —but not the whole orchestra.

Milad now says he can tell Murphy something. Everything takes more time than estimated. And everything you decide to do costs more than first estimated. Also what is happening is often less important than what appears to be happening. It is best to jump on those that appear to be happening. Prevention exceeds maintenance.

I was asking Milad how he came to get his unusual name. He said in Egypt the boys are usually named Sphincter after the sphinxes and the girls are named Sue after the Suez Canal, but his parents wanted to be original. (I have to tell you it took me many hours to find an Egyptian joke.

Mel thinks of everything: In the design of his new home he wants provision for a wheel chair access on the stairs in case he is invalided. So, I suspect he may have seen the possible advantage of an efficient nurse Agnes around the home.

Agnes is versatile and good at everything and does everything except parachuting.

When Agnes was young she played the piano and did a solo at a school concert. When she payed Oh Canada one elderly lady in the audience burst into tears. When she played rock of Ages the same lady put her hands between her knees and cried,. "Oh God."

After the performance Agnes' mother said the lady, "You must be very patriotic, very religious and also very emotional. 'Not really," said the lady, — I am a music teacher." But I understand Agnes has improved greatly and now even plays the organ. Beside music—Agnes is adept at singing, nursing, super sales lady, cooking, etc. Ages spent many hours showing Mel various houses and tried to sell him many properties while Mel enjoyed every minute of it.

Another of Agnes' many talents—is golf. But she has been having trouble with her golf game lately She has been standing too close to the ball —after she hits it. Agnes lays in the low seventies. As for myself I prefer to play in warmer weather.

## Milad and Agnes's Speech Ending

A great speech contains a lot of shortening. So, I end here.

Enjoy your honeymoon. The wonderful thing about a honeymoon is that it makes you feel good enough to go back to work again, but unfortunately poor enough you have to.

We all want to make you honorary members of the 4H club— Humour, Health, Happiness and Harmony

Here's wishing them a life of bliss in their eventual dream house on the escarpment with the spectacular panoramic view.

Note: On the serious side for my memoir readers: I designed the dream 3400 square foot house for Mell for $1500, taking my 600 hours in my spare time for calculations and drawing three large sheets of details and plans. Unfortunately, after all this work and dreams of Mell and Agnes. Mell was laid off from AECL and the house was never built. But I still have the original drawings.

## WRITING

In my early 30's, I used to write a newsletter once or twice a month on the subject of health and fitness. I did this for a couple of years and had a large following of Canadian readers, not customers, as I didn't charge. After marriage I wrote several articles mostly on running training for the Masters National News in the USA also gratis since they (my best customer) were selling my running books and advertising them in large advertisements In their newspaper.

## WINTER SKIING ADVENTURES

In Canada we have a cold climate so it's a shame not to take advantage of the snow and ice. Besides it toughens you up. For many years while I was single, downhill skiing was my favourite sport accompanied by my best friend Ernie Mills a fun loving faithful friend and other great friends like Gene Yaremy, Anne Primeau, daughter of Joe Primeau, a distinguished Maple Leaf hockey player. Sadly, Ernie and Anne are deceased but never forgotten.

I recall some unusual happening on these frozen but exhilarating trails:

Up at 5am on Saturday winter mornings to ski at Collingwood about 20 miles north of Toronto. Smooth sailing usually, except caught in a snowstorm coming home one evening and completely snowed in for the night on the highway with two carloads of friends. Fortunately, we had some drinkable antifreeze with us. Some spent part of the night huddled in a cold school-house. So, it was either antifreeze or schoolhouse.

Only once injured when a lady in the chair in front of me fell out of her chair— fortunately we were not yet in the air— and while tangled up with her and our skis I suffered a sprained ankle. I drove 60 miles home with the largely swelled ankle which surprised the nurse in Toronto.

Every January, the coldest time of the year, but the cheapest accommodation, we would go to Mount Tremblant in Quebec for a week of skiing— or other times for a weekend driving about 300 miles home in the dark after the lifts closed.

We would often stay at the bed and breakfast, Auberge de Penguin, in Ste Jovite, Quebec. I remember arriving late one night with a group of friends, for some reason we couldn't stop laughing. I recall the owner of Auberge de Penguin watching the Montreal hockey team losing and his moaning, "La pauvre Canadienne." We would indulge in the local fare, like delicious tourtiere and poutine, either tasting twice as good after skiing all day. Also, why does alcohol taste so fantastic after skiing. Is that why people love snow skiing so much?

At Mount Tremblant ski resort mainly and also in Austria Switzerland I witnessed some unusual happenings:

Someone up stream of a steep long hill had lost a ski. It is travelling down the hill at about 60 miles per hour towards a ski class of 12 or more and the instructor. The ski rams into the leg of a female in the class doing a demonstration for the instructor.

A male skier has been injured and is strapped into a sleigh for safe transport to the bottom of the hill, by the ski patrol, but the situation was going to get worse for the injured skier. The ski patrol loses their grip on the sleigh and it hurtles at high speed down a steep side hill into the woods.

While skiing with a good friend Gene Yaremy flying over some huge moguls. We made many up and downs on the same hill but just one too many. Gene fell and suffered a bad broken leg requiring a steel pin in his leg and two weeks stay in the Quebec hospital.

On a trip to Austrian and Switzerland on my first outing a fellow Canadian went off the trail into some woods and the ski pole went into his eye. So, skiing has its ups and downs.

I also loved the slalom skiing in the hot summer at Lake Rosseau in Muskoka while staying at Cleveland's House with my friends. But there were no mishaps to report. I usually found I was proficient at anything involving the legs. Oh, happy days of yore when I was young and sometimes foolish. On my further recreational activities after marriage see also Chapter 13, on Karaoke, Hiking, and Coaching.

# 5

## MARRIED LIFE

AFTER OUR WEDDING IN DECEMBER 1966 WE LIVED TO AN APARTment in Port Credit by the Go Station tracks. I recall my father came to our apartment to celebrate the day Melanie was born. It was a happy occasion. We were proud of our beautiful daughter as were our grandparents on my mother's side. A year after Melanie was born, Kathi took a teaching position in Mississauga teaching secretarial skills, as she was an efficient legal secretary for many years. An attribute that may have gone against me in later years, while I continued at Atomic Energy Company Limited (AECL) at Sheridan Park as a section head design engineer.

The Port Credit apartment superintendent was Mrs. Gamble who appeared to be about 60 years old. In those early days I thought 60 was old, but not now at 89. She was a source of amusement for some time since she had had an encounter with the main furnace in the building and had lost her eyebrows and some of her hair. The funniest things are often at the expense of others. A calamity is humorous as long as it is not happening to you.

After a few years we moved to a semi-detached house on Shadeland Drive Mississauga. near Station Road. I built a patio using shale slabs found in the area. After we were blessed by the arrival of Curtis and Tyler, just 1.5 years apart, we were looking for a bigger home. We saw and loved a new house, and a huge backyard with a beautiful view overlooking a huge impressive marsh part of Lake Ontario— the Rattray Marsh in Cooksville, a southern part of Mississauga, close to Lake Ontario. The marsh was busy with wild life. The house was an open concept house two story design, 3000 square feet (not counting the basement) with a cathedral ceiling in the living and dining room, and a walk out basement. We enthusiastically placed a bid and went back to the real estate agent a week later to be told someone else bought the house. The agent should have gone back to us as first bidder, and we would have increased our bid. I suspect the agent probably sold it to friend or relative. We loved the house so much I decided to design one just like it. An engineer friend George Romanick had designed a bungalow house so I thought I could design this more complex two story open concept house in my spare time. I visited this above sold house many times taking measurements before the new tenants moved in. The compete plans and calculations to meet building codes took me over 700 hours in my spare time. The finished product was five complete drawings (which I still have), plans and elevations including electrical and plumbing, heating ducts, etc.

After a long search we found a beautiful 25-acre wooded lot on the Niagara escarpment between Acton and Milton Ontario near Highway 25—actually near Speyside a tiny village. The lot consisted of mature beech, fir, birch and maple trees. So, we put in an offer of $25,000 which was accepted, but then rejected. But the owner was unable by law to change his mind. The money for the land was nearly entirely from Kathi's sale of the small house in the east end of Toronto which she bought near Lake Ontario Beaches district when she was 17. She had made a smart move at a young age. I recall doing some renovations on her house before it was sold.

One side of the long country lot was for a future government road. If this ever happened our property would be valuable for selling lots to future home owners. We found a good builder from Burlington for the house on our new lot. It was a big thrill for me and Kathi to me see the house being built to my drafting plans, and we visited quite frequently during the building phase. Our builder claimed later he made only a few % on building our house. He had made a few mistakes but they were fixed up at his expense. For a couple of years, we lived without some frills, like curtains, to make ends meet for the mortgage and other expenses. I recall having a weekly allowance of about $25 for gasoline, etc. from the accountant and banker Kathi. On completion I loved coming home from work each day and surrounded by peaceful Mother Nature—it was good for the relieving stress and good for the soul.

The house had a walk-out basement—to accommodate this a lot of earth had to be excavated from the back by the contractor. Later Kathi and I dug a long ditch about 40 metres in length, and installed a weeping tile to take away any excess water from the back patio just outside the walk-out basement. And we spent many enjoyable hours cleaning up the surrounding bush. When Kathi wasn't working which was most of the time she had a project of clearing an area to make a future pond. Since this was a country home a well was dug for water and of course there was a septic bed provided also by the builder.

Curtis and Tyler had a great time on our lot climbing too high in big trees and roaming around in the woods. Melanie made some female friends in the friendly neighbourhood. And Kathi and I made friends with some neighbours. In the spring we tapped maple trees for the sap, and in a large cauldron boiled the sap to reduce it to maple syrup. However, life wasn't all idyllic since our neighbour on our right side, Mr. and Mrs. Comfort, insisted on parking is large trailer on our property although he had 10 acres of their own. Very odd unneighbourly behavior. It is difficult to understand some people. A court case would have been expensive and stressful so we tolerated their bizarre behavior It didn't bother me as much as Kathi. Even after I surveyed his side of the property they continued to park on our property..

Two years after we move to the country we bought a trailer camper suitable for sleeping five of us—and towed it on a family trip to visit Kathi's relatives in Los Angeles. Before leaving I was told the station wagon car needed major engine repairs and would not make the trip. But it was reliable there and back through the United State. But the trip from Los Vagus was through a torrid desert without air conditioning.

En route one day on making a slow 90 degree turn...yler only about two years and fell out of his chair and out the unlocked door onto the highway. The people in the car behind were shocked as we were. Fortunately, he was very resilient as a rubber ball and not injured, but he had been eating a hot dog and frightened us since he looked like he had gum damage. We learned to keep doors locked in future.

Then it was time for Curtis to have some excitement on our trip. In Los Angeles on our trailer trip we attended a big pool party at night in honour of our visit. Curtis about three years old, walking on the crowded pool deck in the dark …fell into the pool. Fortunately, I was there to pull him out. We returned home safely without further mishap. The trailer was a happy playground for the children many years. One year all the neighbors brought their trailers for a night corn roast. It was a beautiful sight to see all the many trailers lit up under the stars, and around a blazing fire. It was a happy- carefree- gypsy experience.

A few years later when Tyler was older Kathi, while disgruntled about something, backed up the car, knocking him underneath. Fortunately, I was able to pull him out in time from under the moving car. Later he had a car door nearly close partly on his hand. Again, he was blessed with no injury.

One sweltering hot summer day after we had been clearing brush for several hours our neighbour Frank came with a tray of alcoholic beverages —they really hit the spot as alcohol can do when one is dehydrated.. One winter day I invited about eight friends from work to visit and since the property was huge and new to me, we got lost for a short time. But we headed for civilization, the sounds of a barking dog.

One memorable I took my three children to the Exhibition in Toronto in September. After a whole day of exhibits and mostly rides and food, when we were tired and ready to leave—they started complaining about no stuffed animal to take home. I had no money left, just a 25 cent coin. There was a stand where one could win a huge stuffed anima for a near impossible coin toss—.the coin had to travel a large distance land in a small spot and not bounce away, the usual problem. I figured intuitively the coin had to travel in huge semicircle to say put. Soon somehow I did the impossible— with my last coin we had a huge blue and white bear up to my belly button to shut them up.

One summer day Kathi and I attended an auction in Burlington—a sale of used tractors. I got a bit carried away with all of these seemingly good bargains. We could start them up but not run them, so little did I know of any major problems. To help clean up our huge 25 acre wooded property I purchased a large diesel tractor with an automatic front loader, and also a smaller gasoline tractor with a fixed loader. (Later one of these tractors was a factor in a major calamity as discussed later.) I immediately found that both tractors had no brakes, hence needed brake repair. This posed a problem since it required driving them about 20 miles to home over some hilly sections. My neighbour Frank volunteered to drive the large tractor leaving inexperienced me for the smaller tractor, I believe the experience added a few months to my life. Later I had to drive the larger tractor to a garage between 8 or 10 miles away for the brake repair. I asked the garage mechanic what route to take to avoid any large hills. Following his "good" advice I came to top of a huge hill leading sharply down into a village. This heavy tractor had plenty of momentum. With my hair flying behind me, heart pumping, and Kathi in the car behind, very concerned, I sped down this steep hill into the village—ready to jump off at any moment if necessary. But fortunately, no one impeded my rapid progress.

Then the smaller tractor was an instrument in a major calamity. One day my neighbour across the road volunteered and insisted to repair my small tractor. He may have been drinking beforehand. Maybe he wanted to make amends for damaging this tractor in driving it recklessly through the woods one afternoon. He and I towed it up the road about a half mile and then he went back in his car to his home right across from my home— to get some tools. Shortly after, I heard a large explosion. Extremely worried I raced back as my children had been playing on the road when we left. I immediately saw that his car, now in the ditch, had collided with an oncoming car of a new neighbour. While I was looking into my unconscious neighbour, some spectators pulled the unconscious female driver from her car. She and her husband had just moved into this area just a few days before. This country gravel road had many small hills easily obscuring oncoming traffic, and perhaps one of them or both had not kept to the right side of the road. Sadly, the female neighbour died the same day. No charges were laid.

Speaking of neighbours. One day another neighbour came to my driveway. He was showing us his prized large set of tools in the trunk of his car. Kathi asked, "What is your favourite tool? He immediately responded," I would be afraid to tell you."

One sunny day I was moving rocks with the large diesel tractor on a rather steep hillside. Suddenly, the tractor tipped over, but I was able to jump clear. Shaken up I went back to the house, heart still pounding and l breathing hard, telling of the mishap. Kathi's first words were, "Is the tractor Ok? But I got some revenge later when a medium sized tree I was felling…dropped and bounced on the hood of her sports car—quite accidently I assure you. Another happy day our good neighbours delivered gratis an old upright piano in perfect condition right to our home. So, we had quite a few sing songs around the piano played by ear by Kathi.

I loved the country living and was proud of our house and property. Our wooded lot was the perfect setting for relaxing after work. We had a wooden mailbox on which I carved the names of all the family. It was very invigorating working on improving the lot at all times of the year. And the children were happy in this environment. For example In the winter they would jump from a low roof into the deep snow. The boys loved climbing the tall tress. But unfortunately, Kathi tired of the country living and marriage after 11 years. We were not getting along as she had the habit of going off by herself on weekends when I was available to look after the children. She wanted an open marriage— meaning we could carry on married but we could have other partners. This was not for me. My lawyer told me to get custody of the children, I would need a divorce. So, I told her I wanted a divorce which infuriated her. I had a family law lawyer, one of the best in Toronto, to help obtain custody of the children. It all came to a head one fine summer day: I went to the neighbours to pick up the children, as Kathi was also working at the time—and was told Kathi had already picked up the children. At home, as I entered, my heart went into a high beat at the sight of the inside … I was shocked to see the house was entirely cleaned out of furniture except for the refrigerator and stove— maybe too heavy or provided in her new house. But ironically, Kathi's expensive/ cherished gold bracelet had been left behind in her haste to leave before I arrived home. I thought this is social justice, at least, for all the furniture she pilfered. About 35 years later I thought it best to forgive and try to forget —so I returned the precious bracelet. Obviously she was overjoyed.

Fortunately, I had a good clue where Kathi might have moved to. Near the likely location was a community park and I rationalized the children would eventually come out to the park to play, I waited a couple of hours—and eventually all three of them fortunately, about ages 5, 6, and 10, came out to play, and all without shoes. Fate was on my side. At home I phoned the police that I had the children, but was told they don't get involved in family disputes. The children told me later they were very distraught, stressed and shocked to be taken suddenly way from me, their friends, home, and their school.

The divorce involved the selling of our country home and the 25 acres for $175,000 in 1977. Now in 2018 this would sell for about $1.5 million or even more I suspect. However, our homes in the city have also greatly. I rented an apartment on Islington Avenue for myself and the children— near the 401 highways and overlooking the Weston golf course. It was not far away from Kathi's house. I learned years later to my chagrin Curtis and Tyler and friend would sometimes ride on top of the apartment elevator. No need to go to the Exhibition for the carnival rides. To help with care of the children part time I hired a pretty young English girl which the children were fond of. She was difficult to retain as she was not a permanent Canadian resident. I had to reject several female Canadian helpers from the government agency for various legitimate reasons.

In the winter the boys were involved in hockey; Curtis was six and a half and Tyler was an unsteady five-year-old. Some of the Italian boys on the team were two years older and much bigger than hesitant Tyler. Tyler was not an official member but allowed to train with the older team members. Of course, that hesitancy all changed a few years later when Tyler got his legs. At Ryerson he has a record of seven goals in one competition game. Later Curtis became captain of his team— no one on the team had scored for about five games… until he scored. The long cheering could be heard for miles away. In winter there were also some exciting times skiing in northern Ontario. The boys were particularly daring travelling at hair raising speeds straight down with minimum turns from top to bottom.

After a year of wrangling and legal letters back and forth my lawyer made a big mistake one day in front of a new trainee lawyer. He said in front of me and the trainee: "Mr. Fee has a 50% chance of getting custody," where a year before he had told me I had a 75% chance. Up to this time I had spent about $25,000 (this was in the 1970's when everything was much cheaper than today in 2018). Nothing concrete had been accomplished by my lawyer, just phone calls and letters back and forth. A pure waste of money. Kathi was a legal secretary with lots of legal experience so she carried on without a lawyer. I decided to fire my lawyer; I had learned my lesson about lawyers the hard way. I thought if I carried on I would have little money for a down payment on a new home—hence, we decided we would have the children alternately one year at a time. This worked out for two years but the education authorities thought it best to have them at one school and one parent. I agreed with joint custody, but let them stay with Kathi and in particular Melanie would be better off with a mother. Another deciding factor in this big decision was that I had met Shirley Stevenson, the tall beautiful blond school teacher and we were thinking seriously of getting married but she had two children and I had three, so five was just too big to handle.

When the children moved in with Kathi it was the beginning of many frequent trips to the courts to fight increasingly higher maintenance requests from Kathi. In the end it was high enough for her to quit work. To avoid exorbitant legal costs, I spent a lot of time in the York University law library preparing affidavits, etc. for my divorce and subsequently for the higher maintenance requests. On one occasion in court I was disputing that bonus was not salary. My divorce judgement was that I would pay a fixed percentage of my **salary** for maintenance. At years end AECL was giving a bonus for good work. I contended that bonus was not salary ("fixed payment at regular intervals"). The judge asked, " Where did you get your definition of salary." I said, "From the dictionary." He said, " I am the dictionary here." I was taken aback by this affront. Technically I was correct. But, I learned from several bad experiences that the judge is always right.

Kathi was an expert at these court sessions. Always dressing appropriately, it seemed for these sessions and usually appearing in a dowdy old overcoat; the coat had poverty written all over it but not in letters. On another occasion in the judge's chambers. The judge said to Kathi," I am giving you $1200 a month." For a second or two I was ecstatic— but then I realized it was *my* money he was giving her not *his*. Fortunately, I could see the humour in these situations. This arrangement of the children— a year at a time with Kathi and me was not the ideal situation for education and sports teams.. One year when Tyler was scoring a lot of goals on his elite soccer team In Mississauga at about age seven the coach came and asked for return of his uniform. According to the coach Tyler was off the team for not passing the ball. On his previous team Tyler while staying with Kathi in east Toronto,he was allowed to take the ball all the way from one end to the other without passing. So maybe he had acquired a bad habit. But the new coach should have corrected that habit. But I strongly suspect newcomer Tyler was not popular with the other long established parents. Politics was rearing its ugly head.

About 1980 I had the good fortune to meet Shirley Stevenson—an attractive, tall, blond, school teacher—at a singles dance. I asked for her phone number but was rejected. Later, she had a delayed reaction and searched for me, making enquiries about Earl Lee, which didn't help. But, after meeting up and dating for a couple of years we had plans to marry. Shirley's children Brent and Sherry were about the same age as mine—so during the 10 years as Shirley's partner, with our five children we had many enjoyable ventures, including mainly to the Muskoka's in Northern Ontario. Brent was a hard worker and even when less than 16 had often two or three part time jobs at a time —and in his teens started a strong interest in buying and selling used cars at a profit. Sherry was an exceptional athlete in gymnastics and track and field —and even had a high jump pit and standards and a gymnastics beam in the basement for constant practice. Now as an adult Brent is continuing in the car buying and selling in his spare time —while Sherry is a Crossfit athlete and impressive at weight lifting, and with husband Jan has two children excelling in (you guessed it) gymnastics. In her early 70's Shirley passed away from ---pancreatic cancer—a difficult disease to defeat. I am happy to remain in close contact with Sherry and Brent and their families.

Curtis and Tyler while living with Kathi lacked a father's daily influence— and were up to pranks with fire crackers, etc. at their public school. A neighbor told me he saw them one day hanging and travelling along my 2nd story eves troughs. But both were excelling in athletics: soccer, hockey and track and field. I enrolled them in the North York Track and Field club. For several years I drove Tyler and Curtis for training at York U: about 50 km to pick them up, then 25 km to York U, and back 25km to Kathi's home, and 50 km to my home—about 150 km total. This also resulted in a week each year of training camp at Florida usually and one year at San Diego in the USA. And I was pleased to accompany them as parent or as an official of the North York Track Club.

Tyler at age 13 was first in Ontario in the 400m in 55 seconds. But his best event was the 800m. I recall him telling Curtis before a 800m race, "I am going to win this race for you." Another time Tyler was in 3rd position with about 50m to the finish —two tall runners probably older were running abreast in front of him. He ran into the small space between them, pushing them aside to come in first. Fortunately, not disqualified. Tyler had sufficient talent in hockey (e,.g., 7 goals in one league one game at Ryerson)—to win a scholarship in hockey to a USA university, but lacked interest in scholarly pursuits, although intelligent. And also, in his teens won a few cross-country races in fields of about 150. As an adult Tyler often says, "You only live once." So now after over 40 years I am beginning to suspect Tyler may be an atheist.

Curtis at age 14, won a 10K race for 14 year old's and under in just over 41 min with little training— and also excelled in the 3000m—and in the javelin had a personal best of 26.6m at about the same age. In a soccer game at the sidelines he would throw in the ball between his feet in a backwards flip. As an adult he now has an exceptional standing vertical jump of over a metre. This suggests he has lot of fast twitch muscle. Perhaps that is why he is a good sprinter, Both Curtis and Tyler of muscular builds and near six feet tall have the genes and ability to excel in master's track and field if they so desired.

Melanie raised her three boys, James, Alex, and Andrew, on her own for about two decades when separated from her husband, who offered no support.

After a failed marriage, life must go on. But I remain happy with good memories and the loving relationship with my three children and four grandchildren.

After the children moved in permanently with Kathi, in 1978 I purchased a new house on Sir John's Homestead, where I presently for 39 years still reside, which was ideally just five minutes away from my work at Atomic Energy of Canada at Sheridan Park, Mississauga. With a $150 down payment I secured the largest lot of over 100 homes in Sir John's Homestead and made a choice out of five different designs. The house was built in 1978 and 1979. The house cost $90,000 initially, but in 2018 it was valued at over a million dollars, partly because of the ideal/convenient location and traffic free streets—actually somewhat less value than a lot of my neighbours who have done extensive interior renovations. Instead of renovations I have taken many trips to the USA and around the world to compete internationally—or you might say I invested more in longevity rather than luxury. I am one of the few in the neighbourhood living happily by myself. in 2014 the community home owners organization in my neighbourhood honoured me with a bench in a parkette down the street. The plaque says: 'In honor of Earl William Fee, resident, multi world record runner, and author." I have been blessed with the name "The Great Earl" for many years in the USA and sometimes in Canada, many Hall of Fame Awards, a photo of me on the cover of a 2006 booklet (the last issue) on World Masters Records, and a prestigious male World Masters Athletics award of the year in 2005. But, to be honoured by your neighbours and fellow man is indeed special.

# 6

# MY LANDLORD DAYS

## Landlord Adventure Number One

I DECIDED TO RENT MY HOUSE FOR A YEAR AFTER THE CHILDREN WENT permanently to Kathi's home. A real estate lady found what I thought was the ideal young couple from the USA with two young children. I liked that they were particular and wanted to paint some of the halls and rooms in off-white and other acceptable colours. But it was a bad choice of tenants. And I found later that the real estate lady was related to them, hence her choice was heavily biased.

One day, I arrived to do some minor repairs when they were out: I was in the basement replacing a light bulb when the infuriated husband came home and practically threw me out of "his home "—even though I had notified them I would be over.

They complained of all the windows frosting up in the winter which blackened the window sills; the wife blamed it on poor insulation in the walls. But I found out after they moved out —they had a humidifier in nearly every room for the children's "allergies". When they vacated I found a huge hole had been burnt in the living room rug. My insurance company suggested a patch up job, but I insisted and they fortunately agreed on new carpet in the living room and up the stairs. Also, the glass on the stove was broken. And one of my dressers had been taken away. And before I knew of these problems, I had recommended them to a colleague at my work who was renting his home. He told me that they caused about $2000 in damage. These problems were a learning experience resulting in my speedy departure from further renting.

## Landlord Adventure Number Two

To meet ever increasing maintenance payments for the children when they ended up permanently at Kathi's home in the East end of Toronto— I rented three spare rooms in my four-bedroom house. The children's maintenance eventually went up to $1200 a month. The good news about this was it made my ex-wife, Kathi very happy— she was able to quit work. Of my ten roomers at various times only four were satisfactory, and all were males except for one young lady. Most stayed for less than a year and none left any forwarding address. Two of my best roomers were teaching at the nearby University of Toronto Mississauga branch. I have changed the names of most of my roomers discussed below, but believe you me they are real characters.

While with the Toastmasters I gave a humorous speech about my rooming experiences. But below I give the more serious version.

Jacob was a congenial doctor from Israel, but without a licence to practice in Canada. His room soon had many small mountains of professional articles stacked on furniture and the floor. He was recommended by a close friend — but contrary to the management (me) he persisted to smoke amongst these piles of paper. Also, he didn't want the screen on his window which would have prevented insects entering the room. And he had the healthy? habit in the bathroom sink of inhaling and discharging salt water through his nasal passages which infuriated Damion, (an accountant), another roomer.

Damion asked to store "a few things" in my garage when he moved in—this took about one quarter of the garage space. He treated this space as his cottage which he visited quite frequently. Darion took to playing his radio extra loud to annoy his neighbour Jacob mostly when I was not around to complain. Darion and Jacob argued frequently. I came home from a holiday to find food jam was all over the kitchen ceiling. They had

had a jamboree physical argument. I was mulling over in my mind which one to discharge. In the meantime, one winter 's day they jousted outside in the driveway— one with a shovel and the other with an ice scraper. The resulting court case was thrown out by the judge as there was no witness to the jousting and the resulting torn coat. I decided Jacob was slightly more serious trouble than Darion so gave Jacob his short notice. A few months later Darion was discharged too.

Brad was a tall young likeable construction worker. He even built for me some shelves in my basement without payment. It was an amazing operation as he worked around the piles of junk already in the room. Brad went to an auction and he couldn't resist some of the big bargains —a chesterfield and matching chair, an end table and a large rug. When I came home, his furniture was in my family room and mine was in the basement. But, the last straw occurred one winter night when I was out and he had his drinking buddies over for a party. They had the fireplace going merrily—but when the wood ran out they had the bright ideas to break up one of my tables, a gift from my departed mother. It was a case of the show must go on at all costs. See my poem "The Party" in Chapter 17, My Books, which was inspired by the above incident. I gave him notice to leave, but he was long overdue with his rent. I have had in my garage now for about 20 years a souvenir left by Brad, a long iron pipe about 12 feet long —too long to move or put in the garbage.

Franklin another short-term roomer and turned out to be a fraudster (I learned too late) setting up a computer sales company in Mississauga. I should have suspected in the beginning as when he moved in, he said that his suitcase had been stolen. But he was the superb actor; he could have won an Oscar with his believable well-worn stories. I even went with him to two warehouses for rent which he was considering to store his incoming computers shipments. I realized later it was all an act to convince me of his validity. He also had a good reference (that I spoke to) at a bank in the USA most likely an associate in crime. I first bought a computer from him that never arrived. And invested about $10,000 in his company for a "quick return on investment deal". Always acting as a friend, and I learned later he had hoodwinked many in the US and Canada. He was turned in by a lady he was engaged to, who became suspicious of all his many claims and schemes. Some of my own investigations also helped convict him. It had a happy ending for me since the money I lost I earned back many times over working for a friend Robert Chun as a nuclear consultant with Ontario Hydro, after I retired— a position I sought to make up for the monetary loss. In the process the extra money on top of my pension meant my maintenance for the children increased in direct proportion. Making the recipients very happy. And also, as a result of this employment— I made several good friends as well. Now I have become very philosophical. I can't trust myself so why should I trust anyone.

Afgi (my unaffectionate name) for a young artist from Afghanistan who in the beginning seemed a quiet and reasonable type. In his initial interview he said he had no car, but the very next day he has a car. So, I could see storm clouds coming. Although I was friendly with him he soon took exception to the time I spent conversing with two U of T professional type roomers whom I had more in common. He started messing with other's food and started scratching the furniture and garage doors. I reported him to the police who said: "You have to catch him doing it." After I insisted, a constable went to his work to speak to him. Afgi said, "If I lose my job I will kill you." Then he refused to move out. I expected a physical problem and even resorted to hiding a baseball bat for possible protection. It was a happy celebration day when Afgi eventually left my humble abode. Not long after he left my home the police came to ask where he had moved to as he had been acting up again. But not a single roomer ever left a forwarding address. It was as if everyone was running away from something the law, some debt, some past problem, or an ex wife.

Charles was a friendly supervisor that I had worked for at Atomic Energy Company Limited AECL for a couple of years which gave him some leeway in our relationship. He came with a lot of unexpected baggage resulting from his divorce—his antique car in the garage which he worked on noisily on Sunday mornings —a trailer and a canoe on the lawn and anther car in the driveway, He even talked of buying another car. I said, "Where do we put it," as I had my car as well. (On looking back, I was not a good neighbour.) This kind of nonsense would not be permitted nowadays. (I am one of the few original owners since 1979 in this respectable Sir Johns Homestead.) Now getting back to Charles who had two lady friends named Sheila —this caused considerable confusion when I passed on phone messages to him from these Sheila's. One day after a short holiday I found his huge wet tent drying out on the living room carpet. Unfortunately, his congenial personality did not make up for all his baggage. And I suspect the neighbours did not shed a tear on his departure to more spacious "digs".

Kenneth, a young fit man, lived exclusively on protein powders and surprisingly looked surprisingly healthy. He left owing for two months rent. I had two not- sufficient- funds- cheques from him. he bank had notified me by mail of one rubber cheque but he had intercepted this notification. On departure he left me with his huge water bed for payment which I never used. I spoke to his parents, but they were no help. I came home after work one day and found he had moved my deceased brothers 120 acrylic paintings from the living room to the basement. I realized much later, in view of his crooked tendencies, it was quite likely he had helped himself to one or more paintings in the moving process.

Other tenants were normal, but in the minority, and do not make for colourful description. Such was my second adventure as a landlord. It appears I was not a good judge of character. Usually, I did not bother with references. But when I bothered with references they back fired on me—it would have been necessary to get references on the reference. I learned from these and other experiences that at least 1 in 5 people are crooked. At income tax time the number goes way up. Now I have learned: to trust naught and hence lose naught. Farewell roomers and tenants, you have aged me but hardened me to life's vicissitudes.

My residing in Sir Johns Homestead since 1979, as one of the very first in the area, involved some interesting facts and adventures. About a year before 1979, I put down a $150 deposit for my choice of house design and lot (I chose the biggest one in the area), The year I moved into my house there was the famous Mississauga rail disaster. The 33rd. car of a 106 CPR car freight train on November 10, 1979 had an improperly lubricated bearing which caused a wheel set (two wheels and an axle) to fall off resulting in all the cars behind to derail, resulting in a huge explosion and propane cars to burst into flame (a fireball a mile high) and spilling many chemicals. The main concern was a leaking chlorine tank car resulting in evacuation of over 200,000 Mississauga residents for two weeks in the west and north end.of Mississauga. Other residents were allowed to stay but not enter or leave for several days. I was not able to return to my house for a few days and this resulted happily in the beginning of serious relationship for nearly 10 years with the tall beautiful Shirley Stevenson, a school teacher in Brampton. I saved my friend Ken Cooke's life, since he was suffering of thirst and unable to leave the house for several days --by telling him where he could find some liquor to quench his bad habit.

During the past 39 years at Sir John's Homestead there were also the following happenings in the about 30 homes in an immediate area out of the about 104 homes in secluded Sir Johns Homestead: Firstly, besides the Mississauga rail disaster November 10 1979 described above, there was the following excitement. Eight neighbours in my immediate district in Sir John's Homestead have died, including some close friends. Three non- resident dead bodies were found, one in nearby Sawmill Creek area and two in a nearby Credit River area. Many years ago, I witnessed a huge fire in the garage of a home immediately across the street which destroyed about 25% of the house and part of the house adjacent. Two houses away an innocent mother and a bad acting 17-year-old son lived— one day the son was tied to a chair and questioned while some drug dealers searched for drugs and money. The police were called and the drug dealers were apprehended on trying to escape. Another day, I arrived home to find about 10 police cars in the area. There had been some break-ins in two nearby homes and the police were looking with guns drawn from house to house for the two culprits. Also, in early days although this is a very respectable neighbourhood there were many break-ins, in cars and garages..

The good news the above is all in the past and the Sir John's Homestead Homeowners, an organization that looks after maintaining the quality of the neighbourhood have honoured me in 2014 me with a bench in a parkette down the street. It says, "In honor of Earl Fee, resident, world record holder and author." As far as Abe Lincoln and I are concerned, there is nothing more satisfying than to be recognized by your fellow man.

In later years at work I must have become wiser after my landlord days — since at work I was even asked to interview engineer applicants for full time employment at AECL. Normally there would be about 50 applicants for one or two positions. And the ones chosen turned out to be excellent employees. During one interview with an aspiring candidate engineer with several degrees including a doctorate degree— I said, "You are over- qualified for the position. The job is not complicated enough for you." Quickly he said, "I can make it complicated."

I have learned a lot in the past now 89 years and particularly during my landlord days. Such as—**Never trust:** a sure thing— a person too eager to help you (run away in this case)— a person without a shirt who wants to give you a shirt— a fat dietician or a skinny chef— a man named Doc—and definitely never trust a naked woman. And also ask yourself: can I trust myself.

# 7

# INITIAL WORKING YEARS

IT WAS A BIG THRILL PEERING FROM A PORT HOLE TO SEE THE MONTREAL docks of Canada after three years. To appreciate Canada in a big way— nothing beats being away for a long time. On return from damp and dreary (too often) England to more salubrious sunny Canada, I shopped around for full time employment in the nuclear industry to take advantage of my three years of nuclear power experience in England. In 1957 I was interviewed by John Foster, later head of Atomic Energy Canada Ltd (AECL) Power Projects ( see below) at the General Electric Co. in Peterborough, Ontario. The General Electric Team at Peterborough were involved in the design of the Nuclear Power Demonstration (NPD) reactor—the prototype for the CANDU reactor pressurized heavy water reactor design. The NPD produced 22 MWe —it first produced electricity to the grid in 1962 and was a test bed for fuels, fuel handling, materials and components.) After an interview by AECL at Chalk River Ontario I decided to accept employment there —as AECL appeared to offer a more promising long time future, and I was correct.

Deep River is a remote small town near the Ottawa River and the Quebec border —with lots of extra curricular activities and clubs, but the one main activity involved the liquor store. The weather was a problem—in the winter 30 to 40 below zero quite common, with cars often unable to start in the bitter winter morning, and in the summer the abundant black flies too blood thirsty.

Chalk River, near the Ottawa River is the home of Canada's research reactors and nuclear research. I spent an exciting year there before a golden opportunity to move to Toronto to be a pioneer designing Canada's first nuclear power reactors. Meanwhile, Deep River the small town near the huge Chalk River plant— with its research reactors— had its advantages and disadvantages. There were two AECL residence buildings in Deep River, one for male and one for female Chalk River employees. It was my good fortune to be placed in the lady's wing—I could be in the lady's wing at all hours if I desired in spite of a curfew. I was up late one night when a security guard asked me. "Earl Are you coming or going."

Now I will reveal one of my secrets: Across the hall from my room were two young and pretty French-Canadian nursing sisters and also devout Catholics. I became friends with Marie, and we would meet in my room after she finished her night shift. This went on merrily for a few months, but one night she politely suggested it was time to get engaged. I had been introduced to the family and her other married sisters and had even looked into turning catholic. But I was feeling a bit trapped, so consequently with a clear conscience I made a rapid exit, ending these nightly get togethers. It has been said that the Fee's do not marry early. Then about 50 years later Marie contacted me, but the chemistry wasn't there in spite of her million-dollar home, a wine cellar one could only dream for, and being a very helpful nurse. Reminds me when I was single and president for a year of the Trident Club— a 700 male and female young peoples club at Timothy Eaton Memorial Church on Saint Clair Street Toronto. In spite of a majority of single ladies only one really caught my eye. So, Marie— some lucky and worthy man will come along.

One day I went hiking with some male friends and climbed several steep hills at a good pace —and frequently leaving my friends huffing and puffing far behind me. It gave me the distinct feeling that someday I would be able to do something special athletically. My premonition was to come true about 32 years later when after this long period I would take up running training again.

My work at Chalk River involved mechanical design of equipment to handle radioactive material remotely. This involved going into radioactive areas to take measurements; so, there was always the concern of how much radioactivity the body was absorbing on my radioactivity measuring badge. For example, one task was to make changes to an underwater reciprocating saw which cut radioactive materials.

During my stay in Chalk River one of the research reactors had a radio-active spill at the reactor top. I and other engineers were recruited to don special clothing head to foot, climb stairs with 12-foot-long handed brooms or a long-handed shovel to spend a limited number of minutes dealing with this radioactive material. Later while working at Atomic Energy Company Limited (AECL) in Toronto, design engineers were asked to do inspection of radioactive pipes in a dark tight compartment at the AECL reactor at Douglas Point. The operators there had already exceeded their allowable yearly limit. But I declined to participate —in those early days the safety factors for radioactive exposure were not well known about long term effects. And besides, I expected to marry one day.

After a year in Deep River a golden opportunity arose— an offer to join a select few in Toronto to start design of the first Canadian nuclear power plant. John Foster later became president of our branch in Toronto, designing the first Canadian nuclear power plants. This golden opportunity was hinted at when I— with my three year nuclear power background in England— was initially interviewed by Chalk River personnel.

In 1958 in a hut in Toronto at the Ontario Hydro Manby Center near Kipling Ave the Nuclear Plant Division in Toronto — a major branch of the crown corporation AECL— began operation. Initially the Nuclear Power Plant Division had the major project to design a full-scale prototype for larger future CANDU commercial power plants. After design the Division had the responsibility to manage the construction. The smaller 200 Mwe Douglas Point reactor was designed at Power Projects. It served as a teaching tool for the emerging nuclear industry, and the experience was invaluable for design of later larger CANDU power plants at Pickering, Bruce, and Darlington and also for CANDU plants abroad.

Initially the Division had just a few pioneers in this fledgling Canadian industry: engineers Willie Wilson(the leader), Al Hart, John Ingolfsrud (a masters grad from the prestigious Boston U), and myself; and three essential and important administrative executives whose names escape me unfortunately, and a few draftsmen. Willie Wilson had an engineering mathematics background at Chalk River. Al Hart, a mechanical engineer was also from the Chalk River facility and great pals with Willi Wilson— always laughing and joking together. This number soon grew with the addition of president John Foster, more and more engineers and draftsmen, addition of secretaries, and a librarian Anne Primeau. Alice Kavenough was in charge of the typing pool and other administration. Discrete departments were set up, Mechanical, Electrical, Civil, Nuclear, and Safety. Each with a department head, and branch and section heads. After a few years a laboratory was set up to test prototypes and models. I existed by myself under no other supervision as a special case for a couple of years but eventually management reluctantly explained I had to be under someone so was assigned under section head John Ingolfsrud. John was a taciturn dedicated type, never friendly. When we finished a project, we would record the results or ask others for some action in a memorandum. John had the inefficient habit to review my memos only up to the point where he found some minor discrepancy and return the memo for fixing— the remainder of the memo would be reviewed on separate occasions. There was never any objection to the technical aspects—this meant the memo had to be typed entirely over again as there were no computers in those early days. Consequently, in the typing pool I was good naturedly called "Three Times Fee," since ofttimes about two or three nit picking errors and consequently two or three complete typing might be found on separate occasions in one memo. Now I realize I was doing the typing pool a favour creating work and employment. (About 20 years later John Ingolfsrud had a discharge (firing) from our Power Projects Division. This rare occasion would involve a moment's notice and an immediate walking out the door to prevent any possible retribution tampering with computers etc.)

In those early days my duties were mainly related to engineering calculations, or designs related to cooling of equipment. Here is an interesting story: One of my designs was for a manifold inside the huge moderator vessel to distribute incoming water into the moderator uniformly. Heat was generated in the moderator so it had to be removed with incoming and outgoing water. My large manifold was built strongly with many small plates to guide the water universally—so a lot of welding was required. Years later a replicate 200 MWe Douglas Point plant design was sold to India with the express agreement that the depleted fuel would never be used for weapons purposes; India later broke the agreement to the dismay of AECL and

Canada including myself. But my story involves the manifold I designed. After operation the manifold in India broke apart. This was a very serious problem since the manifold inside the moderator vessel, was near impossible to fix in view of the inaccessibility and radioactivity. The failure in India was attributed to inferior welding. My Douglas Point manifold did not have this or any problem.

After about six years when the Douglas Point Reactor had been designed—the management was surprised —since I had been one of the original engineers—when I told them I would be quitting AECL to take a master's degrees, I enjoyed the work but wanted to get my master's degree. I told management this was my reason to leave but there was another supervisory reason. This was a bold move and involved cashing in my retirement savings as well. But I was to return a year and half later— after obtaining my Master's degree at University of Toronto. I was pleased to work under Bill Morrison a very clever engineer who I had great respect for and who rose high in the AECL and Ontario Hydro nuclear ranks. I subsequently bought back my previous working years so my retirement would not be affected.

My time at McGill University taking the Masters degree did not go well. Firstly, before I left AECL I had arranged an appointment to talk to a professor at McGill University (my advisor) in Montreal about my master's thesis. I arrived on schedule from Toronto at his office. He promptly said: "I don't have time to talk to you right now. See me at a meeting downtown." After the meeting in a crowded noisy room he outlined in a few hurried minutes his one-sided idea for my thesis. During the summer I worked on this idea for many hours: "Boiling of an organic liquid," although I was not enthused since It would be like dealing with molasses. After a couple of months at McGill I finally contacted my advisor again only to find out I had been working on boiling whereas he had meant condensation—a problem arising from our short hurried meeting in a noisy room. I decided to leave and take my masters at Toronto U, although he pointed out the courses I had passed with all A's would not be counted at U of Toronto. I also did not like that my McGill advisor had been treating me as a green student although I was 33 with a lot of good engineering experience. So I terminated before Christmas. Unfortunately, I had signed a year's lease for my apartment nearby to McGill on Catherine Street, and they would not let me break the lease. Leaving my furniture intact behind in the apartment I left for Toronto.

The day I left I met a very attractive single lady who lived just across the hall. Further bad timing, not helping my morale. I like the joie de vivre and accent of the French Canadian women. It was like two like minded ships passing in the night. But I had had some good times at McGill studying with a genius Indian friend Arjun Kapur, who still keeps in touch.

A month after leaving McGill I was fortunate to receive a paid Fellowship to take a masters degree at University of Toronto. My advisor was professor Hooper who had a good reputation in heat transfer technology. I asked where do I study? —he showed me a dingy and dusty laboratory, only suitable for experiments. And he paid me little or no attention until after his exam on heat transfer— my speciality when working — where I answered correctly 100% as well as all the bonus questions. Then he came up with my thesis subject—an electric analog showing how electric voltage can simulate temperature. I was not enamoured with this subject— similar to my reaction to the thesis subject offered at McGill. It was an experiment with a multitude of vertical wires. I frustrated with the experiment since I could not get any stable voltage readings for a month or so— until working late till past 2 am one morning. This was the time when the local TV station stopped its daily transmitting. I had been picking up electric waves from the TV station. In the end I was complimented on an exceptional thesis and offered a position teaching university students. Since I could earn significantly more in industry I politely declined this academic offer.

During my year at U of T working on my master's degree I rented a room in a boarding house not far from the university. Further adventures. I woke up one day and was told by an enterprising individual he wanted some money for waxing my car. It was the worst ting for a newly painted car. When it got too noisy and I wanted to sleep I would turn on my electric hot plate— this normally would blow a fuse in the whole three story house and quiet things down completely. An elderly lady in the rooming house said when things needed fixing," Leave it— they normally fix themselves." One lady resident was after me, but I had no time for romance. In retrospect I should have stayed with my mother during this time and later visited her more.

My working life for 35 years in the nuclear power industry with talented congenial engineers was not like work and never mundane—but challenging, exciting in a pioneer field involving new and novel designs. I supervised several engineers as a section head in several different departments at Atomic

Energy Canada Ltd.: engineering design, safety analysis, project engineering, process( involving pumps, piping, valves, heat exchangers) and heat transfer and fluid mechanics analysis (these my favourite). Now just some worn and tattered text books and a slide rule from university days six decades ago providing distant memories...oh happy days of yore. I feel grateful and fortunate, working for a good company, AECL, a crown corporation, now providing a good pension for life.

# 8

# FURTHER WORKING YEARS

*SOME OF THE* FACTS BELOW MAY BE TOO TECHNICAL FOR SOME OF MY *friends, but do not dismay there are also, in this chapter, some of my interesting personal experiences in the Canadian CANDU nuclear industry, since I was immersed in it for 36 years. So, I could not help also indulging somewhat in the history of the Canadian nuclear power industry.*

They were exciting times, the early days at AECL (Atomic Energy Canada Limited) Power Plant Division in Toronto —mostly young engineers taking on a gargantuan task— (1) to build an engineering organization—2) to design an original 200MWe CANDU (Canadian Atomic Nuclear Deuterium Reactor)— (3) and finally, to build and operate this electric power plant at Douglas Point on the shores of Lake Huron—(4) Finally, design future forerunner plants that became Pickering, Bruce and Darlington, and many CANDU exported nuclear power plants.

Lorne Gray, head of AECL, obtained government approval for the project in 1958. Also, in 1958 the Power Plant Division team started at Ontario Hydro's Manby Center on North Queen Street, Toronto. Those early days for me were to turn into 34 years working at AECL. I was the youngest at the start—as part of a small design team of five initially working on phase

2 above — just age 24 with three years of pioneering nuclear experience in England. At the top of this Power Plant Division was Harold Smith initially from Ontario Hydro. Eventually John Foster would assume command of the growing numbers: from Chalk River, Ontario Hydro, some Ex AVRO engineers and technicians (from the AVRO supersonic jet plane sadly cancelled in late stages by John Diefenbaker our prime Minister), and other experienced engineers and technicians from industry in eastern Canada. Many industries such as those specializing in pumps, valves, heat exchangers, steam turbines, piping, electronics, etc. were eager to get involved in this new growing nuclear industry. Based on a black and white photo in front of the huts we worked in initially—by 1963 in six years the Power Plant division had grown to: a total of 34 engineers, draftsmen and technicians and several administrative head women including Alice Cavenaugh. Willie Wilson, a mathematician from the Chalk River laboratories. was in charge of the design group and the laboratories where mock ups of the design were built and tested. Willie Wilson seemed a strange choice, but the likeable Willie proved to be very versatile and capable in the many diverse areas of the design while directing a multi faceted diverse team of electrical, mechanical, civil engineers, draftsmen and technicians.

Starting in 1954 a separate team of engineers at Peterborough a design team involving Canadian General Electric and Ontario Hydro designed under John Foster the 22 MWe Nuclear Power Demonstration reactor (NPD). This was to be the proving ground for research and development for the larger CANDU system for generating electric power. However, the NPD had vertical pressure tubes containing the uranium fuel — the Douglas Point designers changed this to horizontal pressure tubes for ease in fueling from both ends of the reactor.

W.B. Lewis, the head of Chalk River Laboratories had a big influence in the original design concept of the Douglas Point Reactor, the forerunner to the Pickering, Bruce and Darlington, and CANDU exported nuclear power plants. The concept of choice was a horizontal reactor with unenriched uranium, moderated and cooled with heavy water in separate horizontal pressure tubes as opposed— for example, to the American design of enriched uranium in a vertical pressure vessel with light water cooling and moderation.

# The Basic CANDU Reactor

I include here the basic operation of a CANDU reactor for those technically interested.

Uranium 235 fuel pencils of sufficient size and proximity when bombarded by slow neutrons will produce more neutron, energy, and radioactive products. At shutdown neutron absorbing shutoff rods of barium or
cadmium prevent this reaction. During normal operation the shutoff rods
are removed and a control system ensures neutrons are produced at the same
rate as they are removed. To ensure this steady state operation the neutrons
have to be slowed down to cause more fission; this is done in the heavy water
coolant in pressure tubes and the surrounding moderator which have the
properties of high slowing down of neutrons and low neutron absorption.
To further reduce the inefficient neutron absorption the fuel sheaths and
pressure tubes are made from zircaloy.

Visualize a huge horizontal cylindrical tank holding the moderator.
The huge tank has hundreds of horizontal pressure tubes each containing about 40 small fuel pencils which are surrounded by the heavy water
coolant. At each end of the tank, fuelling machines replace the fuel when
it is depleted; this is done without reducing power of the reactor. Through
the top of the huge tank a multitude of vertical control rods insert the tank
to control power or shutdown the reactor rapidly. Everything around the
tank is shielded with metal barriers or concrete to reduce the radioactive
products from the fuel to acceptable levels for the operators working in the
vicinity. Incidentally, one of my main jobs at AECL was to devise cooling to
surrounding equipment due to their absorption of heat from fission products
produced in the fission process.

In the unlikely event of rapidly increasing power the metal control rods
are inserted rapidly to shut off the super critical runaway reaction.

During steady state operation the heat from the nuclear reaction in the
D2O pressurized (about 100 atmospheres pressure) high temperature coolant
is pumped to the steam generators. This heat is transferred across a barrier
to a light water coolant which is turned into high temperature pressurized
steam in the steam generators. The high temperature steam drives steam
turbines. The turbines turn generators producing electric power.

Nuclear power stations have negligible pollution compared to coal fired stations. A typical household for a year can be supplied with energy from just ½ kilogram of Uranium 235 compared with 6000 kg of coal. Also Candu reactors have a safe containment to withstand high internal pressure in the event of an accident involving possible radioactive products.

As of 2017 a total of 48 CANDU reactors are in operation around the world e.g., in Canada, Argentina, China, India (16), Romania, South Korea, and Pakistan.

On returning to AECL after my master's MASc degree in mechanical engineering. I was occupied for example, with cooling of the end shields—the neutron barrier on both end of the reactor between the fuelling machines and the reactor itself. The neutron bombardment produced heat which had to be carried away continuously. Similarly, the heavy water moderator surrounding the pressure tubes containing the uranium had to be cooled. The moderator had to be cooled and the inlet and outlet pipes judiciously located. I estimated by hand calculation the heavy water currents and temperatures in the moderator. The calculations were complex, since they involved opposing thermal currents and jet currents from the incoming flow. Years later an expensive versatile computer code checked my hand calculations. For about four years the sophisticated computer code indicated my calculations were in error. The computer said the overall current was opposite to my hand calculations. But, in the end the complex computer code was found to be in error and I was right after four long years.

I worked for many years conducting safety calculations for operation of the safety containment system. The containment system consisted of a huge circular building serving four or more reactor buildings such as at Bruce, Darlington and Pickering buildings. In event of a postulated rare burst header releasing steam and radioactivity this high pressure mixture was directed to flow to the containment building normally kept under a vacuum. The resulting higher pressure in the vacuum building would be lowered by a huge dousing system inside the roof of the vacuum building. Following a make belief accident involving a burst high-pressure header released steam and radioactivity to the containment system where the steam was condensed and lowered to safe values. The containment building was built to withstand an earthquake and also the impact of an airplane.

At one point in my carrier I was sent to Paris after a meeting in Rome with some slides to demonstrate the workings of our containment system at a large conference on nuclear safety. I recall during my presentation my microphone fell apart during my presentation. While in Rome I stopped briefly at Italian Government Nuclear Department. I asked the taxi driver to wait for me. Ten minutes later I returned but the taxi was gone with a brief case inside. I was way too trusting in a foreign country. Fortunately, I had the slides with me that were essential for my presentation at the conference in Paris.

As a matter of interest there is a containment building at each CANDU reactor site and the number of reactor buildings connected is as follows: Pickering A and B: 8 reactors of 515 MWe each—. Bruce A: 4 reactors of 769MWe.—Bruce B: 4 reactors of 860MWe each — Darlington: 4 reactors of 881 MWe each..

After the Bruce reactors were in operation, a test at the Bruce site in Port Huron was carried out to simulate a burst header. I went with one of the engineers I was supervising to witness the test. We were told to stand in a safe area. But the test was much more violent than our calculations by my team had predicted. The velocities, I recall were several hundred feet per second and the deafening air currents were so violent a huge door, about 12 x12 feet, was ripped from its hinges and devoured by the rushing air to the vacuum building. Many instruments to measure the flow were swept away. Fortunately, I and my colleague were standing well upstream of the flying door, It was a dangerous frightening but exciting blood rushing experience. On return to work the next day I was reprimanded for attending the test. But the experience was worth the reprimand.

I worked in several different departments at AECL during my 34 years at AECL: mechanical design of reactor components— process design (involving piping, heat exchangers, pumps— heat transfer and containment analysis—. safety and licencing— and project engineering. One of my tasks was to design a small reactor. It was to be in competition with a design from Chalk River and another type of design at Whiteshell a similar research establishment to Chalk River. My design consisted of just essentially a few vertical pressure tubes cooled and moderated with heavy water. My design had the highest overall efficiency. But the study showed small reactors to produce electricity to be much too expensive in capital cost, so were never built. Now in 2018,

Chalk River reactors have been shut down and I understand there will be a major effort there to study small reactors. But based on my earlier studies on small reactors at Power Projects, and also at Whiteshell and Chalk River this seems like a lost cause.

Usually, I supervised about five or six engineers and had two engineers with doctorate degrees, two intelligent trainees from Italy for a couple of years, (one was to become a good friend, Franco Mammarello)—another good friend was Andy Beck. I found a few I supervised were very tight about revealing some of their hard-earned knowledge— perhaps to retain a feeling of power, hence difficult to work with. After 34 years the opportunity came up to accept an early retirement involving a small monetary incentive. II I had stayed on for a few more years I would have received an extra 2% per year in retirement. When I left I was made to believe they would greatly miss the wide knowledge and expertise I had accumulated over 34 years. Suddenly, I was a genius on leaving the company.

While heading the heat transfer and safety (containment) analysis section in the early days about 1970, the engineers in my section using computer analysis would prepare a stack of punched cards several inches thick. This would be sent to Chalk River where the cards would be fed into a huge computer about the size of a large bathroom. Each computer run would cost about $20,000 so *we were told*. To avoid a misrun just a few seconds on the computer was done to check initially for errors in the punched cards. Even a comma out of place could result in a useless run and large expense. Later on, I could see that eventually each engineer would have their own compact computer on their desk. And this was soon to be the case. Then secretaries were not required to type our memos. While working as an Ontario Hydro safety consultant under Robert Chun at the Bruce Reactor Plant site in a building designed to withstand an earthquake —often if heavy equipment was being loaded into the building, it would shake and a day's work on the computer would be lost.

I have the following advice for your ambitious engineers wishing to get promoted and move up rapidly incompany ranks. When leaving your desk during working hours always carry a piece of paper in your hand and move quickly like you are on urgent company business. Little will they know that you are actually on the way to the washroom.

On one occasion at work I was off with a bad cold or the flu. While away someone cleared off my desk and threw out an urgent report that a senior engineer had worked on for about six weeks on pump design. On return I was told the original engineer a pump expert would not be available to do the report again. I was to produce the report that took him six weeks and complete it in two or three weeks and along with my own supervisory duties. It seemed impossible as I was not a pump expert. But somehow, I was able to do It. It is like running: you can always do more than you think you can.

At work I became an expert in heat transfer calculations. For example, I had all the important properties required for air and water in my head and at my finger tips. Other engineers from other departments would come to me and I would do their calculations in a few minutes and they would go away happy. Eventually, after a few years of this — my superiors said I have to stop this, as it was supposedly interfering with my supervisory duties. Their hidden reason was— I was robbing the department of computer work. They wanted to make a big thing out a small thing essentially.

Overall, AECL was an excellent place to work and I especially enjoyed working on all the original designs. Although sometimes working a tight schedule could be stressful. There were awards for 25-year service, a gold watch, and for 35 years service, an Eskimo carving, although I had only 34 years. They say a gold watch on retirement is not appropriate since now you have excess time on your hands. I was ideally situated just about five minutes drive from Sheridan Park, Mississauga, offices. I could go home for lunch and have a short 15-minute nap —maybe one reason I look younger much than my age (according to friends and strangers). AECL has a yearly Christmas banquet, an opportunity to visit friends of old and compare wrinkles. At the 2017 banquet with about 200 ex- employees present I was introduced as a world record runner, only one of two introduced as some sort of celebrity. A great honour in fact.

Here are some important highlights in the Canadian nuclear power industry:

**1952**: Atomic Energy Canada Ltd (AECL) formed, a Crown corporation

**1954**: AECL, Ontario Hydro, and Canadian General Electric together formed to design and build the Nuclear Power Demonstration Reactor (NPD) —a team headed by John Foster.

**1957:** Nuclear Research Universal (NRU) reactor started up at Chalk River laboratories.

**1958:** CANDU Nuclear Plant Division was started in Toronto at Manby Center, Ontario Hydro.

**1962:** NPD reactor was commissioned.

**1967:** Douglas Point produced first electricity to the grid.

**1962;** Plans to build Unit 1 and 2 power plants at Pickering.

**1971:** Unit 1 and 2 at Pickering produce first power.

**!973:** Unit 4 at Pickering produces first power. Ultimately 8 reactors produce power at Pickering and serviced by one containment building designed to contain any radioactive material during a nuclear accident.

**1977:** Unit 1 and 2 at Bruce at Port Elgin Ontario in operation.

Up to **1983** many CANDU nuclear plant are in operation in the world including Argentina, and Korea.

**1987:** CANDU reactors, CN Tower in Toronto, and Alouette space satellite are ranked as one of Canadas's top engineering achievements in the past 100 years. Canada is also the world's leading exporter of uranium.

**1989:** Unit 1 at Darlington is commissioned.

**!992** Unit 2 at Darlington is commissioned.

**1994 to 1996:** Pickering A and Bruce A break world records for continuous operation.

**2002:** 32 CANDU nuclear reactors in operation in the world. And 40 years of nuclear power in Canada.

My working days were not all work, oh not at all. After work I belonged to the Toastmasters International for nearly 10 years and progressed to near the highest level. I have given many speeches outside the Club, e.g., to high school and public school students, at sports banquets, and retirement homes. And at Central Technical School I was the valedictorian at graduation. And I was even asked to speak at a small church during the Sunday service, and even the entertainment at a friend's wedding (see chapter 4).. When someone retired at work I was asked to roast them —that is find out what unusual or funny things had happened to them, or they had caused, then exaggerate these tales in a humorous way. I found that after the audience had a few drinks and were in a jovial mood, I could be very funny. See Chapter 4 for more on Toastmasters.

After 34 years at AECL I thought my working days were over, but something happened shortly after that resulted in employment as a nuclear consultant: Shortly after retiring I was inveigled out a sizeable amount of money by a shrewd operator who posed as a businessman setting up a computer sales operation in Mississauga. We found out later he had hoodwinked many people in the USA and Canada with his smooth talking. He even supplied references at a bank in the USA. An accomplice I suppose. I invested in a new computer which I never received and invested $10,000 in his make belief computer sales company for a supposedly quick turn around of my investment. There were actually several other potential opportunities for investment that he mentioned —later I realized all were illegal frauds. Eventually, I helped to catch him after a lady he was courting and engaged to became suspicious and reported him. This loss of money was a lesson and prompted me to seek part time employment to recoup the money. In the end I met many new friends and recovered the money many times over from my new employment. Consequently, soon after retiring I worked as a nuclear consultant for two years at Ontario Hydro on University Avenue and at the Bruce power plant at Port Elgin Ontario in the Safety Branch under Robert Chun. Robert Chun was a distance runner, friend and a brilliant engineer. Together we joined the highly reputable Saugeen Track Club under Earl and Geordie Farrell. I am a lifetime member of this highly reputable club. This club has produced many top runners who have received scholarships to the U.S. universities in the past 20 years. Training with these young runners with excellent coaching helped me win three gold medals and break three world records at the World Championships at Buffalo USA in 1995. Of course, I also owe a lot of gratitude to David Welch coach at the North York Track Club for over 15 years of coaching. His workouts were tough but they paid off in world records. See many of these tried and proven workouts in my running books and Chapter 9 mainly.

The day I left work there was farewell lunch for me. When we returned I had a phone call from Casey House in Toronto,the home for terminal HIV patients, saying my dear brother Maurice had passed away. He was 64. I thought it just like him always considerate among his other attributes. I will miss him forever.

I started soon after retirement to write about 150 poems over about two years and to train twice a day on most days —In addition I was training twice a week with the Credit Valley Marathon club and would run up to 1.5 hours on Sundays.

In 2018 at age 89 I attended a University of Toronto reunion —65 years ago I graduated there with a BASC in mechanical engineering, and 56 years ago also at U of T with a MASc—and after enjoyed a great free lunch in a huge tent on a sunny hot spring day I recall my parents, not wealthy, had given me $500, their last savings in 1948, to get me started at university. At this reunion, there were only a few in attendance in my 65 group out of the more than 150 graduating 40 to 70 years ago.

# 9

# MY RUNNING TRAINING
# PAST AND PRESENT

TO GIVE SOME APPRECIATION OF THE TRAINING INVOLVED—I LIST SOME of the workouts from my yearly detailed training manuals, but further details are in my books: "How to Be A Champion From 9 To 90" Body, Mind and Spirit Training, self- published in 2001, now out of print— and "The Complete Guide To Running," published in 2005 and 2007 by Meyer and Meyer.

This is a brief summary of how my training changed over the past 23 years as I went from age 57 to age 88. Basically, I am a middle distance (800m,1500m and mile) runner, hurdler, and 400m sprinter— but also have competed with success in the 100, 200, cross country races, 6K up to 8K. and 5K road races. My world records are in the 200m hurdles and 300m hurdles, 400m, 800m, 1500m, and mile events. I have avoided short hurdles to prevent injuries.

After my comeback to running at age 57 I was competitive in the 100m from age 57 to about age 70 years but found it interfered with the 800m training so gave it up after about age 70. I found it best to specialize in the 400m, long hurdles and middle distance events. In the early years I ran twice a week with the Credit Valley Marathon club up to about age 72. This helped to give me a good aerobic basis for future years. During the competitive indoor and outdoor season my training has always been three days a week on the track doing short (150,200,300,400 metre intervals usually close to race pace— or later in the season time trials at race pace or a meet on the weekends— with a complete rest or an easy day once per week. I came to believe that intense short interval training was better than long slow aerobic running to age slower than my rivals—and a good alternative to long slow runs to build endurance.

## Running Clubs

I found it advantageous to belong to various running clubs mainly for the camaraderie, coaching and timing, training partners and regularity in training sessions. For instance, I was with the North York track and Field Club from 1986 to about 2003, the Etobicoke Huskies Track and Field club from about 2003 to 2010—then with Mississauga Track and Field Club for about 3 years. Also, I trained with Saugeen Track Club for two years in my sixties, chasing the teenagers, and continue to be a lifetime member there. Also over 15 years with the Credit Valley Marathon Club starting at about age 58 providing me with good endurance. I learned by watching the workouts of the various coaches. For instance. while acting as my own coach I observed and learned the effective methods of coach/friend Bruce Mitchel in guiding Karla Del Grande to several sprint world records.

With the North York Track Club I attended four training camps in Florida and one in San Diego, California—either acting as a manager or just accompanying my young boys who trained with the North York Club for several years. The club travelled in rented cars on these training camps. On one trip to Florida the teenager athletes at night took without permission our two rented cars on a spin around a local golf course—resulting in damaging the cars. During the San Diego trip our club president and coach/friend David Welch was wrought with worry. He was under suspicion in the murder of a young girl in Toronto who was a friend of David. For two long years his phone was tapped by the police, then the killer was eventually identified by DNA.

**Age 60, 1989.** I list below some noteworthy workouts and races. I believed; you race as you train and in working hard in training so as not suffer in a race— but enjoying the process— keeping in mind what I'm trying to accomplish during the workout, and how it will payoff later. The body will adapt to practically anything if reasonable and gradual over time. The following typical workouts indicated no physical laziness although my training log was blank for six weeks in January and February before I was completely sold on the benefits of a daily log.

- 4x 800m in 2:32, 2:30, 2:30 and 2:32 with 6min. rest in between. (It always amazes me how successive repeats can be so similar).
- 10x50m 90% effort and 13x50m, rest walk 50m between, working on form. (I include this here since there was a lot of emphasis on running form— and always a few medium speed 150m at end of each workout, working on relaxed form and good arm action. (I was rewarded by a lot of compliment on my running style. Pete Taylor, the legendary US masters announcer, remarked that it looked like I wasn't really trying, which I took as a compliment.)
- Run 3.5 miles (25 minutes), next run 750m,750m, 300m, 200m, 600m, 600m, with 2 minute jog in between each— total 7.5 miles in 67 minutes.
- 3x 600m, 1:46.5, 1:46.2, 1:45, 8 rest between reps. until heart beat reaches 96 bpm —400m of 40m fast and 60m slow jog repeats— 3x150m, 20.5, 20,6, 20,7; 4 starts. (Note a 600m in 1:42 is the pace for a 2:15 800m).
- 2 sets (4x200m average 32sec. with 50sec. rest between) walk 200m between sets. (It was usual to do three sets at race pace or slightly faster than race pace, total 2400m at this age, but in this case the pace was faster than normal.)
- Weekend runs up to about 1.5 hours but not too close to a race— always starting with a strong cup of coffee. (In retrospect this is too long for an 800m runner.
- Weight training two or three times a week, but not close to a race.

As I savour the above workouts I think re-finding or remembering a good past workout is like a prospector finding a misplaced gold nugget.

## Typical Workouts at Age 61 in the Indoor Season

January to March training on 200m indoor tracks concentrating mainly for 400m and 800m and 1500m and mile events:

- Lots of mile repeats at about 6:15 pace. For 5K training 3 x 1 mile at about 5:45 with a 200m walk + 90s. rest between. Best 5K 18min:18s.
- Long run once week on road or trail between 45 to 90 minutes.
- 25x100m at 19s. average with walk back +30s. rest between.
- 4x1000m 3:30 pace average walk 200m between, Rest 7 min. Run 5x500 at 90s. average with 60s. rest between.
- 6 x1000m at about 3:30 pace with 200m walk rest between.

Sundays; warmup on 200m track, stretch weight training on 12 machines usually I set, row for 2000m, Run in pool for 1 hour with younger partners (Louise, Mike, and Nanci — repeat intense intervals in deep end with or without flotation belt usually to simulate 800m on track with same effort and total time.

## Indoor Workouts at Age 62, and 63

**At age 62** when I retired from my engineering job at the Atomic Energy Canada designing nuclear power plants— I often trained twice per day. Usually this involved about 35 miles of running per week until about age 70. Countless times this consisted of running in the pool in the mornings and running on land later in the day. **In the deep end of a pool to simulate a running distance on land —run in the pool at the same perceived effort (or heart beat) and the same length of time.** To simulate a 800m race on land I run in the deep end of the pool 5x12.5m. At about 12.5 from the pool edge my feet start to touch the bottom in most pools so I turn around.

After interval training at night at York U track I would often have a coffee and when I got home I would do more running in the dark but slower— there is a mile long gradual hill, a street, Collegeway, near home, that I would often run down. Basically, I had plenty of energy and found as others have found that the more I exercised the more energy I had. I stayed relatively injury free up to about age 70. But not like now in my 80's when it seems the older the more injuries and the longer to recover. The 200 metre or shorter indoor tracks I use in the winter with their tight bends are an injury hazard.

The following were some notable indoor workouts from my detailed daily training logs— training for the 400m, 800m and 1500m in January, February and March—mainly at York University on its banked Mondo 200m track and at the Mississauga YMCA 200m rubber flat track (no spikes allowed, and not suitable for fast sprinting in view of the sharp bends). The indoor training was designed to peak near the end of March at the Ontario championships and often at the Canadian indoor championships. The three months prior to January were for base building. i.e., mainly outdoor training in spite of the colder weather, and a concentration mainly on the aerobic energy training, hill training and weight training (twice per week) to be ready for the intense indoor interval training starting in January. Also the three months prior to January involved cross country races which I participated in with good success. Note the long runs during January, February and March were done outside on the roads or on the indoor track. And rarely any days off.

The workouts are in order of January, February, March, April. All with a good warmup and cooldown. Some rest between intervals and sets are missing, if not in my training log. Also, in many cases there was some cross training just before or after the running training, particularly running in the pool and swimming, but not shown here in all cases for brevity.

# 1991, Age 62 Typical Workouts

- 3 miles: 1st mile 6:07, 2nd mile 6:08, 3rd fartlek fast on straights jog bends, Run in pool.
- 3 sets (5x200m @39s avg.) rest 49s between reps, 3 min. between sets.
- 6x500m. @1:36 avg., rest 2 min. between reps. Rest 8 min. 6x 150m @ 24s avg., walk 200m between reps.
- 3x 1mile Fartlek, fast on straights, jog bends @ 6:20, 6:30, 6:30., rest to 70 beats per min. of heart between each mile. A tough workout, so speed on straights cannot be overfast.
- 2 sets: (Run 100m, jog 100m, run 200m, jog 200m, run 300m, jog 300, run 400, jog 400m, run 600m jog 600m.) Run times set 1: 18s, 36s., 55s, 75s, 37.5s per 200m for 600m. Rest 10min. Run times set 2: 18s, 36s, 55s, 75s, 37.5s per 200m for 600m. Rest 10min. 4x150m @ 24.5 s avg.

- 4x 400m @73, 70, 70, 72s Rest 6min. 6x150m @22.8, 22, 21, 21,5, 22, 23.5s walk 200m between reps.
- 3x300m@ 50s avg. rest 90s between reps. Rest 6min. 3x300m @51, 50, 50s avg., rest 90s between reps.
- 8K race outdoors minus 4 degrees C, 31:42
- 7 miles indoor typical @ near 6:45 per mile usually on Sundays.
- 5x 400m @69s. to 72s, rest 2 min. between reps. Rest 6min.. 3x400m 67.6, 68.6, 69.6s, Jog 3 laps. 3 laps, fast straights jog bends.
- 4x800m at YMCA, 2:33, 2:28.5, 2:30.6, 2:33.8, rest 2 min. between reps, heart at 96 b.p.m. The times were estimated to be several seconds faster if run at York U. track in view of more generous turns on the track.
- Warmup 1 mile. 3x600m, 1:30, 1:25, 126, rest to 100 b.pm. of heart between reps. Rest 8 min, 6x150m, 21.75 avg. Cooldown I mile.
- 3x600m 144.7, 1:45, 1:43.5 rest 6 min between. Rest 6min 2sets (3x200m @ 33s. avg), rest 30s. between reps and 6 min, between sets. Rest 10 min 1 mile fartlek fast on straights, jog bends.
- Coach David Welch ladder March 14 (and March 21): 400m 76s., (rest 90s.), 300m 53s., (rest 2min.), 800m 2:32, (rest 90s.), 500m 1:34, (rest 3 min.), 1000m 42s. per 200m, Rest 10 min 4x200m 33.5s avg., rest 30s between reps.
- 400m 72s, rest 60s, 200m 32s, rest 90s., 800m 2:30. Rest 10min,4x200m 33s avg., rest 30s. between, 300m 50s. Rest 10min., 2x200m 31 and 33s, rest 30s between. Jog 4 laps, 3 laps fast straights, jog bends.
- 2sets x (6x200m @ 32 s) rest 45s between reps and 9 min between sets. Rest 12 min, 1 mile fartlek fast on straights, jog bends.
- 3x500m 1:30, 1:27,5, 1:27,5, walk 100m + rest 2.5 min. between reps. Rest 10min, 3x300m, 49, 48.8, 48.8s, rest walk I lap between reps. Rest 4.5 min., 2x300m, 49, 51.5s, rest walk 1 lap between reps.
- 2x1000m 3:12 avg., rest walk 3 laps between reps. Rest 10 min, run 1mile fartlek: fast on straights, jog bends.

# 1992, Age 63 Typical Workouts

- 4x(200m x3 @ 33 to 36s), 45s in between reps.
- 6x300m @52s average, 2min. rest in between. Rest 8min., run 400m @ 65s rest 1min. run 400m @70s.

- 3x1000m @3:27 avg. pace, walk 200m between. Rest 6min. run 1200m fartlek. Swim and run in pool.
- 4x(400 + 60m fast)@73s avg.) walk 140m between reps. Walk 2 laps, 1 mile fartlek @6:40s, Cycle 10min. Level 2. Run up 25 stairs.
- I mile @5:57, jog 300m, 1 mile fartlek @6:30s, jog 200m, 800m @ 2:57.
- Swim 5x25m @2:25. Run in pool deep end 10 sets (3x12.5m) @ 2:14 to 2: 24, rest 30 to 40s between reps.
- 6x100m @15s, jog 100m between reps. Rest 8min., 4x200m @31s, rest 30s between. Rest 8min. I mile stride straights and jog bends. Later weight training.
- Run outdoor 38min. @7min. pace with last mile 6:30 pace. Later at indoor YMCA 5:30 mile.
- 4x800m @2:37avg. rest 4min between., Rest 10min. 3x 200m @33s avg., rest just 10s between reps, Rest 8min. Repeat 3x 200m @34s avg. Later cycle 10min.
- 4x500m @ 88, 89, 88 and 92s, rest 4min. between reps. Rest 10min. 6x150m @23.5s, rest between to 108 heart beats per min. Jog 4 laps, fartlek 800m. Massage.
- 3x600m @1:57 avg. rest 3min between reps. Rest 8min. 3x600m @ 1:54 avg. rest 3.5min between reps. Cycle 12min + 8min.
- Cycle 5 min level 1 and 2, run 6 miles 42min. Cycle 15min level 1and 2.
- 4x400m @69s. avg., 3 min. rest in between reps. Rest 8min. 3x400m @68s. avg. Rest 6min. 6x150m@ 24, 23, 23, 22, 22, 21s, rest to 96 bpm between reps.
- Coach David Welch's tough multi interval ladder workout (see also 1991 above) usually once or twice per month: Warmup 7min. mile, stretch, ABC sprint drills, 8 fast strides. Ladder February 6 and 23 also similar on January 6 : 400m 76s, (rest1 min), 150m 23s,(rest 1.5min), 800m 2:36, (rest 2min), 300m 49s,(rest 3min) 1200m 4min. 7s, (rest 10min), 400m 78s. Rest 8 min. 4x200m 34, 33, 32, 31s, rest 30s between reps. "Getting easier now than 1 month before." Jog/ stride 1 mile cool down. (*On February 6 had a Tachycardia episode after finish of similar workout while suffering from a cold.*)
- 3x800m @2:35, 2:33. 2:29, walk rest 1 lap + jog 2 laps between reps. Fartlek 800m @3:12. Cycle level 2, 12 min, walk 2 laps, repeat cycle 12min. level 2. Pool run intervals in deep end without flotation belt.

**Age 65, 1994** I was still running with Credit Valley Marathon group on weekends—typically about an hour and 30 minutes —and a shorter run-mid week. Also, my training involved a lot of running intervals in the pool. My coach, David Welch, at the time was an ex-marathoner, so there was negligible emphasis at the time on sprint speed training, Some speed training came only a week or two before a competition—actually a coaching mistake—I learned this is too late, one has to work on speed always or it is lost. **You will race according the training about a month before the competition.** Some typical indoor workouts were:

- 8x400m at about 72 seconds avg.with one minute rest between
- 3 sets (4x200m rest 50 seconds between reps) 5 minutes between sets
- 1 mile fast and 2x1 mile fast on straights jog the bends
- warmup I mile. and 3x600m and 6x100m accelerations
- 1000m time trial at mile race pace
- 1200m time trial at mile race pace
- 2x1200m fast and slow (100m fast, 100m slow repeats)
- And the coach's favourite ladder workout, but usually slightly different each time : 400m, rest 1min.— 150m, rest 2min.— 800m, rest 3 min.— 1000m, rest 10min.— 6x200m, 800m pace, rest 30sec between.

The above workouts seem difficult now at age 88, but not at the time—they were quite manageable.

**Age 66,1995.** I had quite a few world records previously, but I believe I reached a peak after 9 years of training and broke the 400m and 800m age group records and a specific age record in the 300m hurdles at the WMA Championships at Buffalo NY in 1995. ( see Chapter 11 for details)

At about age 70 I was still doing long runs sometimes as long as an hour to 1.5 hours and competing in 5K road races, or 8K cross country races —and still training with the Credit Valley Marathon Club. In the cross country I was undefeated in Canada in my age group for many years. I loved to pick up the pace when I had the wind at my back.

Below I examine some of my workouts at age 69, 75, 78,80 and 85 to see some trends such as when I had to eliminate long runs and when Tachycardia became a more frequent happening. My daily detailed training logs, one for each year since age 57 have been very helpful to see what worked, and what didn't, i.e., lessons learned and to see trends. Also, it is motivational and indicates that my training was and is taken seriously.

**Age 69,1998. A specific age world record can sometimes be more impressive than an age group world record.** For example, I had a particularly impressive indoor **specific age** world record 800m of 2:17.05 at the US National Masters Indoor competition at Reggie Lewis track in Boston on March 29, 1998 at age 69 —just a week after my birthday—this was equivalent to the open world record on the age graded basis. This was just 0.25 sec. slower than my **age group** world indoor 800m record **five years** earlier at age 65 in 2:16.80 (broken by Joe Gough in 2:16.65 (IRL) in 2018).

Indoor workouts **at age 68** below are selected below because I wanted to see what workouts and habits in 1998 in the three months before my 69th birthday contributed to the above good indoor 800m performance: Leading up to the indoor training starting in mid December, 1997— a good aerobic **base** was achieved from many sessions of 1, 2 or 3 minute repeats on hilly grass loops at the huge Earl Bayles Park in Toronto in September, October, November and December, often in the snow and chilly darkness, but also often by the light of the moon. In addition there were also aerobic warmup runs of 2, 2.5 and 3 miles at about 7 to 7.5 minutes per mile. But also, there were long land running most weekends, and the occasional 5K race and 8K cross country races. In addition two or three times a week running in the deep end of the YMCA indoor pool and some swimming and cycling, plus weight training twice per week provided for recovery and variety in between running days— and sometimes on the same day as the land and treadmill running. Some recovery was provided by self massage most days on the legs. My first book, "How to Be Champion from 9 to 90," had a detailed chapter on Self Massage. In those days there was no convenient roller which I use at night at age 88 most days, All the above contributed to: a gold medal in my age group for a Canadian Championship 8K cross country race November 29, 1997 in a muddy rainy course in Vancouver Stanley Park, and also provided good conditioning to withstand the intense/fast repetitions indoor.

I trained at the 200m indoor tracks at York University or the YMCA in Mississauga, a total of three times a week. At the younger age of 69 I was able to run most days in succession whereas at about 78 and older it was necessary and smarter to have hard and easy days, i.e., recovery cross training days in between running days.

# Specific Typical Training leading up to my 2:17.05 800m indoor race at age 69

The following are typical indoor workouts used in January, February and up to 29 March,1998 my 2:17.05 800m race. I do not mention warmups and cooldowns. Usually a warmup involved about 1000m to a mile of slow jogging, stretching and ABC drills, and a cooldown with less jogging but more stretching. My coach, David Welch, in these early days had us running some slower 150's in good form ( good arm action) during the cooldown. Note numbers in brackets are actual times achieved in the workouts.

## January

- 5 x 400m indoor (67 to 68s), 4 min rest between. Later, 10 x 50m on steep hill, recover 1 minute and jog down.
- Run 4 miles (7min. 20 sec. per mile)

## February

- Cycle 30 min. Rest. L2, L3, L4, L5, L6, L&,L8, 2 min. each. Rest between as required.
- 4 x 400m (72 to 77s), Rest 2min. between). Rest 6min., 3 sets (3x 200m, rest 1min. between), rest 2min. between sets. Cycle 15min. Walk 30 min.
- 5 x (3x200, 30s rest between) 1 min. rest between sets.
- 800m race 2:22.9. Rest 15 min. race 3000m 12.04 min.
- 5 x 400 (75,74,73,73,76s) rest 90s between.
- 4 x 500m (1min 44, 1 min 29, 1 min 39,  1min. 40, walk 100m between reps. Rest. 1 x 600m, fast on straights, jog bends (2 min 26.

## March 1

- 3.5 miles at 7min. 20s/mile pace, Cycle. Swim, 6L Kickboard, 1L=25m.

## March 3

- Cycle, and weights. On treadmill, 21 min. at 7min,/mile pace. Rest, 25 min. at 8 min./mile pace.

## March 4

- Weights. 4 x 250m (42 sec), 1 min, rest between. Rest 6 min. 6x 150m (21 to 22s). 1 min. rest between.

## March 6

- 3 x 2L swim fast (53 to 56s), rest 40s between. 3 x 2L kickboard with flippers. Run in pool shallow end 20 min. Some weights. This is considered an easy day.

## March 7

- 2 sets (2 x 600m, rest 2 min. between reps) 4 min. rest between sets. Actual time 2:02, 2:00, 1:58, 1:59. Rest 5 min. 2x600 fast on straights, jog bends ( 2:24 and 2:28). Cycle and walk 28 min.

## March 14

- 800m race 32s, 33s, 35s, 38,7s= 2:18,7. Too fast initially, legs tired last 150m. 30 min. later 200m race.

## March 21

- 2 x 600 (2:03 and 2:00), walk 200m (1 lap) between reps. Walk 2 laps, 1x600 (1:58). Walk 1 lap, 1x400 (78s), Walk 100, 1x200m (38s), Walk 2 laps, 1 x 600 fast straights, jog bends (2:20).

## March 24

- Walk 30min. Run 3 miles 1st mile 7 min. mile pace, 2nd mile 6:40 mile pace,and 3rd mile 6:20 mile pace.

## March 25

- 5x50m accels., 5 x150m (23s, 23s,30s, 30s, 30s) 2.5 min. between reps.

## March 26

- 1L kickboard, 2 x 2L swim (57s, 59s), run in shallow end + ABC sprint drills: total time 26 minutes, 24 lunges,. stretch. This type workout in retrospect too close to race, not recommended.

## March 27

- Travel to Reggie Lewis indoor US national masters meet in Boston.

## March 28

- I mile in 5:26.43, a specific age 69 world record. 90 min. later 200m in 28.31.

## March 29

- 800m in 2:17.05, March 29 a specific age 69 world record, (33s, 34s, 35s, 35s). Note near perfect pacing compared to March 14.

**At age 69** the above indoor performance helped me to run an outdoor 800m in 2:19.48 (a gold medal) and 102 % age graded at the Nike World Masters Games in Eugene Oregon in August 13, 1998. My training log says 98 degrees F and very windy. At this well run meet I had 3 additional gold medals in 3 other events : 200m in 28.28,— 400m in 61.63, beating all 60 year olds — 1500m, missing the specific age record by over a second.

**Age 70,1999** leading up to a memorable experience at the US National Masters Indoor at the Reggie Lewis Track in Boston —a wide variety of longer and shorter repeats, but particularly a lot of 150m repeats often with 100m, 200m or 250m repeats in the same session. Some of the typical indoor workouts in January and February were:

- 4 sets (3x400m, rest 60sec.between 83 sec. repeats) rest 4 min. between sets = 4800m total
- 3 sets (run 38sec. 200m, jog rest— run 19 sec. 100m, jog 200m,— run 80sec. 400m, jog 400m) rest 4 min. between sets = 2100. Rest 8 min. repeat above = 4200m grand total
- 2x1000 (3:40 avg. pace), rest 8min., 3x600m (fast on straights jog bends, 2:30 each) = 3800m total
- 5x150 (24 sec. reps. rest 90 sec. between reps), rest 5 min, 5x100m (15 sec. reps.@ 400m pace, rest 90 sec. between reps)
- Run 600m time trial 33.0 sec./200m pace=1:40, rest 8min., 5x100m 16 sec. avg., rest 60 sec. between reps, rest 8 min., 4x250 50 sec. avg. 3 min. rest between reps.
- 12 laps (1.5 miles) at an average of 6:30 per mile followed by a workout in the pool swimming, and running in the deep end..
- 10x150m (23 sec. reps @ 400m pace, rest 70 sec. between reps), rest 8 min., 5x150 (repeat 23 sec. reps).Stretch 4x150m slow.
- 10 lengths (25m) kickboard in pool, This is hard work. 4 lengths swim on back

For a world class master or a good national competitor the above at about age 70, the **total anaerobic workout (intervals) in a typical session** would be less than 4800m for 1500m training — 2400m to 3000m for 800m training —1200m to 1500m for 400m training— 600 to 800m for sprint training. And the total varies inversely with age. i.e., at age 88 I am running mush less than above. These are rough guidelines —always train within your present capabilities. Less is more! Too much, too fast or too soon leads to injury.

My aerobic conditioning came from: cycling, a few long runs of 2 to 3 miles, frequent pool running in the deep end, four indoor races in January, February and March, plus less than a mile of slow running as part of my warmup on running interval days, and from the 3 times a week HIIT interval training.

**At age 70 my 800m world indoor and outdoor age group records were practically identical at 2:20.5,** and just 1 second increase from the outdoor 800m in August of the previous year. This indicates the importance of good performance the year before arriving in the new age group.

# At age 75 my world indoor mile age group record in 2004

My preparation in January and February had been good involving some 600m trials at 800m race pace: and time trials at mile pace for 800m (once), 1000m(once), 1200m( twice) — also, a 1000m race, 1200m race and a 1500m race. There was only two long runs (3.5 miles) but a mile warmup run before each workout. The main emphasis was on mile training, with 800m training secondary, and with negligible 400m training. The following are some other noteworthy workouts prior to my success at the Reggie Lewis Stadium March 27 and 28:

Workouts in Categories The workouts are listed below in categories and showing typical workouts. The percentages represent the emphasis during the three month period leading up to my mile record. Notice the emphasis on the mile training with little emphasis on 800m and speed training.

**World record mile race pace 800m to 1200m runs (7.5%):** Jan 1, Feb 21, Feb 28, Mar 19. Mainly about 4:11 to 4:17

for 1200m. at 42 s per 200m target mile race pace.

**Races:** 1500m Mar 6 and 1000m Jan17 and Feb 8 (**7.5%**).

**One 800m repetition (HIIT) workout session (3%)** at mile race pace or faster: 800m 2:41 (40.5 sec. average per 200m). Walk 250m. Repeat 2:50 (42.5 sec. per 200m).

**600m repetition (HIIT) workouts (8%):** 3 x 600m at 800m race pace 37 sec. per 200 in training session, Or, 3 or 4 x 600m at mile pace 42 sec. per 200m, walk 200m between.

**400m repetition (HIIT) workouts (5%):** usually 4x400m at 800m race pace in 75 to 81s, walk 200m between repetitions

**200m repetition (HIIT) workout (2%),** at 800m target race pace, 4 x 200m (36 sec. per 200), Rest 3 min. 2 x 200m (36 sec. per 200). Rest 3 min. 2x 150m (26 sec). 1 min. between all reps.

**100, 150, speed repetitions workouts (13%):** These repetitions were at about 95% full sprint speed, hence less than 600m to 700m total in a training session and much less close to a meet.

**Aerobic runs for endurance workouts** between (2 to 3.5 miles) (**12 %**). Since this was in the Canadian winter these runs were all indoors, in view of the cold climate here— with about 2 out of 3 on the indoor track and 1

out of 3 on the treadmill. I was starting to see some circulation problem in my left calf— becoming tired on long runs, but after about a minute of rest I could go again faster to make up the lost time.

**Easy days (16%).** These days at this age usually involved about I day a week rest day—e.g., walking, dental visit, physiotherapy treatment for injury or travel or return from a meet to the USA.

**Cross training (26%) workouts:** in order of emphasis, running in the pool, cycling, kickboard in the pool, rowing, walking and swimming. In many cases there was a longer run with the cross training.

# Typical indoor workouts at age 75

- Simulate 1200m on track with equivalent time (4:00) and effort in the pool deep end.
- 3x400m, 82 sec. avg., walk 200m in between 400m reps., rest walk 400m + 1 min., 3 sets ( 250m 48 sec. avg., walk 45 sec. run 150m 26.5 sec. avg., rest walk 400m between sets.
- 2x800m 2:41 and 2:50, with 200m walk +45 seconds in between
- 2 or 3 sets (600m, fast on the straights jog the bends), between sets walk 200 + 45 sec.
- 5x 600m at slightly faster than mile pace, walk 200m at medium pace between reps.

At an Ontario masters meet in February 2004, during my warmup, before an 800m race I had a tachycardia episode— my heart going into a high continuous beat, up to about 120 bpm in my case, and chest feeling tight— I took my prescribed pill. Just before my race I returned to normal —so I thought. But, before I had completed one lap I was filled with lactate and stopped due to heavy arms and legs. Some weeks later, after submitting a Tue form I found the propranolol (Indural) pills I took "as needed" were not a sport enhancing drug— but I had learned that on my own.

# Year 2007 Age 78

At about age 78 I started having a amore frequent circulation problem in my left calf muscle, a condition called "Intermittent Claudication" due to partially blocked calcified arteries. I am grateful.to Dr Galea, sports doctor, who sent me in mid 2007 to Dr. Wooster, a specialist in vascular problems, who diagnosed my problem as Intermittent Claudication. After about 6 to 8 minutes of slow running my left calf would become too fatigued to continue. But after a short rest of about a minute or two I could go again at even a slightly faster pace until it happened again. Fortunately, there was no problem with short fast intervals.

As one ages it is necessary to adapt. Hence, I found from my own training that intense short interval training can develop aerobic endurance (oxygen uptake VO2max) and speed at the same time— and high intensity interval training ( HIIT) became my new training method without long slow runs. To be clear, I continued doing HIIT, as since age 57 but the long aerobic runs on land were now replaced with more aerobic cross training (running in the pool, swimming, cycling, rowing, and elliptical). Research by Gibala at Mc Master U and others (for example Dr. Tabata studies) have shown that HIIT can provide similar oxygen uptake (VO2max) as long slow running in much less time —for example, a few minutes of HIIT can produce the same cardiovascular improvement as 15 minute of long aerobic running. I have broken world records in the 200m hurdles, 300m hurdles, and 400m and 800m, in the 75-79 and 85-89 age groups since eliminating long runs in my training. Jeanne Daprano of the USA, eight years younger than me, has also had good success without long aerobic runs also — e.g., a WMA mile record at age 75 under 7 minutes, and other middle distance age group world records — she is also an enthusiastic rower doing intervals on the rowing machine. I also believe rowing is an excellent cross training method working most muscles of the body unlike for example cycling. See details of Jeanne Daprano's workouts in Chapter 16.

Getting back to year 2007: At age 78, in addition to my Intermittent Claudication problem revealed in this year —my Tachycardia started to occur more frequently. Fortunately, it is not life threatening as Atrial Fibrillation where the heart can go into flutter and which can lead to a heart attack— and I have never had Tachycardia during a race. But it occurred right before a 800 prelim at the Worlds in Brisbane Australia when I ran with it —not recommended (see Chapter 11 on World Masters in Brisbane Australia). Also it occurred at an awkward time just before a 4x400 relay in Riccione Italy where I was running in the anchor leg. (see Chapter 11 on World Masters in Riccione in 2007). But, now I have adapted to this problem and know how to avoid and reduce the frequency and get rid of an episode by relaxation proper diaphragm breathing, and "mindlessness," a word I invented—thinking of nothing —like daydreaming.

All in all, in spite of the above problems I consider myself fortunate—as many my age have prostate problems, heart attacks, stroke, diabetes, knee and hip replacements, etc., which I have fortunately avoided. So I count my blessings every day and I recommend this habit to you also.

With the above problems and the adaptation I have continued to break age group world records at age 80 and 85 and hope and plan to do so at age 90. Basically. it is important and essential to keep active and age slower than your rivals, and working on reducing strength loss which occurs every year. Hence, as one ages it is important to keep up with the usual activities. It is so true: use it or lose it. For instance, up to about age 70 I frequently ran on the treadmill with no problems. But now after leaving this for over 10 years It seems much harder than running on the track. Also, with swimming: prior to age 70 swimming the crawl was no problem and I could go smoothly for many lengths but after leaving it for about 10 years now, the kicking is difficult and tires me out. So I have resorted to using the pool buoy float between my legs which has the advantage to rest the legs in between running days. Also it is most important for older athletes not to take a year off. This would result in a major loss in performance for the year and a slow return to competition fitness.

## Typical Training Sessions at age 78

Here are some of my high intensity interval training (HIIT) workouts for anaerobic and also aerobic conditioning, without long aerobic running used in 2007 **at age 78** prior to the world championships in Riccione, Italy in August 2007:

- 4 x (250m, walk 75m, run 150m, walk 50m, run 100), Rest 3 min. between sets
- Run 600m ( 2:00 or 40 s/200m), rest 5 min., run 400m ( 72.8 s), rest 4 min., run 300m (56 s), walk 100m, run 100 (18 s).
- 9 x (200m (42.5 sec. average/200m), walk 50m + 20 sec., run 150 (28 sec.)). Walk 200m +30 sec. between repetitions.
- 350 m@600 race pace, walk 50 m, run150m at 600m race pace. Walk 200m plus 75 seconds. Repeat 3 times.
- At 800m race pace run 200m, walk 50m, run 200m, walk 50m, run 150, walk 50, run 100, walk 50, run 50. Rest 6 min. Repeat.
- Run in pool: 5 x 12m in deep end in 2:46 average pace. Rest 1 minute between repetitions. Simulates 800m race. Repeat until tired.
- Run in pool deep end L=12m: 5L, 6L, 4L (2:45), 8L (5:27), 4L (2:45). Rest 1 min. between repetitions.
- Row: 2:22/500m for 7.5 min. Rest 3 min. Row 2:24/500m for 6 min. Rowing on indoor Concept machine.
- 800m time trial: 600m (38 sec. per 200m or equivalent 2:32 800m), Rest 7 min. repeat.

In addition, in 2007 there many local indoor and outdoor races, 200m, 400m, 800m and 1000m, too numerous to mention—and including the US Masters National at Reggie Lewis,Boston indoor meet— prior to Riccione Worlds in August. There is nothing like a race to build fitness and reveal your true fitness or weakness.

# Typical Training Sessions for Sydney World Games 2009 at age 80

For the Sydney World Games at age 80 in 2009 I entered 5 events:100m, 200m, 300m hurdles, 400m, and 800m. I planned to train on the track for sprints (100m, 200m), 400m, 800m and 300m hurdles on 4 separate days on an 8 day cycle with cross training providing aerobic endurance and recovery in between these more intense track running days. This 8 day cycle is much more convenient than the usual 7 day cycle to accommodate 4 separate training days and proper recovery between the intense sessions. If training with others on a 7 day cycle one is forced into the same routine on each day of the week. But I was training alone —my usual routine at this age.

Note times in brackets are actual times achieved. Rest times are not always included below since these details are often missing from my logs. Everyone is different, but in 800m and 400m training I usually start the next repetition again when my heart returns to about 85 to 90 bpm. I recover quicker than most athletes. When doing sprint training at 95% speed start again after about 7 minutes— or take 5 or 6 minutes rest for speed endurance training. As conditioning improves the rest is shorter. As you get older the rest is longer.

Also, some of the workouts below are not complete, i.e., some less important aspects were not described.. At age 80 I recommend for a complete workout **total** metres: for sprinting 600m, for 400m training about 1100m, for 800m training about 1500m. (For instance at age 60 I was doing about 2400 to 3000 total metres at near 800 race pace.) For hurdles always quit before too fatigued to prevent injury, and before form drops off with fatigue— usually clearing in a session a total of about 16 hurdles.

# Sprint Workouts

Based on target times: 100m 16 sec., 200m 32.5 sec., 150m 24 sec., 50m 8 sec.

- 2 x 50m ( 8.1, 7.9), 1x80m (12.8), 1x100 ( 15.99), 1x120m (19.25), 150m (24.33)

## 400m Workouts

Based on target times: 400m 71 sec, this relates to 200m in 35.5 sec., 300m in 53 sec., 250m in 44 to 45 sec.

- 4x 50m (8.8 sec. average), 2x200m (35.3 and 34.3), 150m (25.3), 100m (16.9) Rest as required but not complete rest.
- 2x 50m (8 sec.), 200m (36), 200m (36), 250m (44), 250m (44). Rest walk back +30 sec. between each.

- 3 x 50m (7.8 average), 3 sets (300m (53 average), rest 4 min. between.
- 4 x 250m (44 sec. average), rest walk back + 1 minute
- 3 x 50m (8 sec. average), 2 x (300m 53 sec.), rest 4 minutes, 150m (24 sec.)
- 4 x 50m ( 8.6 average), 2x200m ( 35.3,rest 5 minutes, 34.3), Rest 6 min. 250 (44 average), Rest 4 min., 1x100m (16.9)
- 250m (43.7), Rest 6 minutes, 250m (42.7), Walk 250m, 200m (35.2)
- 200m (36), 2 x 250 (44, 43,5), 300m (53), rest walk back + 30 sec.

## 800m Workouts

Based on target times: 2:49, this relates to 400m in 84 sec., 200m in 42 sec.,250m in 53 sec., 300m in 63 sec., 600m in 2:06

- 3x250 (53 sec. average) Walk back + 1 minute between repetitions. Rest 5 minutes. 3 x 250 (53 sec.) average)
- 3x 50m (9.3, 8.6, 7.6), 3 x 200m (42, 39.3, 39.1), Rest 4 min., 2 x 200m (39.1, 39.6), 150 m (27.3), 100m (18.3), Rest between repetitions: walk 100m.
- 600m time trial in 2:03, Finish with 4x150m at about 600m race pace.
- 3x 50m (8.5 sec. average), 400m (83), Rest: walk 100 + 30 sec., 400m (81.7), Rest 6 min., 300m (58)

## 300m Hurdles 27" height

Based on target time: 56 or 57 sec.

After warmup run several 50m at hurdle race pace. Start with hurdle drills over 4 or 5 hurdles. Then practice on grass over one hurdle. Then on track over 1st hurdle to establish which foot is forward in the blocks to get favored lead leg at this first hurdle. During practice hurdle space between hurdles is about 1 foot less than 35m regulation to account for less speed in training and when training in running shoes not spikes. At beginning of a training session, hurdle height may be about 3 inches less than regulation to establish good rhythm and confidence over the hurdles.

3xH1 @27", 1x 5H's @ 24", 1x4H's@ 27", 1x4H's @27"= 16 hurdles total. After running over multiple hurdles walk back + take several more minutes.

# Typical Cross Training for Sydney World 2009 Games

Typical cross training is mainly to build endurance and provide recovery from running sessions. Usually a combination of the following in a session— Not overly strenuous.—Aim to save energy for next day running. (Recently in 2018 I over did it one day and swam 20 lengths too strenuously (and longer than usual) —which resulted in a bad rare cold.)

- Run in pool deep end wearing flotation belt. E.g., 1x 5L where L is 12.5m when usually feet start touching the bottom of pool —to simulate effort and time of a 800m race. Note: A rest between intervals in the pool is less than1 minute usually, which is much less than on land due to the buoyancy of the water assisting the heart.
- Swim 18L. Rest then swim 12L where l L= 25 m, length of regulation pool. I use a pool buoy to save the legs since cross training days are recovery days.
- Float board kicking for 2 L ( where L=25m) is intense and strengthens legs.
- At end of a pool session I stand at shallow end of pool and swing my legs, 9 different movements, and 12 to 24 repetitions per leg. taking about 5 to 7 minutes. See explanation below
- Run on grass or artificial loops (soccer field), if weather permits, short intervals of about 1.5 min. each
- Row 2 or 3 times about 2:20/500m for about 5 min. repeats or continuous 2000m on Concept rower.
- Bike outside for 30 min. or inside at higher rpm for short intervals. Usually 10 min. indoor cycling at near 100 rpm during warmup.
- Elliptical machine 15 to 20 minutes.
- Weight training once or twice a week on 12 machines, usually just one set since running next day.(At age 88 I now use about 20 machines and usually just 1 set of 12 reps on each.)

**Leg swinging at shallow end of pool.** This recommended exercise increases leg strength and flexibility is described in more detail in my book, "The Complete Guide To Running." Here are some (7 out of 10) of my exercises. When finished with right leg do same number of repetitions the left leg. Faster of course provides more resistance.

Standing facing the pool edge and holding the pool edge

EX 1: Imagine a hurdle in front of you and execute a trail leg movement with your outer leg.

Ex2: Reverse trail leg movement.

EX3: Mule kick.

EX4. Straight leg moves parallel to wall out and up while keeping back vertical, then down back to side, repeat without stopping.

EX 5: Straight right leg moves parallel to wall and to the right out and up ending right foot near the surface, back to center then to the left out and up with right foot ending near the surface, back down to center, repeat with no stopping. After repetitions with right leg do similar with the left leg

Standing sideways to pool wall, holding wall with inner hand.

EX 6: Move leg smoothly in an exaggerated running stride.

EX 7: With straight leg outer foot moves out In front parallel to wall then traces a half moon shape, then back moving parallel to wall to center. Continue with no stoppage. Do half the reps in clockwise direction then revers and do the other half in counter clockwise direction.

EX8: straight leg moves parallel to wall outwards and up as high as comfortable, then down to start and back as far as comfortable, then return to start. Repeat without stopping. Back should reman straight at all times or you are going too far forward or backward.

**See Chapter 10 for Sydney World Games 2009 results from the above workouts at age 80.**

# My Age 88 Training

I am writing this now at age 88 in 2018. For the past few years I have found I can run much further at a slow pace before my left calf fatigues due to calcified/blocked arteries. Perhaps I have developed some new capillaries in the area from the HIIT sessions for many years now and/or from weight training, Or this improvement is from just pushing on after fatigue sets in. Also I started taking vitamin K2 in 2018 to reduce calcium build up in my arteries. I highly recommend this vitamin for others. I do not take K2 for increase in bone strength since I know from research at McGill U I have the bones of a 30 year old.

My running training at age 88 for the 200m, 400m and 800m is briefly as follows: Note, unless otherwise stated the running pace is at race pace or leading up to the competition pace.

- Run 3 times a week, e.g., Monday (200m training), Thursday (400m training), and Saturday (800m training). (This is the usual situation, but sometimes I will concentrate on one event for several weeks and still three times per week. I did this in prior to 400 race in March 2018 and had an age graded percentage of 107% in an indoor 400m at our Ontario Masters Indoor championships in March 2018. See also Chapter 12 where I concentrated on the outdoor 800m for about two months in 2017 with good success.)
- Weight training on Tuesday since training for sprints Monday, 400m Thursday, on and 800m Saturday.. Also when it is a couple of months before Malaga Spain Worlds I will likely start some 200m hurdle practice on some of the above days to help maintain my readiness for a possible age group world record when I turn 90. Another weight training session following the Saturday running session (the same day) is ideal, giving ample recovery time before the next running session — otherwise on Friday or just once a week. I occasionally, miss some weight training sessions depending how my body feels—but on non-weight training days before bedtime I do a brief routine when healthy; 24 or more pushups, about 30 squats with the big rubber ball at my back, and one arm rows with a 25 or 30 pound weight, and 24 medicine ball (10pound) throws up a wall catching in squat position. Or I miss some of the above and include massaging the muscles with the big roller for about 7 minutes. In practice. the above schedule can be affected, and more frequently as one ages, by injuries, physiotherapy sessions, and sore muscles.
- Before getting out of bed in the morning I do another brief routine about 50 pelvic tilts, massage and shake legs, rotate feet, stretch legs, groin, hip flexors and gluteus muscles,and a back exercise all while lying on my back.

- Another routine is frequently massaging, stretching the fingers a few times during the week or put them under a strong jet in a shower (a habit it I picked up from friend/swimmer Migal). I have some arthritis is in my small fingers
- In between running days—cross training mainly in order of preference: swimming and running in the pool, rowing (2x800m, or 1x2000m), fast 100 rpm cycling (at least 10 min.), elliptical machine, if available make big waves with two big ropes, usually 24 reps, and fast walking or hiking. And usually one easy day or day off once a week depending on how my body feels. The total time spent on these motion machines in my case is usually a total of 30 to 40 minutes. See also the above cross training for Sydney World Games
- Total intense running volume not counting warmup and cooldown, per session— 600m (for 200m or speed training) at 95 % speed— 900m to 1100m (for 400m training at 400m race pace)—about 1400m (for 800m training at 800m race)..
- 200m training: 4x150m, rest 2 to 3 minutes between. Or separate workout: 50m, 50m, 80m, 80m, 100m, 100m, 150m., Rest: walk back plus 2 or 3 minutes between reps. Both workouts 600m total. All at 95% speed..
- 400m training: After several weeks of conditioning.Week 3: 200m, 200m, 200m. Week 4: 200m, 250m, 250m. Week 5: 250m, 250m, 300m. Week 6; 250, 300, 300. For these workouts walk back + 2 or 3 minutes between reps, or go again when ready. Race times for the above sessions can be slightly slower than competitive target times in initial weeks.
- 400m training on some weeks:6 to 10 x100m,walk back plus take another 30 to 45 seconds rest. Run at 400 race pace.
- 400m training:. It is essential to be able to run 300m at 300m race pace, ideally 2 or 3 weeks before competition. — so some training should be devoted to this later in the schedule but not too close to competition.
- 800m training: 400m at 800m race pace, walk 100m + 60 to 75 sec. run 300m or 400m at 800m race pace.
- 800m training: 2 sets (3 or 4 x 200m), 60 sec. between reps., rest 6 min. between sets. Pace in initial weeks is slower than target race pace,

later weeks pace is at race pace, later weeks pace is slightly faster than target race pace. As condition improves shorten the rest between reps.

- 800m training: After a few weeks of the above training, run a 600m time trial at target race pace. A week or two later another time trial 650m and so on for later weeks. The last 50m accelerate. Complete the workout with some slower 150m.
- Build a good aerobic base in October, November and December (In the Fall in Canada) in preparation for competition (the indoor season in Canada and the USA) —build this aerobic base with sessions of swimming, running in the pool, rowing, elliptical, hiking, hill training, and weight training—or the occasional long slow outdoor run. High Intense interval training (HIIT) also helps to maintain or increase aerobic as well as anaerobic power —in my case I use HIIT instead of long slow running. During this base building phase, although mainly aerobic condition speed should not be neglected.
- Keep a training log of the timed workouts. These records help to assess what works and what doesn't.

# Summary Training Targets for 85-89 Age Group

- Note at this age total meters in a session is about 1400m for 800m training, 1000m for 400m training, 600m for sprint training. Compared to training at 80-84 age group in this 85-89 age group there was easier cross training between running days and usually a day off, or an extra easy cross training day once per week:
- **800m.**Target 3:10 which relates to intervals 200m at 47.5s, 250m at 60s,, 300 at 71s, 400m at 95s and a 600m time trial at about 2:22.
- **400m.** Target was 80s which relates to intervals 100m at 20s, 150m at 30s, 200m at 40s. 250m at 50 sec, 300m at 60s.
- **200m.** Target was 36s which relates to intervals 50m at 9s, 80m at 14s. 100m at 18s,120m at 21.5s, 150m at 27s,

**Good luck, and enjoy your training.**

# *10*

# COMPETITIONS ON YEAR OF NEW AGE GROUP

I STRESS HERE THE YEARS WHEN INDOOR AND OUTDOOR AGE GROUP world records were most likely in my case, namely: age 60 (1989), 65 (1994), 70 (1999), 75 (2004), 80 (2009), and 85 (2014— years at start of a new age group, **but not including World Masters Athletics Championships (see chapter 11).**

I mention just a few specific age records —the 2006 edition list 30 of my specific age records. Since there was no other edition of specific age records there was no way to determine if one had a specific world record after that, so I stopped submitting my race times to Pete Mundle USA). In view of many Earl Fee races above 100% age graded after 2006, usually several each year— these would likely have been good candidates for specific age records too.

**AGE 60, 1989** I competed in a total of three indoor meets in February March and April, and a cold outdoor 5K race (in!8:36) in February and another 5K on May14. At a Corporate All Comers indoor meet I ran the 800m on February 25 in 2:15.0, Two hand timers, (33, 67.5. 1:42.5, 32.5=2:15). Had I submitted the proper forms and with three timers it would have been a world indoor record at the time, but in those days, I was not yet familiar with the process of taking the correct form to the starter the meet director etc. for signing. I sometimes would do this for world records, but in the last 20 years or so I leave it all to the officials. For a specific age world record a copy of the meet results was sufficient.

## Ontario Masters Athletics Indoor Championships

In the indoor season in March I ran the 200m in 27.12 seconds while recovering from a cold, the 800m in 2:17.71 and the 400m in 58.30. Little did I suspect that in six years I would run the 400m faster and would break the age group 65-69 outdoor world record in less than 58 seconds— and run another age group outdoor world record in the 800m in 2:14.43.

In April of that year I competed in the 400m, and 800m at an indoor meet in the north east USA — I'm unsure of the exact location but according to my training log I was again recovering from a cold and the air in the arena was poor. (Nowadays I rarely catch a cold.) In the 400m the legendary Jack Greenwood was in my race. Before the race the announcer said Jack Greenwood had never been beaten— but with 100m to go I felt strong and finished ahead of him in 59.82. (But I had run 58.30 at our Ontario Masters indoor meet a few weeks before.) The race took it out of Jack for some reason— after the finish line he was down on his knees. In the 800m after starting too slow and passing two runners, including Jim Sutton(USA) I managed to win in 2:17.84. But I was to get several seconds faster in the outdoor 800m.

## Ontario Masters Outdoor Championships

In the outdoor season on June 18 and prior to the World Masters Athletics Championships in Eugene Oregon —in the 800m I ran 2:14.40, just 0.2 seconds slower than the world record, but was named athlete of the Ontario meet.

## All Comers outdoor meet at Centennial Stadium

In Toronto on July 6th, running alone a large distance behind a younger runner I ran an age group outdoor world record in 2:12.85, my 1st lap 400m in 65.5 and the 600 in 1:39, and finished the last 200m with a good kick.

I recall, I had to rush from work to get to the race on time, so my warmup was rushed, but it all worked well out for me.

**AGE 65, 1994**. At age 65 in my new age group I competed in the USA National Indoor Championships in Columbus Missouri in March 1994 just four days past my birthday— what could be better timing?. After a rushed warmup from not realizing that the races were alternately men and women in the same age group— I ran the 1500m on a fast track. My first lap was 35 seconds, way too fast — a stranger told me later; he thought I would never keep it up—but I finished in 4:47.11 lowering the previous indoor age group world record by about 5 seconds. (The outdoor record by Sien Herlaar (HDL) broken later in the year was several seconds faster). The next day at Columbus Missouri, my age group world record in the 800m in 2:16.80 lowered the previous record by about 5 seconds. Joe Gough (IRL) lowered this in 2018 by a fraction of a second, but my record had lasted for 24 years.

In July at a Belles (ah yes) and Braun's outdoor meet in Buffalo NY—after running the1500m and the 400m on the same day — I had a specific age 65 world record in the 400m hurdles 30 inches high in 68.5sec... which bettered the old record of 71.4sec.. and the age 63 and age 64 records. My travelling buddy Chuck Sochor from Michigan had the age 66 specific age world record in 70.8 seconds. At the famous Hayward stadium in Eugene Oregon in July —I loved running there— I had an age group outdoor world record, finishing strong in 2:15.23 in front of a large loud cheering crowd. At this historical stadium of Steve Prefontaine fame, the track is fast, the crowd enthusiastic, the announcing exciting and the meet efficiently run. This race indicated good forebodings for the **World Masters Athletics Championships in Buffalo** next year in 1995. See details in Chapter 11.

My record keeping shows also a mile age group world record indoors in Detroit Michigan in 5:13.3 at age 67. It was a large field of women and men together, which didn't help my time.

## NIKE Portland/Eugene World Games 1998

**AGE 69,** I gathered in the summer of like ...1998 I gathered four large impressive gold medals in four events: 200m,400m, 800m (2:19.48, 100% age graded) and 1500m—apart from this nothing colorful or extraordinary to report. But I impressed one competitor in my age group.who remarked: I was from another planet. I missed the 1500m specific age 69 world record by a few seconds. I learned it is always best to plan well in advance when trying for a record.

Also at age 69, I had one of my best 800m races ever in March 1998 in 2:17..05 indoor at Reggie Lewis track Boston. It was just 0.25 sec slower than my indoor age group 65-69 world record 4 years earlier.

**AGE 70,1999** lead up to a memorable experience at the **US National Masters Indoor at the Reggie Lewis Track in Boston** on March 27. In my 400m—at the start my blocks slipped. We were called back, but I had a slight cramp from this—so my start was cautious... I'm not sure if this slowed my overall time or not, but it made for a more even paced race and perhaps saved some energy for a fast finish. It was a world indoor age group record in 1:01.31, lowering the old record by 5 seconds. (About ten years later the great American sprinter speedy Bob Lida missed breaking my record by 0.1 seconds.) The next day March 28 at Reggie Lewis was the 800m. In the previous two months I had three 800m races, all about 2:22 to 2;23, but I peaked at the right time with an age group world record in 2:20.45. I have to give some credit to the cheering/ supportive crowd, the announcing by Pete Taylor and for the track itself which feels fast and springy. About 75 minutes before this 800m race I had run a 200 prelim. There again, it is not clear whether this hindered or helped me. In my following 200m final I finished 2nd in 28.49, to the winner in 28.36. Considering my sprint training consisted mainly of 150m repeats, I was happy.

My record keeping shows also a 300m hurdle age group world record in 49.07 in Orlando Florida at age 70. I recall a sweltering hot day and having to wait outside in the blazing sun while they set up the hurdles. This record was lost to the great Guido Muller 10 years later.

**AGE 74, 2004** leading up to my birthday on March 22 I was in unusually good shape from building a good base in the previous 3 winter months, October, November, and December. There were more frequent sore left calf muscles during long runs due to my circulation problem, intermittent claudication. But I was able to lower the world indoor specific age group 1500m to 5:19.34 at York University from the previous 5:26.50. I recall two other

1500m specific age 74 world record attempts at York U; one where I lowered the record by just 0.10 seconds and another attempt where I failed when I got completely confused about laps to go and lost concentration —when my coach yelled out some unintelligible numbers as I passed by.

On my birthday, March 22, some running friends, mainly Louise Soucy Fraser, Mike Carter, who I had been coaching, and also John Powell, arranged a huge surprise birthday party for me. I arrived at a dance which I attended twice per year with my dancing partner Louise. On opening the door to the dance hall I was surprised to see hundreds of my friends and family. It was a great surprise although some of my friends had been acting rather strange in the week or two before— now I know why.

**AGE 75, 2004 At the US National Masters Indoor meet on March 27** shortly after my birthday, I was fortunate to break three WMA age group world records in the 75-79 age group at the Reggie Lewis Track in Boston, Mass. It was my good habit and good fortune to compete at this meet most years, usually about a week after my birthday on March 22. Pete Taylor— the great masters announcer—would announce me as the "Great Earl" and the races stirring up the enthusiastic loud crowd while the athletes sped around the fast track—that seemed to give extra life to each stride. Pete would soon become a good friend.

My main preparation in January, February and March was to break the indoor mile age group world record in the 75-79 age group. My training involved some 600m trials at 800m race pace, but mainly time trials at mile pace for 800m (once), 1000m (once), 1200m (twice) — also, a 1000m race, 1200m race and a 1500m race. I was never so well prepared for an age group world record attempt.

On the first day of this Reggie Lewis National Masters meet in 2004 I ran the mile at the pace I has trained for. The crowd was very loud and encouraging me, a Canadian, on each lap —I have to love those Americans. With about 100m to go on the last curve I lost a fraction of a second in lapping two runners side by side.— but a new age group world record. It was at this congestion on the track that my main competition in the race, a five years younger runner, passed me. He had timed it perfectly just before I was passing these two slower runners, when I was blocked in. A very clever move. But I finished within a fraction of a second to my target in 5:41.95.

The legendary Ed Whitlock, my late friend and fellow Ontarian, has the world outdoor record in the same time within 0.1 seconds. My method for training for this record to run a time trial at world record race pace once a week and increase the distance each week by 200 metres proved to be a good method. My last time trial was at 1200 metres, I reasoned that with the adrenaline, the rest in days before and the crowd encouragement and wearing the lighter spikes I would continue on at race pace for another 200m. A similar method should work also for 800m and 400m training.

About two hours later, after my mile race I warmed up for the 400m. My lethargy from the mile suddenly disappeared when in the large and busy warmup room I was suddenly kicked in the most sensitive male area by another athlete doing some backward "mule kicks." I have had a few of these kicks in my lifetime and I can remember each one even many decades later— and these resulted in an operation in England in1954 to cure a hydrocele (excess fluid in a testicle). This time at the Reggie Lewis track I decided not to visit the nurse on duty, but Ice was required. Then I was fully awake —running an age group 400m world record in 66.28 seconds—this was based mainly on my mile strength training since there had been minimum speed training in the months before. This indicates mile training, or aerobic training, can assist 400m training as it enables one to maintain the speed. Bob Lida, USA, would smash this a decade later as he was specifically trained for sprinting.

Next day at Reggie Lewis, feeling refreshed... my 800m was an age group world record in 2:32.48 (99.0% age graded)—I love this track and the enthusiastic friendly crowd, cheering me a Canadian. In the outdoor season I was not able to get close to my indoor time; for example my indoor and outdoor times at age 70 were practically identical in 2:20.54 and 2:20 47. In August I ran to a world outdoor age group record in 2:37.68 and didn't last long in the WMA record books. My outdoor time, 96% age graded (lower than usual) should have been about 5 seconds faster.i.e., closer to my indoor record. I had been taking treatment in previous weeks on my right hip and felt I was not running smoothly. Also, my mile record and the 400m the day before had taken something out of me. These are my excuses. A well respected runner, Jose Rioseco, from Spain lowered my record by several seconds in 2016, but now seems to be retired early from running. I would love to know his training secrets.

I shouldn't complain, but in the summer of 2004 my problems started on April 24. I was selected for an Alliance Insurance TV commercial involving me running over some hurdles at Varsity/Stadium track— where I was the one and only athlete. This video eventually was shown with some other seniors athletes doing their favourite thing. One was a 75 year-old who was shown doing his 1000th jump from an airplane and another senior of similar age flying around on his motor cycle racing in the mud. My TV shoot involved four huge trucks of equipment and about ten photographers and technicians. I even had my own personal female helper. First, with muscles rippling I was kept crouched in the starting position for about 10 minutes while they took umpteen photos of me from on high and low. This photo about 12 feet high graces the entrance of The Alliance Insurance lobby in the USA and appeared in a full page in many newspapers with their slogan " The best is next." Unfortunately, I should have known better, but I was kept in the crouched position too long— since when I eventually started my left hip flexor and groin seized up, I felt obligated to continue over the hurdles and also did a repeat run as if nothing had happened. The $2200 US they paid me was some consolation. Three other injuries followed that summer— hampering my training— so my short- lived (for three years) outdoor 800m world record of 2:37.68 was not impressive in my opinion. I should have been close or lower than my indoor record of 2:32.48.

# AGE 80, 2009

This was a busy eventful year for Earl Fee since it involved several competitions: a the US National Masters indoor meet in Landover Maryland — a southeastern Masters outdoor meet in Raleigh NC —and a World Masters Athletics Championship in Lahti Finland, and The World Master's Games in Sydney Australia —and the usual frequent injuries from indoor running particularly in January and February.

The first five weeks of the year consisted of no running, but lots of rowing, cycling, swimming and running in the pool —necessitated by a left calf injury. In the next six weeks I had 13 running workouts: 150m, 200m, 250m, 400m repeats, and two 600m time trials at 800m race pace; and weight training twice a week, but no long aerobic runs or sprint training. But still I was not fit enough to race; and so missed competing in four local meets.

Later in 2014 I realized after a lot of research on my part—my injuries were most likely largely affected from taking statin drugs for high cholesterol. So I stopped this prescription. I also realize that most heart attack people have acceptable cholesterol.

On March 14, I was honored by a huge 80th birthday party in my finished basement. I ordered seven large tables and fifty chairs for the occasion. My friends Louise and Mike had arranged a special gift from all my friends: a cheque about 8 feet by 4 feet for $500. I was aghast at this generosity and organization. The only problem being I was up till 2:30 am after more than a few celebration glasses of wine, and an 800m race early in the morning at York University. I surprised myself —running 2:54.10—just a few seconds slower than my world record a week later at Landover Maryland. The frequent cross training particularly the swimming sometimes up to 40 lengths and the intense running intervals in the pool and the rowing had provided the necessary aerobic endurance. And there is always muscle memory from the year before.

# AGE 80, 2009 HIGHLIGHT MEETS

## US National Masters Indoor Championships in Landover Maryland, March 21 and 22, 2009

A week later at the US Masters Indoor Nationals in Landover, Maryland on March 21, the day before my birthday, I ran 73.35 with the 75-79 age group. The next day, March 22nd, on my 80th birthday my 800m, after lapping several runners from 75 to 90, was announced as an age group world record lowering the old record by 17 seconds. Pete Taylor, my announcer friend, provided further excitement during the race, announcing me again as "The Great Earl"— a very honorable moniker indeed for a Canadian competing in the US, and mentioning my name several time on each lap. But two hours later, I learned the official timing device was not turned on during my race. (I heard later that the official in charge of the timer was called away at this time by the police to answer some question about an assault occurrence in the meet hotel.) The hand timing was 2:49.80, and a professional video gave a time of 2:50.1 (see You Tube for this exciting race), but the officials decided no world record. I would have to break it next year when I could be 1 or 2 seconds slower due to aging effects..

Although a professional video of the Landover race showed a time of 2:50.1 this was not accepted by the officials. I was able to break the record a year later in 2010 at the US National masters indoor at Reggie Lewis track in Boston a time of 2:52.57 —this was slower by only 1.4% compared to the year before in Landover. The reduction in yearly performance for an 80 year old age group world record holder is normally much higher at about 3% or 4% per year. A 60 year old age group world record holder typically has a 1%/year reduction in performance. This indicates Earl Fee is aging slower than other world record distance runners.

At this Landover indoor meet some of my friends from the legendary female Athena track club were successfully competing such as Julie Hayden (co-founder), Terri Rath Cheryl Bellaire, and Joan Hunter.

One highlight of this meet was Nolan Shaheed —multi world record holder in middle distance events, and professional musician — thrilling me and the appreciative crowd with a saxophone solo.

## Indoor Ontario Masters Championships at York U Toronto, March 29, 2009

400 world age group record in 71.23 sec. bettering the old record by 4 seconds— and in the 200m a Canadian record in 32.07 sec.

# Southeastern Outdoor Meet in Raleigh NC USA, May 2, 2009

*2 age group 80-84 world records*

400m in 70.64 and 2 hours later 800m in 2:53.29 on a very hot humid day. At the well run meet, I won $500 as the athlete with the highest age graded of all those entered.

(The next day while competing in a seniors soccer game my 60 year old friend John Ward had a heart attack playing with a team of 40 year old's. Fortunately the ambulance arrived within 6 minutes—after this they say it is too late.)

# Ontario Masters Outdoor Championships York U Toronto, June 21, 2009

800m age group 80-84 outdoor world record in 2:48.95 and two hours later 400m in 70.82. This 400m race was a good opportunity to break my Raleigh 400m in May world record as I was in better shape about six weeks later. However, I remember distinctly at about 100 having a back problem that slowed me momentarily and I lost a precious fraction of a second in recovering.

## WMA World Championships Lahti Finland, August 2 to 8, 2009 (See Chapter 11 for more detail)

**World Games Sydney Australia, October 13 to 18, 2009** *5 gold medals:*
100m in 15.68 a Canadian Age group record
200m in 32.41 a Canadian Age group record
400m in 71.29 against a strong wind in the home stretch
800m in 2:49.30 again against a strong wind
300m Hurdles in 56.93—a world age group record lowering the old by about 5 seconds. But I learned when I returned home that WMA does not recognize World Games records although the officials and timing are much superior than small masters meets where records are recognized— also rabbits much younger and faster may happen.. To follow a runner in an 800m race is worth a saving of about 1.5 to 2 seconds. The unacceptance by WMA of my record was very disappointing since the 300m was the main reason for my attendance at the Sydney World Games. Otherwise, it was a wonderful experience where everything went smoothly with excellent officiating.

One interesting fact is that three of my 800m races above were within a second of each other all around 2:49. It is amazing to me. It appears there is only a limited amount of energy in the tank and one reason is that most champions are very consistent. It is interesting to see that the actual times achieved were exactly the same as target times or within about 0.25 seconds difference. This shows **you race as you train**. Perhaps I should have trained for a faster time. This World Games in Sydney as usual was very efficiently run. All my races were documented in detail for me and suitable to present as official recognition in case of a World or Canadian record..

All events at Olympic Park were efficiently run with electronic timing and the very best officials. The closing ceremonies were honored with never ending musical bands and dancers. The legendary Peter Crombie although injured dominated even with his injured knees. Later he and his lovely wife Margose entertained many of us including his friends from Canada and the US at his palatial apartment overlooking the ocean. The great Bill Collins (USA), and US friends including my roommate Bob Cozens (USA) all ran impressive times as usual. I also recall my friend Bob having some dizzy spell one day—maybe the extreme heat. Bill Collins was also injured for most of the meet and finally was taken away in a wheel chair— one of the many injured but participating warriors.

Reluctantly, I left behind Sydney with its magnificent Opera House and Harbour and our four star hotel close to the subway leading to Olympic Park — from our balcony the famous Stanley Park was seen below. I will miss also the ice cold pool on the top floor of our hotel which provided sudden shocking recovery from the many races and scorching sun.

But on returning home the excitement was not over, for a bad rash appeared on my exterior which my doctor promptly diagnosed as bed bugs— thinking I had picked them up while away. On the weekend I was in great pain, and at emergency clinic it was diagnosed as shingles. This painful rash can happen to seniors if they have had chicken pox in their youth, as in my case. With shingles it is essential to start drug treatment early but this was not possible now, so I endured longer. Then— with the heavy pain killer Tylenol T3 (with codeine) —I had an equally painful elimination problem. (Again too much information. But I would suggest to avoid T3 Tylonol, particularly, if taken with an antibiotic.) I see now there is a drug to help prevent reoccurrence or initiation of shingles but there are too many side effects for my liking.

But now 2009 now is just a memory of mostly happy experiences which have never faded. Would I have done it differently? No!

# AGE 85, 2014

This was a good year for me since I was in a new a group 85-89. Conveniently the World Masters Indoor championships in Budapest Hungary would be shortly after my birthday from March 25 to 30.

However, the year did not start well with frequent injuries with the hamstrings and right hip so training was not too intensive — so I missed four indoor meets organized by the Ontario Masters Athletics in Toronto. These problems I attributed to training indoors and the statin pills I was prescribed for high cholesterol— my extensive research indicated for highly competitive athletes statins cause muscle weakness which coupled with intense exercise cause injuries, especially, in older athletes. My research also indicated that statins are not useful for those over 70 even if cholesterol is very high. My doctor did reveal this useful information. In fact most of those with heart attacks don't have high cholesterol. I concluded that there are several other pathways which are more important for elders which cause heart disease. After this experience I wrote an article on this subject to National (US) Masters News. And after May 2014 I terminated the statins and remained mostly injury free for the remaining year.

# Budapest Hungary Indoor WMA Indoor Championship, March 2014

To add to my injury problem in January and February on March 4th, just three weeks before leaving for Budapest I slipped on ice in my entrance walkway to my house falling on some rocks and fracturing some ribs. In Canada this could happen. After five days on powerful painkillers I was able to run slow with discomfort but kept fit with some intense swimming (five laps fast) to simulate an 800m and also by running in the pool. The training I had been doing in the weeks before though not ideal —stood me in good stead. Muscles fortunately have a memory.

At Budapest four days before my 800m I had a good indoor workout— some 200m and 150m repeats at a good pace, and two days before some fast 50m's. At Budapest I was in the bottom of a new age group. The first lap of my 800m was several seconds way too fast. My friend Geraldine Finnegan, a good coach, screaming from the balcony something about world record, said later this too fast first lap had her worried. But it was a world record in 3:11.09 improving on the old record of about 3:31. The 400m the next day was again too fast in the first lap and I slowed considerably in the home stretch, and lapping one runner near the finish— finishing in a world record in 1:21.26 compared to the old record of 1:25.50. Due to injuries and my fall I had done no speed work preparation for my 400m, although I did do some fast 50m repeats on the nearby U of T Mississauga 180m per lap indoor track. Also this convenient track close to my home has tight turns not conducive to fast sprinting. The training for the 800m had enabled me to maintain the speed for the 400m. In view of the lack of 400m training—I had a Tachycardia episode after the race and my heart did not go back to normal until about 2.5 hours afterwards. At one point 94 year old Olga Kotelko joined me laying down with feet up against a wall, for a short time. This was her favourite way to recover. That was the very last I ever saw of my friend Olga.

I was surprised of the two age group world records in spite of my fall three weeks earlier—but the good track, the spikes, the adrenaline, the competition, the cheering crowd and the increased focus provided a boost—and my muscles remembered the decent training before my fall. Also, the few days taper before a meet Is always beneficial.

## Southeastern Outdoor Masters Meet in Raleigh NC USA, June 2014

In early June I competed in the 400m and 200m at the Southeastern outdoor Masters in Raleigh NC breaking the 400m world age group record in 1:19.04. A press release to National Masters News said that I was the first over 80 years to run the 400m under 80 seconds. Also as an athlete of the meet with the highest age grade of all male and female track and field athletes, I was fortunate to win an award worth $500 US. There were some awesome athletes competing including world record holder/sprinter Charles Alie. I won this award also at age 75 so I feel somewhat reluctant to attend too frequently in case I am fortunate again. The organizers of the Southeastern meet stopped this great annual meet in 2017. But they were always happy, as I was to have me compete there and I usually donated a few books for prizes at the banquet. And my good friend Pete Taylor the legendary masters announcer was there making the events much more exciting for all. I left this 2009 meet happy but with a hefty bump on my shin from falling on some stairs while carrying some gift books to the awards banquet. The bump has stayed with me as a reminder of this great experience.

# Canadian Masters Athletics Outdoor Championships Varsity Stadium Toronto, July 2014

At the **Canadian** Masters Athletics Championships at Varsity Stadium in Toronto I ran the 400m and 800m. In the weeks before I believed I could improve on my 400m age group world record in Raleigh and felt a target 77.5 was within my capabilities—two seconds faster than Raleigh. So I prepared by getting well used to running relaxed and slightly faster than this pace for 300m, assuming there would be some slowing in the last 100m. In previous races I had found that my first 200m was usually too fast, but concentrating on the 300m training resulted in a much faster time. The race day was unusually windy but I felt strong —and finished in 77.10 with an age qrading of 106.3.% for my age 85.

The next day was the 800m and very hot and humid. I had prepared to run the first 400 and 600m in a certain time to finish around 3:10. Unfortunately, there was no timer at 600m but my 400m was on target. By concentrating in picking up my knees and swinging my arms— along with some very welcome loud female encouragement. I finished in 3:09.10 lowering the existing world record by about 9 seconds, and 99.24% age graded.

# US National Masters Outdoor Championships in Greensboro NC, USA, July 2014

A week later at the US National Masters Outdoor meet in Greensboro, NC, on a very hot day I had to cancel my 800m due to a Tachycardia episode most likely caused by the extreme heat, no shade, no hat, and too little water. I cancelled the 200m hurdles due to lack of preparation. Just a few minutes before the 200m I had a bad pain in my left foot. I quickly borrowed some Biofreeze ointment from an older athlete and the pain luckily disappeared. The next day I ran a 78.82 in the 400m, not a world record, as some thought, in view of my 77.10, 400m race, in Toronto the week before.. But in any case the National Masters news referred to me as the "ageless wonder", in my opinion, a great compliment.

# North American Masters Outdoor NCCWMA Championships in Costa Rica, August, 2014

Next I competed at the North American Masters Championships in Costa Rica which takes place every two years in years between the WMA championships; this involves Canada, USA Caribbean countries Mexico and South American countries—these are also WMA sanctioned meets. In the previous weeks I had been nursing a plantar fasciitis injury—a problem that had plagued me too often in the past 28 years. My main purpose in Costa Rica was to break the 200m hurdle world record. In the previous two weeks my hurdle training—three sessions, my only sessions this year did not go smoothly; in fact the last session on a windy wet day when I should not have been training, the scissor hurdles were being blown over —I hit a hurdle and wrenched my right groin. It was uncomfortable to run even slowly. But I had eight days to recover. Since the hurdles was my main priority in Costa Rica it was a mistake not to put in more training on the hurdles. But hurdle training is more likely to cause injury.

After running a slow 800m at Costa Rica in running shoes instead of spikes to protect my sore left foot—the following day I warmed up for the 200m hurdles. To break a world record in the hurdle there had to be at least two in the race. At my age of 85 there are few competitors. So was I was happy to have Christa Bortignon W75, a friend and multi world record holder in my race. She clears the hurdles much too high but makes up for it with her speed between the hurdles. (Incidentally, a W75 is roughly equivalent in race times to a M85 according to my own research.) As soon as we came from the declaration area we were taken to the start. Christa immediately complained to the officials that the hurdles "looked too high;" our regulation height was 27 inches. The officials response was not too reassuring, "They are the same height as these hurdles at the side of the track." There was no time to check. We were off. I cleared the first hurdle with not my usual favourite lead leg. Each hurdle after this felt awkward. Some hurdle races go very smoothly even with little or no preparation as in Barbados in 1999, but not this race one—maybe it was my right groin, still stiff from last week. With one metre to go I felt I had won this race— Christa finished strong in 42.66 to my 42.70. I was confused by a double line at the finish about 1 metre apart. I mistook the first line as the finish and let up at that point— a past bad habit of mine. But I was happy to lower the existing record by about three seconds, and Christa was very happy. The hurdles is a race where you can improve even though older since it is a skill event. So I was looking forward to the Worlds in Lyon in 2015.

The 4x400m relay with the M60's was my most enjoyable race in Costa Rica. The officials took us out about an hour too early. In the torrid sun and no shade I was concerned about dehydration and a possible Tachycardia episode which high heat can bring on. But although our team finished third I was pleased with my effort and the comradery, hence, enjoyed this even more than my hurdle record. And so it ended—for me a most productive year of ups and downs.

At Costa Rica I was also pleased and surprised to learn many Costa Ricans, in this corner of the world, who knew of Earl Fee, his books and world records. Nobody can tell me that recognition is not a reason to be modestly motivated. I was happy to meet my new friend Sigrid Gutierrez who knew of me and also happy to spend some time with my friend Joy Upshaw. Two beautiful famous athletes. See below Sigrid and daughter, lucky me, and Joy.

*San Jose party*

# WORLD RECORDS FOR EARL FEE
# AGE GROUP 85-89

## AND RELAY RECORDS AGE GROUP 80-89

| EVENT | AGE GROUP | DATE | PLACE | WORLD CHAMP'S | WORLD RECORD |
|---|---|---|---|---|---|
| 4x400 Relay | 80-89 | March 16,2013 | York U Toronto | No | 6:06.28 WR |
| 4x800 Relay | 80-89 | July 6, 2013 | Toronto Varsity Std | No | 14 min. 24sec WR |
| 400 Indoor | 85-89 | March 30, 2014 | Budapest Hungary | Yes | 1:21.26 WR |
| 800 Indoor | 85-89 | March 28, 2014 | " | Yes | 3:11.09 WR |
| 400 Outdoor | 85-89 | June 7, 2014 | Raleigh, NC | No | 79.04 WR 104% |
| 400 Outdoor | 85-89 | July 12, 2014 | Toronto, ON Varsity Std | No | 77.12 WR 106.33%AG |
| 800 Outdoor | 85-89 | July 13, 4014 | " | No | 3:09.10 WR 99.24%AG |
| 200 hurdles Outdoor | 85-89 | August 23, 2014 | San Jose Costa Rica | No NCCWMA | 42.70 WR OLD 45+ |

# 11

# WORLD MASTERS ATHLETIC CHAMPIONSHIPS

## FROM 1987 TO 2014

### 15 WORLD MASTERS ATHLETICS (WMA) CHAMPIONSHIPS I HAVE COMPETED IN AS OF 2017:

1987 MELBOURNE AUSTRALIA
1989 EUGENE OREGON
1991 TURKU FINLAND
1993 MIYAZAKI JAPAN
1995 BUFFALO USA
1997 DURBAN SOUTH AFRICA
1999 GATESHEAD ENGLAND
2001 BRISBANE AUSTRALIA
2003 PUERTO RICO
2005 SAN SEBASTIAN SPAIN
2006 LINZ AUSTRIA
2007 RICCIONE ITALY
2009 LAHTI FINLAND

2011 SACRAMENTO USA

2014 BUDAPEST HUNGARY

2015 LYON FRANCE attended only, due to misdiagnosed hernia— my doctor had recommended no competition.

2018 MALAGA SPAIN. I will be competing in this meet at age 89, this book published shortly after this meet. Results: 800m 2nd, 400m 3rd.

## WORLD GAMES I HAVE COMPETED IN UP TO 2017:

1998 PORTLAND/ EUGENE, OREGON USA

2009 SYDNEY, AUSTRALIA

# MELBOURNE AUSTRALIA WMA CHAMPIONSHIPS 1987

Melbourne was my first experience at a World Masters Championship. About four months before, I was competing in a small local meet in the 400m. I had borrowed some running spikes from my good friend/training partner Wayne Cosgrove for the race—a middle distance runner, also training with the North York Track and Field Club. After the race Wayne was very impressed and enthusiastic with my performance and said, "You have to compete at the WMA Championships in Melbourne." This was all new to me.

In Melbourne since lacking in experience I had a bad case of nerves jangling throughout the whole days during my two weeks in Melbourne, but particularly, the five days before my first races, 800 prelims and final. The fact that Melbourne was an exciting city with a stunning coastline, where you could even walk down the street with an alcoholic drink in your hand, and had two best friends with me — relieved no stress. I knew of no mental techniques, as I learned a few years later, to quell nervousness and increase energy and confidence.

*Nervous as a cat on a hot tin roof*
*Was I. But now it's all in the past;*
*No longer concern about coming last;*
*This smirking cat is the living proof.*

The visit to Australia did not start well. On arrival at Sydney my travelling friend George Romanick, a fellow engineer at AECL, and I stopped at midnight at the home of Ken Cook, a past friend from Canada. I immediately noticed—I was missing my airplane tickets. By retracing our steps in the dark fortunately…we found my tickets at the edge of the ocean. Needless to say, it called for a celebration drink or two. Later in Melbourne. my luggage had not arrived after a week in Australia— due perhaps to the complication of a stopover in New Zealand— so complete new track equipment was purchased. A month later, I was reimbursed by the airlines with an airline ticket worth $500 which I gave away.

On looking back my inexperience showed— when I see in my training log, in the five, four, and three days before my 800 prelim I did workouts, of 4380, 3910 and 4650 total meters respectively of aerobic and anaerobic runs. This was way too ambitious the week before a major meet and resulted in very tired legs in the last 200m of the 800 final. I learned the hard way— less is more in many cases. Another big mistake was not taking it easy in the prelims.

I made the 800m finals out of 44 competitors in age group 55-59 and finished 7th of the eight finalists with Tony Churchill, GBR, 1st in 2:08.07, David Carr, AUS, 2nd in 2:09.78, Ralph Miller, USA, 3rd in 2:10.02, Bertold Neuman FGR 4th, Unto Mattson FIN, 6th. As I quickly gained in experience in a couple of years, I would later compete successfully in the 800m against Miller, Neuman, and Mattsson— but David Carr being three years younger posed a problem, although we always ran close to each other with me winning if based on age grading. Mattsson and Carr were complete opposites; Unto towering devouring the track with each stride, but David moving smoothly with short rapid strides. Churchill won the 1500m handily. Unfortunately, I didn't see the affable Churchill again at any World meets. He and his lovely wife were very friendly at Melbourne offering me information about training and competing. I noticed and learned—he was one of a few athletes that cooled down after a race.

In the 400m prelim I had the 4th fastest time out of 44 competitors. And 3rd fastest out of 14 in the semi. Finally, I finished 4th in 57.49 after Charles Williams, GBR 1st 53.98. Bertold Neuman, FGR, 54.49 and Churchill, GBR, 3rd 57.05. Nine years later at age 66 I reached a peak and ran just 0.5 seconds slower than Melbourne to break a world record at the Buffalo NY Worlds. The speedy Harry Brown, world record holder in the 200m indoor age group 75-79 and many other USA records) who was to become a friend in later years was also in the final 400m. I always had good success against him in the 400m but he was an uncatchable rocket in the 200m and 100m with a blazing start.

Some distance races at Melbourne were run in spite of a tremendous downpour of rain. I recall the volunteers huddled together all sheathed in plastic from head to toe. Two male competitors in the 100m in their 90s continued to race each other running neck to neck for about 60m past the finish line. Another exciting race for me was watching Ray Tucker from Canada competing against 88 athletes and finishing a close 2nd in the M40 800m, with a time of 2:00.19, close to 1:59.35 for Ron Bell of GBR. I had watched Ray train and race many times in Canada. His prelim and semi times were 2 seconds and 1 second faster respectively than his final time. This indicated one has to train to be strong for three hard races in a few days of competition.

Fare thee well Melbourne, you were a great learning experience.

# EUGENE OREGON WMA CHAMPIONSHIPS 1989

After the experience gained in Melbourne followed by two years intense training— I improved and was able to break a world record in age group 60-64 at an age 60 in the 800m in 2:12.85.

The day before leaving for the Worlds in Eugene OR, I pulled a hamstring doing some fast 100m repeats. Then on arrival I heard that Derek Turnbull the New Zeeland sheep farmer phenomenon had also recently run nearly the same 2:12 something in the 800m. Still a greenhorn athlete l trained one day before my 800 prelims with an icepack strapped to my leg. And my sickly pre-race jitters were still with me but not as bad as in Melbourne. In later years I learned adrenaline is actually your friend. In fact, my best race ever was the 800m final at Buffalo Worlds at age 66 in spite of a bad case of nerves due to a roaring heavy wind.

I learned the following useful information the hard way from my 800-final run at night with the wet track shining under the bright lights. Don't take the lead for most of the way when competing against equally talented competitors. If you have more speed save your energy for the final kick, Normally, the race starts at about 100m to go. Avoid a burst of speed mid race to pass an unknown competitor as I did in passing my future friend Chuck

Sochor at 300m—this wasted precious energy and helped produce a first lap a couple of seconds too fast. With 200m to go the announcer remarked that Turnbull was in 6th place. (Two decades later it is considered wrong for an announcer to give out such detailed information.) This gave me extra confidence particularly since Turnbull had already won the 5K earlier in the day even after stopping to pick up his false teeth. But at about 60m to go he charged past me coming from the back of the pack, seeming to me like a freight train suddenly passing in the night, I lost a fraction of a second in recovering while he won in 2:14.53 with me second in 2:15.12,and Frank Evans 3rd in 2:15.69, Windred Norman, AUS, 4th. Later, I noticed Kelsey Brown, USA, way past his great prime was in one of the prelim heats, and also the popular Don Farquharson of Canada, one of the pioneers of forming International masters athletic meets, a DNF in the same prelim heat.

Derek Turnbull in his prime would normally win five or six golds at these world championships in events from 800m to marathon including many heats over the two weeks of competition. I consider he was the master athlete of the 20th century. He told me he would normally run with his friends on Saturday from farm to farm for many hours over the hilly New Zealand country. He told of running with some fit mates to a pub 20 miles away and returning the same day after many fortifying beers. I figured I had a big disadvantage sitting at a desk all day compared to Derek's active outdoor farming life.

At Eugene I met for the first time Jack Greenwood and Jim Law two formidable American and world record holders. In the 400m final Greenwood was 1st in 57.64, Law 2nd in 58.06, myself 3rd in 58.47 and Chuck Sochor 4th in 59.03. Jim always looked resplendent in his white track suit and would save his energy in the 400m for the last 100m passing his competitors. At a later meet in May in Raleigh North Carolina—Jim, the good sportsman, suggested to me he would help me break his 400m world record by being my rabbit. He dropped out ahead of me at 250 metres and explained to others he had a twinge in his hamstring. But I wasn't up to it that day, mainly due to too early in the season. That was the late great Jim Law who died a year or two later from a heart attack at a track while training after doing some hill training shortly before.

I had entered the 300m hurdles at the Eugene worlds but cancelled due to my recent recovering hamstring. Greenwood was an excellent hurdler and won in 43.49. He told me he was happy and surprised with the fast time. Jack had a triple bypass in later years, but was still able to break American and world records after. At an indoor meet in the USA I attended — before the 400m where Jack and I were both entered, the race announcer remarked Jack Greenwood had never been beaten in a race. After the race he was on his knees and bent over. I recall feeling strong that day even with 50 metres to go and was able to beat him. But I believe in view of his exhaustion he must have been recovering from his operation or an injury.

At these Eugene worlds the beloved Peyton Jordan, USA, multi world record holder won handily in the 100m and 200m. It was obvious he was a very popular champion with the USA female athletes.

Sadly, many of the above greats that I know of are no longer with us: Jack Greenwood, Derek Turnbull, Frank Evans, Jim Law, Kelsey Brown, Peyton Jordan, Don Farquharson. All gone, gone with the wind, and no longer running like the wind, but not gone or lost in our fond memory.

# TURKU FINLAND WMA CHAMPIONSHIPS 1991

The Turku World Veterans Championships in 1991—attended by athletes from 56 countries— for me at age 62 was another learning experience. But it was exciting to visit this far north country with its 188,000 lakes, mainly dense forests, home of the great Paavo Nurmi, rugged sportsmen and beautiful amazons.

There were hundreds of thrilling moments. In the W70 marathon Kaczperczyk of Poland was 2nd in an impressive time but also Dq'd when Polish fans spurred her on from the inner field for almost the entire final lap.

There were the following super performances, to mention a few. Jack Greenwood, USA, always a treat to watch— broke three M65 world records; 100m hurdles in 16.30, 300m hurdles in 45.20, and 400m in 1.00,23. (I would be fortunate to lower the latter time at the 1995 Worlds in Buffalo.) Ron Robertson, NZL) another exceptional athlete, broke M50 world records in the 10K in 31.01,90, and the 3000m steeplechase in 9.43,97.

Before my 800m final I was introduced to Jim Sutton, USA, one of my competitors in this event. He spoke in a belittling way about his abilities and experience in the 800m. But it appeared he was a quick learner and improved tremendously in a short time by winning in a fast time of 2.13, 98. Berthold Neuman, GER, led up to about 60m from the finish with me following comfortably behind utilizing energy. (It feels so much easier following —believed to reduce race time by about 1.5 seconds in the 800m.) At this point Berthold stepped on the rail injuring his left leg. As I slowed momentarily trying to get around him Sutton came flying by. I finished behind him in 2.14,50 followed by Unto Mattson, (FIN) in 2.15.21, and Simon Herlaar, HOL, in 2.16,09. After the race Archie Messenger, a long-time veteran in the USA who had introduced me to Sutton— rebuked Sutton, "Why did you say "that" to Earl before the race?" But Jim just smiled.

The friendly Sutton also impressed by winning the 1500m in 4:32.09. I learned later he trained as I did with good competitive middle-distance runners about 20 years younger. But I was fortunate to keep just ahead of him in four future races in the US. At a US national outdoor meet in Carolina where the temperature was at a dangerous 100 degrees athletes were collapsing— I had to run three races: 200m, 400m and 800m in one day as the meet got backed up due to a lightning storm the day before. Jim was in my 800m and his jovial manner before the race in these torrid conditions relieved me of a lot of stress and nerves.

In my final 400m at Turku on the back straight on an inner lane next to me Wilhelm Selzer of Germany came flying by on his way to his world record in 57.36. This caused me to deviate from my race plan.—and tense up. Hence,

I finished with poor form and tired legs 0.01 seconds behind the 3rd runner. I can't remember running a worst race. I learned an important lesson— to stick to my own race plan. Also, it would pay also to be knowledgeable about the competition before the race—I knew nothing about Selzer until after the fact. However, in the 4x400m relay running with the M50's I had got it together and ran relaxed and nearly 2 seconds faster than my 400m race, indicating hope for the future.

Turku was another learning experience for Earl Fee.

# MIYAZAKI JAPAN WMA CHAMPIONSHIPS 1993

Never has there been such a World Masters Athletics Championship of this magnitude as this in Miyazaki Japan in 1993, —71 countries and 12, 000 athletes competing, over twice the usual and mainly Japanese, and the equivalent of $12M US spent in preparation and running expense in spite of thousands of volunteers. No expense was spared; for example, the heavy impressive medals came in a velvet case. The opening ceremonies involved thousands of dancers, musicians and singers in the stadium bedecked in flowers and flags. One day on the street in front of our headquarters hotel we were treated to a street fair —hundreds of stalls selling food, wares of all kinds in a colorful atmosphere of drums and other live music. The monster closing banquet with it's drums and colorful performers was perhaps too tempting and enjoyable with its unlimited drinks for some who had to compete next day. We saw and experienced the great respect the Japanese have for their elderly. By this time I had broken a few world records and I was honored and pleased to carry the Canadian flag at the grand opening ceremonies attended by over 60 international countries.

The 1st photo is my enjoyable prelim 1500m at Miyazaki—I recall the pace, about 10 seconds slower than race pace, feeling slow, so I was taking long relaxed strides. I was 64 at top of my age group and decided at the meet to run the 1500 instead of the 400 which was too loaded with talent —I envisaged a battle in the 400m for 3rd place as Ralph Romaine, (TRI) and Berthold Neumann (GER) and David Carr (AUS) were entered plus 50 others. But, I had trained only to run the 400, 800 and the 300 hurdles. I decided to skip the hurdles and instead on the hurdle day to do instead some preparation training for the 1500m. Before the 1500m I did not know one of my competitors, Simon Herlaar, (HOL). already had the 1500m world record in this age group, and in 1996 he still had the 150m outdoor world record in the 65-69 age group in an impressive time of 4:38.50 I learned it is wise to know about your opponents strengths and weaknesses before a race. So it was a mistake to lead all the way in the final until about 150m from the finish when Herlaar passed me. I came 2nd in 4.44.86 to Herlaar in 4.42.86. He ran a smarter race; I should have let someone else lead. Definitely the very hardest race I ever ran, in view of my lack of specific preparation— taking me two hours to recover, but fortunately, fatigue did not hit me until after the finish. And fortunately, I had also been training with youngsters at the Saugeen Track club in Port Elgin for two years with some tough young teenagers and a tough female coach named Geordie Farrell. Also prior to Miyazaki I had been doing 8 mile runs once a week up to about mid May 1993 and also the occasional 5K race in the summer of 1993.—and endurance workouts lasting less than 45 minutes: usually two to three times a month in Maple Grove woods in Toronto Scarborough — while visiting my children in the area— consisting of intervals on the many hills and smooth trails.

第10回世界ベテランズ陸上競技選手権大会　平成5年10月7日〜17日　宮崎市にて

The 2nd photo is the 800m final, age group 60-64—150m from the finish. At age 64 at top of the age group I made the mistake of leading until the final sprint after the bend—being a slow learner— finishing 0.2 seconds behind

Carr (AUS) outside left, and one second behind the winner Neumann, (FGR) third from right. In those early days I did not know: when there are competitors of near equal ability it is best not to take the lead. But at Turku Finland Worlds in 1997 I would be fortunate against Neumann and would be also in Durban South Africa Worlds. Some years later Neumann had a serious brain operation, I believe finishing his impressive running career.

The third photo is our 4x400m Canadian relay finishing 4th due to three much older runners: Tom Callendar, Bill McIllwaine and myself with the great Harold Marioka as the speedy anchor. But I would be on a winning 4x400m relay team with Harold at the Worlds in Puerto Rico in 2003.

At Miyazaki, Harold Marioka a strong competitor winning in the 50-54 age group the 800m, in 2:03.42 and breaking a world record in the 400m in 51.76, and also winning the 100m Doug Smith also a fellow Canadian and stalwart executive and president on the Ontario Masters Athletics for many decades— in Miyazaki competed in the following 40-44 age group events: 1500m, 5K, 10K, 10K cross country, 3000m steeple chase and even the marathon—demonstrating amazing endurance in a period of less than two weeks, and he may have had other races too.

I finished the championship competing in the 4x400m relay in the 50-54 age group-—no medal but a Canadian record. My travel companion friend, Chuck Sochor from Grand Rapids USA, had won three golds, in the 65-69 age group: the 300m hurdles and the 4x100m relay and the 4x400m relay with his USA team mates. We had traveled around Japan for a week—it seems like we must have visited a hundred temples — and Chuck who has a total of 10 sons and daughters collected 10 kimonos, one or two from each hotel as souvenirs for his grown offspring. Hence his suitcase was bulging like a fat whale.

Paul Spangler, USA at age 90+ in age group 90-94 impressed the thousands of spectators with his six gold medals, running alone, in the 200m (1:38.50), 400m (2:53.26), 800m (6:19.65), 1500m (14:27.59), 10K (1hr 58:38.00), and cross country (2 hours 41:11). Some medals were given out by the Royal Princess so Paul no doubt was one of the fortunate recipients. In his 200m I witnessed him falling several times, but no one was allowed to help him for fear of a disqualification. In the cross county, they pushed him up some hills. I asked if this was legal and was told, not seriously, by the Americans; "It is, if you are over 90." He told in Miyazaki he was writing his memoirs —hopefully he finished them later as he was a most interesting and colorful character. Considering the number of events and his age, and his grit, his overall performance— although seemingly slow— was amazing.

In the M75 100m first and second were tied at 13.99. Initially the gold medal was awarded to Walter Rennschuh, GER, rather than Bill Weinacht, USA, based on visual observation of the electronic photo. But finally upon review, two medals were awarded. The medals were worth keeping as they were heavy, impressive and came in a velvet case. One of the many reasons the meet cost over $12M.

At this meet as in many others I roomed with my good friend Chuck Sochor from Michigan, USA, a good multi-disciplined athlete and strong as a bull. Chuck had brought a lot of food with him as was his custom, but we preferred to eat dinner at a small Japanese restaurant nearby. We normally ordered Yaki Soba, fried noodles and vegetables, ordering by sign language. After about four visits we were happy and surprised to receive impressive gifts from the husband and wife owners— a fairly common Japanese custom we learned. Chuck at age 66 in M65 group won gold in the 300m hurdles based on practising on a dirt road over make shift hurdles and was a member of the winning USA 4x100m and 4x400m relay teams, comprised of Larson, Sochor, Daprano and Law and — Siefort, Daprano, Sochor and Law respectively. At the airport and on some of the return flight Chuck, justly proud of his gold medals, enjoyed carrying them about this neck — the clattering and clanging on each step reminding one of cowbells. So, there was no concern about losing him or his medals.

All in all, Miyazaki—a great experience and for me a learning one. And it was obvious the young Japanese children worshipped seniors. After this memorable meet I didn't realize I was still improving and learning, and the best was yet to come in Buffalo, USA, in two years.

# BUFFALO NEW YORK WMA CHAMPIONSHIPS 1995

The World Masters Championships in Buffalo New York in 1995 was attended by nearly 6000 competitors from 78 countries large and small, e.g., Canada 317, USA 1830, Great Britain 222, Germany 565.

My best meet ever was at age 66 at this World Championships in Buffalo—our own back yard where friends and relatives could watch. This was in spite of the University Dorms which were like an oven for the first four days. However, the gigantic cafeteria meals made up for this inconvenience—we ate and ate and loads of fruit and desserts—it seemed to help rather than hinder.

At this meet after 9 years of consistent training I reached a peak in performance at age 66 —breaking three M65 records in the 400m, 800m and 300m hurdles. Leading up to this auspicious meet in July 13 -23 my preparation was fortunately, better than normal and injury free except for a nagging plantar fasciitis problem. For example, in the fall of 1994 while working at the Bruce nuclear power plant in Port Elgin, Ontario as an Ontario Hydro consultant I trained happily with the with teenagers at the Saugeen Track Club. This involved long runs on the windy shores of Lake Huron and chasing these speedy runners on steep hills, coached be Earl and Geordie Farrell. This and also training with North York Track Club fortunately toughened me up considerably both mentally and physically.

Back in Mississauga, Ontario during the five months before these World championships I competed in various meets sanctioned in Canada and the US and ran 33 races: 60m, 200m, 400m, 800m and 300m hurdles including three 5K races. In March a 11-day training camp at Baton Rouge with the Saugeen track club Involved a 1.5 mile run to and from the track each day and some hard workouts— for example, a 7-mile run around a large lake, 2 sets (600m, 400m, and 200m); or 3x300m, 3x200, 3x150m; or hurdle training, followed by the tired 1.5-mile jog back to lodgings. I felt strong from the above training and 33 races enabling me to break three M65 age group world records before Buffalo—an outdoor age group 800m record at the Canadian championships in Toronto in 2:15.30, and a 2:!5.23 outdoor age group 800m record in Eugene, OR, and an indoor age group 400m record in 59.53 at Reno — Michael Johnson had broken a world record 400m on this track a week before, but it was later disallowed since official track measurements indicated one foot short. I could see the correction on the track marked with tape. Oddly enough this good track was immediately adjacent to a barn for cattle and the nose could attest to the proximity. In view of my above records the US officials at the Buffalo meet appeared to be ready for me as I was tested for drugs immediately after the final 400m and final 800m. After the 400m it took me one hour and 45 minutes to come up with enough fluid. Nevertheless, my Saugeen coach, Geordi Farrell waited for me. She had arranged my entry long before, so I had bib # 1. It was an exciting time in my life with friends and family there to cheer.

I particularly enjoyed the opening ceremonies as did the other Canadians. Our contingent was well received by the enthusiastic crowd. Then in the company of our energetic cheerleader Marg Headshot we smiled our way all around the track. The meet went smoothly except during the opening ceremonies— the female torch bearer, a famous ex- high jumper, had her hair catch fire in lighting the flame to officially start the meet. Also, for several days it was so hot athletes were collapsing particularly at the cross-country venue. Before my 300m hurdle prelim I waited in mid afternoon for over two hours shaded under a tent, but the heat got to me nevertheless— when I ran over the hurdles, I was unable to concentrate on which leg to lead on the various hurdles. Before my prelim heat the official starter relieved my anxiety by saying, "You are the fastest so you have to pull this wagon," (referring to a heavy 2 wheeled apparatus nearby).

**300m hurdles**. The 800-meter semi only one hour before the 300m hurdle final gave me some concern but I took the two laps easy in 2 minutes and 29 seconds. In the hurdle final one competitor arrived 10 minutes, late but I was surprisingly calm since I had already broken the specific age 66 world record earlier in the year in Lansing Michigan (US Masters Outdoor) the week before. Also, this time, I had rehearsed many times mentally which lead leg on the various hurdles. In my 300m hurdle specific age world record I had a close race with Standing Ariel Levies (CHL). We were dead even at the 2nd last hurdle, clearing all hurdles cleanly. Standing had won the 300m hurdles in Miyazaki in an impressive 46.43. I purposely slowed slightly at the last hurdle to be careful and finished in 45.71 followed by Standen in 46.91. The hurdle training advice from Steve Bogatek our ex Olympic Polish hurdler— and the Saugeen Track Club had helped me tremendously. Also, my 800m training probably gave me an extra bit of endurance for a strong hurdle finish.

**800m.** After a day of rest, the 800-meter final came on an exceptionally windy day— the flags were straight out in a formidable dark sky and the wind roaring roaring like a lion in the packed stadium making conversation difficult. I had never run the 800m in such conditions; this made me more nervous than I had ever been before a race, bordering on a sickly feeling— but gave me extra adrenaline. I thought I'll be happy with a time 2 or 3 seconds slower than my recent age group 65-69 world record of 2 minutes 15.23 seconds (Eugene, Oregon outdoors during July 1995). In the warm up with the wind I felt I was flying. I envisaged a slow race fighting this heavy gale. In these conditions in the other age group 800m races there was a great reluctance to take the lead. But I took the lead immediately, followed closely by my main competition, the tall Unto Mattson, (FIN), until about 500m (see below). At this point with the strong wind at my back

I made a concerted effort to pick up the pace and imagined myself as a big sail. In the home stretch I could see the big clock— the time was fast— but it seemed taking ages to get to the finish against the wind in spite of the encouragement from the roaring, supportive crowd. Later, on TV I could see I was wobbling slightly from the effort but it was a new world age group record time of 2:14.33 and over 6 seconds ahead of the valiant Mattson of Finland in 2:20.93. and over 13 seconds ahead of Tadatoshi Samuda 3rd in 2:27.94. All of the above finishing under the previous world record of 2:27.99 by Norm Windred (AUS) in Miyazaki.

I had reached a peak at the right time and place. The thousands cheering in the stands including about 300 Canucks gave me a terrific boost. After the race and out of breath I was immediately interviewed by CNN before being rushed off for drug testing, but the wind was so loud I could hardly hear the questions. I went through the first lap in 64 seconds in the lead in spite of the wall of wind against in the home stretch. The seasoned veteran runner, Winfred, from Australia said it was the best race he had ever seen. After a brief TV interview, I was immediately rushed off for drug testing. There was no big hurry as it took me over two hours to provide enough liquid.

This 800m was without doubt my best race ever and would have been faster without this wind. Unto Mattson from Finland, sent me a message and a gift at the next Worlds in Durban South Africa two years later via his Finnish team mates: "Tell Earl in our 800-final race I was dead at 400m." The first lap 400m of 64 seconds running my pace instead of his own had done him in. Actually, the same Unto didn't learn his lesson, as he made the same mistake in our 800m final at San Sebastian Worlds.

**400m.** In the 400-meter final, in good weather, I said to myself I am going to do this for the Saugeen and North York Track Clubs, my son Tyler who was in the packed stands on his 23rd birthday, for Canada, and myself. All year I had been getting closer and closer to the world record. The main competition was Switzer from Germany—he had won in record time in Turku in the 60-64 age group and also in Japan in the 65-69 age group. He was in the 3rd lane and I in the 2nd fortunately where I could watch him and see most of the competitors. Selzer had passed me on his way to a world record in the back straight in Turku disrupting my relaxation. Since I heard he had a strong finishing kick I planned to pass him at about 175 meters from the start. It went according to plan and he didn't respond. I recall taking a slight imperceptible breather at about 275 meters to gather myself for the sprint home. With about 20 meters to go I felt my stride shortening and some lactate in my quads - I was afraid someone would catch me—but it was an age group world record in 57.93 seconds in near perfect conditions bettering Jim Law's record of 58.79 seconds. I was followed by Wilhelm Selzer (GER) in 59.37, friend Charles Socher (USA) in 59.76, and Harry Brown (USA) in 1.00.91. My success at Buffalo Worlds in the 400m was based mainly on speed endurance, e.g., 800m training, and repeat 100, 150, 200, and 300 metres, but no real sprint training, or repetitions at 400m race pace,400, or weight training. The 300m hurdles helped my 400m since it is similar to running a 400m race. Also, the 33 races in1995 had paid off. Later, I was taken again for drug testing immediately after my record 400m. I was beginning to feel USA officials were suspicious of Earl Fee as it had been a very successful world record year. But no drug testing after my specific age world record in the 300m hurdles final (actually 0.5 seconds slower than the great Jack Greenwood's age group world record four years earlier. The huge enthusiastic encouraging crowd had brought out the best in me.

Here are some of my other vivid impressions. The Canadian embassy reception, done with class. The parachutists dropping into the dark stadium in the opening ceremonies followed by trails of coloured smoke. A girl from Brampton in the stands cheering and clapping on her feet for the Canadians- she was a joy to behold. Fred Robbins running solo around the track through the rain and 5-inch-deep water on the track during stoppage of events —one of the crazy Canucks. The doping — they got me twice—- negative of course since I am only on the supplements. I had bib number 1 thanks to the early entry arranged by the Saugeen Track Club. The many foreign strangers who came up to me to offer their congratulations and some with gifts. But particularly the company of friends from USA, Australia and Canada, and some family.

At this world there were two ladies also with three world records each: Marg Allison (AUS) in W50 100m, 200m, 400m, and Brunhild Hoffman (GER) in W55, 100m, 200m, 400m. I was happy to be in such auspicious company. But in 2005 in Sebastian Spain at age 76 I was able to have another fortunate meet.

All the above made it all worthwhile. The occasional hard training, my plantar fasciitis, and some stress were soon forgotten. As they say, "The pain is short, the pride is long." Needless to say I will never forget Buffalo 1995.

# DURBAN SOUTH AFRICA WMA CHAMPIONSHIPS 1997

The 12th World Veterans Championships in Durban South Africa in 1997, at that time, was the first and the largest participator sporting event ever undertaken for the continent of Africa.

The weather was kind except for the first two rainy days, and physiotherapy chiropractic's, and massage was free. I recall a well-run meet and a most enjoyable banquet, a wide variety of South African foods and energetic dancing music all of which I enjoyed with my good friend Marne McMillan from Vancouver— and also with her some refreshing dips in the nearby ocean. At the opening ceremonies at a huge stadium many long speeches were given and eventually to relieve the boredom the athletes started the "Wave" in the stands. It was usual to see police patrolling the street carrying machine guns. This seemed like overkill but some Americans were robbed while walking on a street, by assailants with machetes. Another American couple actually had an intruder right in their hotel room, with a gun seeking money. One sunny afternoon on our busy street a taxi van filled crammed to the brim with people overturned right in front of me. I helped to lift the van so people could escape from underneath. Soon, nearly everyone in the van had a white bandage on some body part.

The day after arriving in Durban I had a bad strain in my quad while doing some medium speed accelerations. This was a reoccurrence of an injury I had some weeks before leaving for Durban. I believe this was caused by the long air flight of about 13 hours from New York City to Durban, For the three days before my prelim 800m I constantly applied ice off and on, walking slowing in the ocean nearby, massage from our trainer Jonathon, and frequent massage, stretching and Advil. On the day of my prelim Jonathon applied a four-inch tape around the quad and my body in a figure of eight configuration. It was very restrictive on walking but I managed to win my prelim, although I made a mistake in running too far by following some orange cons that had been placed all around the track in my starting lane. The tape had helped me get through the prelim. The two days after, I ran in a pool slowly with my feet touching the bottom. On the day of my 800m final I warmed up on grass followed by a light massage. Berthold Neumann, (GER), and David Carr, (AUS) were my main competition. Neumann followed me closely but only for about 600m. My legs felt like lead, but I finished in 2:19.08 with Neumann 2:20.10 and David Carr (AUS) in 2:22.17. In retrospect, the tired legs were due to minimal land running training for eight days previous, and the two times running in the pool a couple of days before my race —years later I found pool running should not be done less than four days before a competition as it is similar to weight training.

This meet produced nearly 60 world records. Derek Turnbull (NZL), still going strong, had three records: 800m, 1500m and 5000m. Phil Raschker (USA), not surprising, had seven records in track and field. (Raschker had about 80 world records in track and field, so in my opinion would be the female master of the 20th century.)

While looking at the Durban world records list recently I couldn't help but notice that the phenomenon Ralph Romaine ran 57.64 in the 400m breaking my M65 record at Buffalo Worlds of 57.97 by 0.33 seconds. But then I noticed he broke this M65 record while running in the M60 age group In Durban. He was 60 at start of the Durban meet so he had to register with the M60's, but on day of the 400 final he was 65. He must have reminded the officials of this and that his time lowered the existing M65 record of 57.97 (mine). However, Ralph had an advantage— running with the faster 60-year old's he would be forced to run faster. It used to be the case in Canada that one could not break a world record if there was no one in the race in the same age group. I accept this finagling as water under the bridge and offer Ralph my best wishes in his non-competitive life in Trinidad. I was happy to have this 400m record for two years. (But my 1995 800m record at Buffalo worlds has been there now in 2018 for 23 years.)

In the 400m final at Durban— after the prelim and semi heats on the two days previous— Neumann in lane 5 passed me in lane 6 at about 250 m— going on to win in 59.50 with me 2nd in 62.16 and finishing with "very tired legs" after 300m due to no intense training for 12 days previous. Without the tired legs and cramping in my quads I was able to run 60.8. a month later. David Carr would have been competitive in the 400m but could not run the 400m semi due to a prelim 1500m— but winning the final 1500m by 0.5 seconds in a close race with Herbert Becker (GER).

This was the last big competition for Neumann due to brain health problems. He did show up as a spectator in Brisbane Worlds. It was in Brisbane where I had would have two major problems but some success regardless.

# GATESHEAD ENGLAND WMA CHAMPIONSHIPS 1999

Six thousand athletes from 74 countries competed at the XIII world Veterans Championships in Gateshead in 1999.

Sixty new world records were broken at Gateshead. My 800-world record in 2:21.95 with James Beall (USA) 2nd in 2:34.70— was listed as a world record in Gateshead results but I had actually broken it in 2:20.52 at Hamilton

Ontario in an outdoor meet five week before. Other Canadians breaking world records in Gateshead were: Olga Kotelko in W90 in the high jump and weight pentathlon; past Olympian Debbie Brill in W45 high jump winning in 1.76 m; and Helgi Pedel in W75 high jump. I noticed also the great Canadian Harold Marioka, won the M55 400m in 54.08. In the M60 800m Alan Bradford (AUS) had an exceptional world record in 2:10.42. I finished the meet also with a gold in the 400m in 63.11, with Rodney Brown (USA) 2nd in 66.11 (sadly now deceased). I recall in the 400-semi feeling particularly energetic on a fine sunny day—in retrospect it would have been a good day to try for a world record.

I did not compete in the 300m hurdles although entered and trained for it, since it was too close to my 800m final, and the two events were at two different, faraway stadiums. It is the usual custom at these worlds to schedule the 300m and 800m final within about 2 hours of each other. But at the Riccione Worlds in 2007 I did the double reluctantly and not enjoying the sick nervous feeling before the 800m due to the hurdles before.

I really enjoyed the medal presentation where young topless African females presented some of the medals. I have one photo of myself with one of these ladies. I suspect my times could have been faster as I had made the mistake of a great deal of walking in the days before my events and also too much sitting in the stands. During the latter part of the meet I was happy to have my friend Chris Erickson from Mississauga join me. Unfortunately, this prevented me from spending any time with my good friend Marne McMillan.

*Gateshead Worlds, 800m, age 70*

A highlight of the meet was an interview by Alastair Aitken of England to gather information for his book in progress at the time "Athletics Enigmas" (I gather meaning athletes with rare outstanding talent) He had published "More Than Winning" (1992), and "The Winning Edge" (1998). I didn't know I was an enigma (something puzzling); I knew about enimas but not enigmas. But I jest. In 'Athletics Enigmas"— Aitken covers about 400 athletes, mainly runners, in either a few words, sentences or a few pages for each athlete. He referred to me as a "true Athletic Enigma" in a couple of pages, and also states, "The most astonishing performance in the two weeks of all was when Earl Fee ran a world record of 2:21.95 for 800m, at age 70 (see the attached photo) shattering the age best of 2:27.57; itself a highly considered record by Californian James Lytjen back in 1991." Aitken also mentions my 30 total specific and age group world records broken up to that time, and also my testicle operation in England (too much info as they say) —my excuse or reason for not running for 33 years after University. The book includes a good photo of me running the 800m in Gateshead—looking very relaxed and fluid. When younger l used to receive a lot of compliments on my running style— slightly more lean than most— as I used to practise and strive for smooth relaxed, economical running in my training. I have found simply by thinking relaxed and striving for a longer stride, with greater push off at the back, and on the toes, automatically results in more speed. I felt very honoured and fortunate to be singled out in Aitken's book of "outstanding" Olympians and veteran runners such as Olympian Norm Pirie (ENG) and veteran Gilmore (AUS), etc.

At the end of the meet I recall a happy unwinding liquid event in a tent with Mike Carter, Anselm Lebourne and other friends, and later a visit at the beautiful York Minster Cathedral and the many highlights in London England.

# BRISBANE AUSTRALIA WMA CHAMPIONSHIPS 2001

G'day! Welcome to sub-tropical Brisbane the 14th WAVA World Veterans Athletics Championships with half of the 4900 athletes and officials from nearly 80 overseas countries.

At this meet 19 world records were broken; for example, Ed Whitlock (CAN) in the in the M70 5,000m and10,000m and Ron Robertson (NZL) in the M60 1500m, 5000m and 2000m steeplechase—not too surprising results from these two outstanding and legendary athletes.

I made a wise move on stopping off at Honolulu for two days to break up the long flight to Sydney. Here I met my running friends from Canada Marne McMillan, Maureen De Ste Croix and Linda Findlay. I was overjoyed to socialize with them and train briefly with them. My lovely talented ladies finished 2nd in the W45 8km cross country team event in 104:28. How I wish I was 45 again. OK I would settle for 60.

I had brought 25 copies of my self- published book on running, "How to Be Champion From 9 to 90." It took several hours to clear the customs and pay an exorbitant custom duty. At the main stadium in Brisbane a store sold my books without charge—a good example of the Aussy hospitality and friendliness. But otherwise, things did not go well for me in Brisbane.

Four days after arriving in Brisbane on checking in for my M70 800m prelim, after warming up for the race, the officials told me I was not registered although I did sign in the day before. Now feeling stressed since the prelim was just 30 minutes away— I had to find the head official in a very crowded large tent to get permission to reregister. I was eventually rushed over to the stadium with 15 minutes before the prelim; this stress caused my heart to rapidly speed up, a condition I experience occasionally, called Tachycardia, similar to Atrial Fibrillation. When this occurs, there is inadequate oxygen to the muscles and some weakness. Although not recommended, I decided to run a slow pace; and the fact that it was a prelim, and I already had the world record, gave me some confidence. I qualified 2nd in my heat in 2:40 but finished quite tired with a large dose of lactic acid in my legs, and strangely with very leaden and sore hips.

My heart did not stop its high beat in time for the 300m hurdles two hours l later so I cancelled. James Stookey (USA) won in 51.97; he was a strong hurdler in the 80m and 300m. I had several 300m races against him always successful except one when I had not practised. I especially remember a race at the NCCWMA Championships in Barbados in November 1998. My hurdle training before the Barbados meet consisted of a single run from the blocks and over the first scissor hurdle— which I sent flying. In the Barbados race I cleared all hurdles smoothly; and with about 60m to the finish Stookey was ahead by about two metres. I did not panic. With about 0.5m from the finish I passed him for a M70 world age group record. That is the thrill of sport —the unexpected, for most the pathos and some the jubilation. But win or lose the important thing is to compete.

A newsletter at the Brisbane meet stated, "In the M70 800m prelim John Downey's time at age 70 was 16 seconds faster than Earl Fee's at age 72, the world record holder; so, it is not looking good for Earl." A week later Downey broke the world M70 record in the 2000m steeplechase in 8:03.47. And in the 800m semi his time was 0.3 seconds faster than mine. So, he was my main competition. In the final I followed him (not usual for me) up to the final curve and passed him there— as I had noticed he goes out fast but finishes slower. I finished in 2:27.24 — nearly 7 seconds slower than my world record— with Downey 2nd in 2:27.94, and Hiroo Tanaka, (JAP) 3rd in

2:41.09. Derek Turnbull at age 74, top of the age group, finished 4th— not his usual phenomenal self: I suspect besides the age problem Derek most likely had some other undisclosed problem. Derek was very friendly offering me a sandwich and inviting me to his sheep farm in New Zealand. I didn't take advantage of this kind offer perhaps fearing I would be involved and laid low from one of his all daylight running sessions over hilly New Zealand with his sturdy friends.

My bad luck continued in Brisbane when I was disqualified in the 400m prelim by stopping on the inner line in my lane. I should have known better as I was warned before my race by an M75 athlete from the US that there were many getting Dqd by officials all around the track. But this advice went out of my head as soon as I started. I have been Dqd twice after this: At the **indoor** Worlds in LInz in 2006 while in the lead I crossed the cut-in line at 150m too early— but at least had the satisfaction of winning handily. The Dq in the **outdoor** meet at a US National meet in 2014 was due to by cutting in at a line at 150m from the start of a 400m race instead of continuing in my lane all around the track. My excuses: for the latter—the extreme heat might have affected my thinking, and I had been running too many indoor races where cutting in at 150m is the practice; and besides, after over 700 races in 32 years as a master— there is apt to be some misjudgment.

The final M70 400m was won by Hiroo Tanaka (JAP) in 62.90, Harry Brown, (USA).2nd In 63.38 and Wilhelm Selzer, (GER), in 64.88. Based on my times in training and my past experience with Harry and Wilhelm in Buffalo, I suspect I would have had a close race with Tanaka if not for my disqualification. However, I would have success against Brown and Tanaka at Puerto Rico and Ricionne Worlds. Prior to the Sacramento Worlds Tanaka broke my 400m world record of 70.64 by 0.3 seconds. But I only learned about his recent past success after my 400 final at the Sacramento Worlds where he won the 200m in a blazing time of 31seconds and beat me in final la stretch of the 400m.

But overall Brisbane Worlds and Australia were a great experience, for example, a boat tour on the Brisbane River. In Sydney my good but late Australian friend, Ken Cook, and room mate in Canada for several years, treated me like a King. Paying for my accommodation and splurging on a meal for three at the best restaurant in Sydney overlooking the Opera House and famous Sydney harbour at a cost of over $700 Australia, equivalent roughly to same in Canadain dollars.

**Wedding of Peter Crombie.** Sydney is always a great city to visit. But a highlight of this WMA Brisbane Worlds was the wedding of Peter Crombie (AUS) to his beautiful bride with a magnificent best ever reception at a Sydney castle served by black tie waiters, and no expense spared. In his speech Peter said he had no time to waste as he was getting older, so had to act quickly. Her six children did not deter him.

# PUERTO RICO WMA CHAMPIONSHIPS 2003

The 15th World Masters Championships in Puerto Rico in 2003 brings back fond memories. Although at the top of my 70-74 age group at age 74 — it is still useful to strive for your very best in spite of age, as this leads to a better performance when arriving at your next age group. If your age graded performance is not declining, you know you are not slipping. I was pleased to achieve an average of 100.26% in three events. Winning gold isn't everything, although there was some gold.

My main completion in the 800m was David Car (AUS) age71, holder of many Australian and world records. As we lined up for the start with David in lane one—an Aussy colleague/trainer came out and tightened David's spikes. I thought I am in trouble— dealing with a perfectionist here— and thinking the best I can do today is an 800m specific age 74 world record. I immediately took the lead as my custom, but David passed me at about 450m, then for about 20m he slowed down. I suspected later, he was either taking a breather or had some strategy in mind. Now I think he was encouraging me to take the lead. I continued to follow closely. At 110m before the finish he picked up the pace as expected and finished in 2:26.14, followed by me in 2:25.09. In retrospect, I should have been working on my finishing kick, My 800m was age graded 102% and a specific age 74 world record. I had slowed down just 4.5 seconds in four years since my world record at age 70 of 2:20.52. This is only a 0.8% decline per year where most world class athletes at this age are slowing down about 2% per year. But as Phil Raschker told me long ago— as we get older— a big heap of decline can suddenly happen in one year. For example, at age 69 I went from 2:17.05 to 2:20.52 a year later (a 2.4 % decline). And I went from 2:25.09 at age 74 in Puerto Rico to 2:32 a year later (nearly 5% decline). For example, If you haven't seen some senior friend for a year or two you can sometimes notice a huge change in appearance and shrinkage in height which indicates big changes within. Enough of these happy thoughts.

In the 400m in Puerto Rico I finished in 2nd place in 1:04.50 and pleased with my age graded 99.95%. The phenomenal Ralph Romaine, (TRI) at age 70 devouring the track in each monstrous relaxed stride— finished 1st (as expected) in 1:01.01, Harry Brown 3rd in 1:06.39 and the diminutive Hiroo Tanaka 4th just 0.02 seconds out of 3rd in 1:06.41. Hiroo would get his revenge later in the Sacramento Worlds by improving his speed every year..

In the 300m 27" hurdles, I was happy to break a specific age 74 world record and with a 99.98 % age graded performance in a golden finish in 50.78 coming from behind Bonfield at 45m from the finish— with Bonfield (USA) 2nd in 51.45, and Przyborowski, (POL), 3rd. Stookey had an off day in the 300m hurdles finishing 4t h — while warming up on the track just minutes before the start, he hit a hurdle injuring himself—— but winning here at Puerto Rico in the M70 80m hurdles in an impressive 13.70.

I ran with the M60 in the 4x400m relay; all were 60 except me at 74. Tony Badowski handed off to me. I made a mistake in not cutting in at the cut in line as the 2nd runner is supposed to do and continued on in my lane two when a frantic official waved me into the inner lane just before the final curve. I thought now I must pick it up to make up for this extra distance. So, I pushed mightily and handed off to Bruce Mitchel in 1st place who held his own in 1st place. We all knew that with the rocket Harold Marioka, although injured, as anchor. the game was over for the other teams. Harold also won gold in the M60 400m and 800m and went home in great pain with his Achilles injury which took forever to heal. All in all, Harold the Great had five operations on his knees with little success and also a near death open heart operation, followed by another heart operation a year later. Although he tried, and tried, and tried valiantly, also in Budapest Indoor Worlds, but even with his iron will, he never regained his brilliance and continued to run slow and in great pain.

Some other highlights of this meet for me were; My sales of my self-published book, "How to Be a Champion from 9 to 90." Unfortunately, some copies were stolen overnight from my book stall. The visit to the rain-forest— some getting lost. And unwinding by snorkeling over the coral reefs; and I remember vaguely but fondly the unlimited rum drinks on the snorkeling boat with its Caribbean music. My 100.30 % age graded for my three individual races. Two gold medals and two specific world records. I had a Tachycardia episode but it was after the relay and the end of the meet— the most convenient time.

But the meet was over and another adventure was ended. But, my next Worlds in San Sebastian, Spain would be a new age group for me, 75-79;. I was to have great luck there and age 76 would be one of my best years ever.

# SAN SEBASTIAN SPAIN WMA CHAMPIONSHIPS 2005

The 16th World Masters Championships in San Sebastian Spain was extra special for me in the M75-79 age group at age 76. I stayed at a fine apartment with Chuck Sochor (USA) and six Canadian friends including Mike and Myrtle Carter who arranged this great accommodation as usual. Just across the road was the fabulous San Sebastion beach featuring many nonchalant pretty topless females in an ideal bay frequented in the past by Kings and/ Queens. I remember fondly that beach.

One rest day at the main stadium I was shocked to l see on the bulletin board a book cover of an advertisement of a running book showing me on the cover in good running form. It appears that my Myer and Myer publisher of my book, " The Complete Guide to Running," had allowed this for another author since they had the copyright of the photos in my book. This great Photo was taken by Canadian friend Bill McIllwaine..

In my first race, the 300m 30" hurdles I finished in 52.91, and smooth over all hurdles, to break the world record with Jerry Prazyborowski, (POL), 2nd in 59.97. Jerry seems to be following me around like my shadow.

The next day I visited with friends including Peter Crombie (AUS) the modernistic Guggenheim museum—a masterpiece of architecture. During this visit I have a bout of Tachycardia. And another episode during the meet mainly from dragging around a suitcase on wheels with my books for unsuccessful sales, and also due to the fact that our accommodation seemed like two miles to the bus stop to the stadium.

The final 800m seems like a rerun of my Buffalo 800m final with the likeable Unto Mattson (FIN) apparently not having learned his lesson in Buffalo in1995— following me closely again for about 500m. I'm feeling strong and finish in world record time of 2:36.28, with Ramirez Francisco, (MEX) 2nd in 2:44.41 and Unto Mattsson 3rd in 2:47.21. To add some humour to the race— Jack Castel, (CAN), in a photo at the finish line shows Jack ahead of me— but he has only run 400m to my 800m.

In my 400m final in this stately main stadium I had lane 4, Don Cheeks, (USA), lane 3, and Wolfgang Reuter, (GER), lane 5. Little did I know at the time Cheeks had finished 2nd in the 200m, and Reuter had won the 100, 200 and long jump, all in impressive times. At 200m I could see I was losing ground to these two speedy sprinters, especially Reuter who was flying like he was in a 200m race. But past 300m I was gaining slowly on Cheeks and leaving Reuter behind. In a frantic finish I win in 1:07.67, Cheeks 2nd a close behind in 1:07,82, and Reuter in 1:09.88.

A day after my 400m final Brian Keaveney our Canadian Masters Athletics president at the time leaves me a phone message — asking me if I would accept the 2005 male Master of the World WMA award. I was surprised, shocked and on cloud 90. It took me five unsuccessful attempts from five faulty phone booths before I could tell Brian, "Yes." I learned later It was a close call as Reuter (GER) had broken at least two age group world records in 2005, but it is important to break them at WMA meets if possible. Also, I had three age group world records in the previous year 2004 in this age group which may have had some influence on the vote. Reuter is a kind gracious athlete. I know his friends were disappointed. The 2005 female master of the World WMA award was Reitje Dijkman of Holland who had broken sever WMA records track and field events.

My good friend Geraldine Finnegan from Northern Ireland competing with GRB— a long time multidiscipline athlete— later told me an amazing inspiring story of her participation in the W35 heptathlon at this 2005 WMA meet. She had 10 competitors and after the 100 hurdles (2nd), high jump (1st), shot put (2nd), 200m (2nd), long jump (5th), and javelin (2nd) —only the dreaded 800m remained. Dagmar Imme, (GER) was the favourite with four 1sts in six events. To beat her— Geraldine had to finish about 20 seconds ahead of Imme in the 800m. Like her past Irish father, a professional boxer, Geraldine personified determination. Before the 800m at the first aid tent she asked, "Do you have oxygen? "Have it ready for me after my race." With her asthmatic condition she knew from past experience how her body would react. After the race she lay on the inner field breathing oxygen. The final results of the M35 heptathlon: Finegan 6663, and Imme 6637. Geraldine had finished first in a terrific effort in 2:20.61 to Imme 4th in 2:38.00.

When I arrived home from San Sebastian in Mississauga, I recall having a rare glorious feeling of euphoria come over me like a shot of morphine, I would suppose. Five days later I flew to Monaco. for an all expense paid flight, expensive hotel and meals with wine— and a huge banquet with the world's best open athletes. When I left the hotel after three nights, my total bill was just one euro for a bottle of water from the mini- bar. Oh happy, happy days! 2005 I was sorry to see you leave.

# LINZ AUSTRIA WMA INDOOR CHAMPIONSHIP 2006

Some of the highlights of this indoor meet are:

This was the best track I have ever raced on. It had an obvious fast feel about it, and adjustable banking on the curves, from shallow to steep. But in the outer lane the six feet or so drop to the surface below was a bit scary for the outer lane runners. Warmup and cooldown was done in a huge tent on a grass surface adjacent to the track. For me the track was a short walking distance from my hotel. In my experience Austria has the worst wine but the best breakfasts and pastries.

I entered in the 200m but with little sprint training— in the outer lane I did not see my competition until about 60m to go and finished a close 3rd to Manfred Konopka 2nd, with Wolfgang Reuter 1st, two fine German gentlemen. In fact, all the competitors in my 200m were from Germany. I had had some success against Wolfgang in the 400m in the Spain WMA championships in 2005. In the 400m in Linz I won by about 2.5 seconds but later was Dq'd for cutting in a few inches too early towards the inner lane at the 150m line. (I have had 4 Dq's in my past running career, the above Dq in Linz, stepping on the inner 400m lane, at Brisbane WMA championship, and at two USA national masters meets.) In my sleep the night before the 400m in Linz, I recall I had dreamt of something bad happening in a race. It was weird like a premonition of disaster. In the 800m at Linz there was only one runner in my age group finishing about 10 seconds behind and I recall lapping the 80-year old's in the race. I was 77 in Linz.

Kerry Smith, a speedy Canadian friend, had a great 60m race in the final against 59 entries finishing just 0.01 seconds ahead of the 2nd runner. Nanci Sweazey another Canadian friend, a world class race walker, medalled in the women's age group 50, 3000m track walk race. The officials put all or many age groups in one final race so there were about 35 in her race, all jostling and elbowing for position —and I suspect many escaping Dq under these conditions.

At this meet I met some attractive Great Britain female competitors and the cheerful Sid Howard was there from the USA, 10 years younger than me, to add life to the party.

During the meet I was presented with a plaque for my 2005 WMA Male Master Athlete of the year 2005 award which was not given out at the Monaco banquet for the open athletes. At the same time at the Linz track, the legendary and inspiring Guido Müller of Germany was also given a male WMA of the year award. As of 2018, Guido has actually received three such awards. At this meet he was not at his best since recovering from an Achilles injury. I have been fortunate to receive many letters from Guido, and usually with a good photo of him in action. He is 10 years younger than me. I hope he keeps going.

One of my German competitors in the 200m said: "You have power." (I like the 200m but don't often enter it. But I intend to enter more in the future, unlike the 800m there is no suffering.)During my warmups in the big tent I had a compliment, from a male athlete saying, "I was admiring your great flexibility." Actually, apart from stretching before and after a race, or running, or cross training, or weight training— I stretch in the whirlpool also before swimming and after in the sauna, and also every morning before getting out of bed. All this helps reduce stiffening that can occur with age— to reduce the loss of stride length that occurs each year.

In my spare moments in Linz I took some great photos of large boats on the nearby river and inside an impressive cathedral. But my greatest memory is of the superb and fast track.

# RICCIONE ITALY WMA CHAMPIONSHIPS 2007

The Riccione Worlds in 2007 went smoothly enough for me except on my flight from Italy to Greece as I will explain later.

In late 2006 the World Masters Age (specific) records booklet came out covering the past years up to August 21 2006 and to my happy surprise they had honoured me with my photo on the cover. I have 30 specific age records listed there in 400m, 800m,1500m, mile and long hurdles. It is pity that specific age records are no longer kept.

As usual I was happy to be accommodated with my friend Myrtle and Mike Carter from Trinidadian descent— a superb apartment accommodation arranged as in Puerto Rico Worlds and San Sebastian Worlds and in 2011 in Lahti Finland Worlds by Myrtle. Tom Callendar, another Trinidadian and a speedy sprinter also in my age group stayed with us in Riccione and provided a lot of humour.

One highlight of this meet was my meeting Geraldine Finnegan, a multi-disciplined athlete, W40, from Northern Ireland and with the GBR team. She introduced herself and her two male friends one sunny afternoon as I was shopping for wine. In her skimpy outfit she looked like a pretty teenager. In Riccione it was the custom for locals and particularly visitors to roam the carless streets day and late night visiting the various interesting shops and restaurants. Geraldine said that my book, "The Complete Guide to Running," was her "bible", which she used to teach her track and field athletes in Ireland, and so she was big fan of Earl Fee. I had a photo taken of us together at our apartment where I gave her a new copy of my book to replace her "worn out" one. We became good friends and I visited her twice in Ireland for weeks of training and enjoying the emerald green countryside, some pubs and nearby ocean viewed from her home. I continue to recall the great hospitality, the pubs, the fresh air by the ocean compared to Mississauga. and the infinite brilliant stars that are absent in my city.

Geraldine told me while she was taking a massage at the Riccione Worlds high above the track— some colleagues shouted *Earl Fee is running,* I thought later: it's a good title for my autobiography book. Geraldine jumped from the massage table to see me following closely behind the small, but quick- stepped David Car from Australia, three years younger and with some world masters track records of his own. See 800m results below.

Geraldine had her 10 year old daughter, Nicole, with her— a very intelligent physically strong girl, but also too adventurous, strong willed, rambunctious and with a mind of her own. So, while competing in the 80m hurdles, 400m hurdles, steeplechase and heptathlon Geraldine had also this supervising distraction to contend with. Nevertheless, she had a 2nd in the 400m hurdles and won the W40 heptathlon again (having won the W35 heptathlon in 2005 in San Sebastian) this time in Ricionne with 4886 points compared to Makarova's 4724, For example, Geraldine won the final event, the heptathlon 800m again—this time in 2:30. 67 giving her the necessary points to win the heptathlon. In 2018 Geraldine had further great success—a world record in the heptathlon (7 events) in Holland in with 4880 points—and a few months later another world record in a tetradecathlon (14 events) in two days in 10,274 points. In June 2018 her world record in the decathlon in Stendal Germany was confirmed—6898 points compared to the old record of 6712 points—by a good margin. In 2018 she had three world records in the decathlon, and in Edinburgh broke through the 7000 points barrier. All this in spite of poor training facilities in her home area. All the above amazing, requiring everything—strength, skill, speed, endurance, versatility and loads of spirit. I call her the female Jim Thorpe, who won the pentathlon and decathlon in the 1912 Olympics in Stockholm, Sweden. And all the more amazing for Thorpe while competing in shoes he had found in the garbage— since just before someone had stolen *his* shoes.

In Riccione, I particularly enjoyed USA Anselm Lebourne's 800m M50 race where he dictated the race and the race pace —winning in 2:02.63 with Engholm, (SWE) 2nd in 2:04.43. Anselm led for the whole race, saying he could tell where his competition was by observing their shadow behind him. I noticed Wolfgang Reuter won the 200m in 29.38. Jeanne Daprana had a world record in the W70 running the 400m in 77.92. On this basis I concluded that a world record female at age 70 is close to equivalent to a world record male at about age 85 —since at age 85 I had an outdoor 400m world record of 77.10.

My 300m hurdle final went smoothly in 53.63 followed by Ichida, (JAP) in 56.88, Flora, (IND), in 57, 70, and Konopka, (GER), in 1:01.80. Flora told me this was the only the second time he had run the 300m hurdles, the first time was the prelim— this is truly amazing if it's true. After the prelim 300m hurdles Fields GBR had said. He had the European record and we should try for the world record in the final." I said, "Good idea." But just before the final the next day I thought I don't need to try for the world record, I already have the record. The attached photo shows him following me in the final but field finishing a disappointing 5th.

Just two hours after the 300m hurdles was the 800m final. The warmup area was like a farmer's field of ruts and overgrown grass, and a small rubber stretch near the track. Even in 2007 I was nursing my left calf, for the past 10 years or so and with it always feeling tired after long slow running, but not after fast interval running — due to a lack of circulation —diagnosed as Intermittent Claudication. (Fortunately, now at age 85 this condition has improved somewhat.) So, my warmup at Riccione for the 800m to keep the legs fresh consisted of a reduced warmup of 100m runs with short walk between. Seeing my amiable friend Sid Howard the popular USA middle distance champion helped me to relax— thinking I am not alone in this. Still I was feeling sickly with nerves with the prospect of running the 800m against the AUSSY David Carr, a strong competitor. David is three years younger which makes for some advantage at my age 78—performance deteriorates about 2 to 3% per year for most world record holder distance runners in this age bracket. It is always easier to follow, so I followed David closely until about 60m from the finish line when he surged ahead finishing in 2:38.99 to my 2:39.67. I had made the mistake of pulling up beside David instead of pushing past. And I should have been working on my finishing kick, knowing it would be up against David Carr.

A good friend, John Ward, had come all the way from England to watch me and some of his countrymen race. John is the CEO and developer of condo villages in England and Wales. I had met him in Mississauga. We had similar interests, namely, both runners and interested in writing poetry. He flew to Rome, but although a millionaire CEO he slept in his rental car on the way from Rome to Riccione I believe just for the adventure of it. We toured the beautiful country side one day during the meet. A couple of years previously John invited me to the opening of his new condo village development in Wales ( previously the location of summer resort) and paid for my plane ticket from Canada. At this grand celebration (banguet, dancing, etc) I sold my self published running book, participated in a mile race, flew in a helicopter over the new condo village and was treated as a celebrity —and had a couple of women chasing me. Needless to say it was an awesome experience.

Back to Riccione. There was no nerve problem in the 400m as I was up against my old competitors: Rueter, (GER), Tanaka, (JAP), and Brown, (ASA). I ran nearly the same time as in San Sebastian in 107.50, with Rueter,

1:09.24, Tanaka 1:09.34, and Brown 1:10.11. At the Worlds in Sacramento in 2013, Tanaka made a big improvement in the six year interim and finished ahead of me in the 400 having previously, unbeknown to me, also broken my world record of 70.64 at age 80. Tanaka used to run the 800m in my age group, but in recent years he must have concentrated on the sprints since his 200m and 400m time were now very impressive.

The day of the relays was more exciting than I would have liked. During my warmup Geraldine, a heptathlete arrived from another stadium after finishing one of her many events—dressed in a revealing bikini. She had some excuse as it was very hot. Soon after, not due to her appearance, I had a Tachycardia episode, a rapid heartbeat came me out of the blue during my warmup for the 4x 400m relay. This was due to the extreme heat.(Now at 88 in these conditions I normally drink a lot of iced water and keep in the shade to help prevent these episodes.) I was reluctant to mention this to my teammates who were eager and excited with possibility of winning a medal. We had reasonable team with the speedster Tom Callander, born in Trinidad, running first leg and me running anchor, and we had good support with Bill Thompson and Joe Gregorich running 2nd and 3rd..I received the baton in a close third place, with my heart still in an excessive high beat. It is actually dangerous to run in this condition although I did in an 800m prelim heat in Brisbane Worlds to make the final but won later against the world steeplechase world record holder from Australia. This time I took off at full speed not knowing what would happen —but could feel my heart come back to normal and not in distress, then running fast to achieve a bronze medal. In future I would back out if Tachycardia occurred beforehand.

Riccione had a beautiful beach with thousands of coloured umbrellas, but September sun tanning was fast declining. All in all, Riccione was a wonderful experience, except for the crowded buses usually rammed overfull like sardines in a tin, if you could force yourself onto the bus. Another problem was several hours to receive a medal and long waits to catch a crowded bus back to the hotel. But Myrtle Carter as usual had arranged excellent lodging in an apartment close to all the scintillating night street action.

Oh yes, my flight adventure from Riccione to Naples on the way to Athens, Greece. My happy disposition turned negative when somehow, I missed my flight from Naples to Athens. I still cannot fathom how this happened, but I recall enquiring at the Naples airport why I should have two boarding passes to Greece, to two different departure gates. After I missed my flight I went to the Customer Assistance desk where the were calling me. Later, I politely complained that I had a flight to catch today in Athens to fly to Mykonos in Greece, one of the favourite islands in Greece. Another male passenger and I were kindly accommodated by flying us way back up north past Riccione to Milan, and then a long ride in a limousine to another airport. When I got on the plane to Athens I was so relieved I was euphoric. As I boarded the plane they were plying "Summer Wine" by Vile Valor. Music never sounded so good— now it is one of my best Karaoke favourites. My luggage showed up in Athens, but I missed my flight to Mykonos. In retrospect, sometimes it is good to experience the out of the ordinary.

Mykonos was a great island with magnificent beaches but September is too late in the season for any exciting night life.

Before leaving 2007 at age 78 I had decided to coach myself although, my coach David Welch an ex- marathoner had brought me a long way, I had acquired a lot of knowledge since I started back at age 57 and in writing my running books, knew my body well, and hence I did not entirely agree with some of the workouts. Also, a big problem was the training sessions starting usually at 7:30pm after coach David's work and I was free all day having retired now for 15 years. While writing this my memoirs I became more aware and appreciative of the superb coaching of David Welch and the favourable transformation in my body resulting from his training.

"Arrivederci Riccione!" You were exciting and unforgettable, and I will miss your rich red wines so unbelievably cheap.

# LAHTI FINLAND WMA CHAMPIONSHIPS 2009

The year 2009 at age 80 "was a very good year," as Frank Sinatra would sing, since I was in a new age group. That is why competitive master athletes love to get older. So, the 2009 season was kind to me leading up to the Lahti Worlds.

At the Lahti Worlds, as usual, Myrtle Carter has arranged great accommodation, a large house with super amenities, also for Mike her husband (my training partner), and temporarily for their daughter Jarnal, Karla Del Grande and husband Al, and me. The main stadium is a mile away so there is plenty of walking everywhere, but it posed no problem. At this meet I am still recovering from a left calf injury, so I cancel the 300m hurdles due to lack of training. I also felt running the hurdles might jeopardise my 800m and the 400m.

The 800m final is not at the main stadium which is the usual practice, but at a smaller stadium. The regulation 400m track looks small since the stands are sparse —psychologically this gives me a confident feeling. I am assigned a lane with an Asian partner— who was unsure of the pace. He leads in my lane then slows in front of me before the cut in at 150m. At 400m I see from the clock that my time is 84 seconds, about 2 seconds slow, as I usually run about 4 seconds faster the first lap—so I immediately and noticeably picked up the pace. At the final bend, outside the track my friend/coach Bruce Mitchel urges me on, along with the cheering crowd, injecting some encouragement and urgency into me, saying I am way ahead. Surprisingly, I finish in 2:49.92 just a second slower than my record in Toronto. The officials thought it was a world record but they didn't know about my World record in Canada in July which was actually about a second faster. I was happy with this time in view of my calf injury and lack of preparation training. I noticed in the lower age group M75, 800m my Riccione competitor friend David Carr, (AUS) at age 75, finished 2nd in 2: 44.90 in a close race to Kociszewski, (POL) in 2:44..23.

The 400m final could have gone better except for the semi just few hours before. We were the only age group of men and women, and also the oldest age group, to have to run a 400m semi and a final on the same day. I win in 1:13,23 with Osorio, (COL) 2nd in 1:20,27. The semi was necessary, since the officials had qualified nine athletes from the two prelims for the eight lanes. While near the starting blocks for the final— Geraldine threw me a green Irish bunny for good luck. I decided to leave it behind for now. Geraldine is fast— she then rushed over to the final bend outside the track to cheer me on. My Canadian friends later were jokingly, but insistently saying she threw me some lingerie. I say let them have their little jokes. At the banquet in at the stately Sibelius Building Geraldine was stunning, as usual, in a flaming red gown accompanied by her pretty daughter Nicole.

After the meet, I signed up for an overnight voyage on a huge cruise ship from Helsinki to Sweden. I spent my time mainly exploring the ship and its many floors, a sauna visit, a pub visit, and two great meals on board. The constant exercise over many flights of stairs created a thirst necessitating a visit to the popular duty free wine shop. The highlight of my trip to Sweden was an organ recital at a beautiful cathedral. The sound reverberated in my heart strings. Later In Budapest I experienced another great organ recital in their main cathedral.

# SACRAMANTO USA WMA CHAMPIONIPS 2011

> *"Behold through the gates of a New Year 2011 the distant variegated declarations of future achievements glimmering at you and daringly luring you to give pursuit.* **Anon**

The 18th World Masters Athletics Championships in San Sebastian CA in 2011 produced the following medal count for the top 6 countries.

USA. . . . . . . . . . . . . 184
AUS. . . . . . . . . . . . . 142
GER. . . . . . . . . . . . . 135
GBR and Ireland  . . 123
CAN . . . . . . . . . . . . 105
MEX . . . . . . . . . . . . 60

Our legendary Canadian Olga Kotelko from Vancouver, in the W90 group entered 12 events producing mostly gold..

At age 82 and staying mostly injury free I was well prepared with some impressive workouts as seen in my training log for that year but I was not prepared for the desert heat. For example, the inner field was at 100 degrees F, and there was no shade in the stands or warmup area.

I finished the 300m hurdles with a 1st place in 37.31, just 0.36 seconds slower than my age group record of 36.95 in Puerto Rico at age 80. Before the race I had a Tachycardia episode due to the excessive heat, causing some stress, but fortunately it cleared up in time after I laid down with feet up in the shade of a tree. On the same day, but in the evening several hours later I ran the 800 final in a respectable 2:53.70 with Michio Kumamoto, (JAP), 2nd in 3:03.67.

The 200m is usually a stress free event for me, as I don't train for it specifically, and since I am not expected to win. My time of 32.55 for 3rd was just 0.12 seconds slower than 2nd place in 32.43. Hiroo Tanaka, (JAP), won in and impressive time of 30.78, having also won the 100m in a blazing 14.70. The legendary Payton Jordan still has the world record in 14.35. Payton, now sadly missed for many years, wrote the Foreword in my book, "The Complete Guide to Running." See Chapter 16, which includes information about Payton and his thoughts on sprint training.

Before my 400m final I had another Tachycardia episode in view of the high heat and humidity but again was fortunate it cleared up in time. Before the 400m final I did not know that Tanaka had broken my M80 age group world record of 70.64 by about 0.3 seconds —but I knew of his super fast 100 and 200 wins here. My past experience is that these fast sprinter types like Rueter for example, usually fade a bit in the homestretch after 300m. So my strategy was to catch Tanaka in the last 100m. At 300m he was about a meter ahead of me, but I should have known he was in my 800m race in Brisbane, and had endurance as well as speed. He finished strong in 1: 11.53 to my 1:12.73. He graciously said, "You gave me the gold.". In retrospect, I had the wrong strategy and was too relaxed and confident before the race against this 80 year old youngster.

However, I hoped for some revenge in the M75, 4x400m relay where our competitors were a Japanese team with Tanaka, and a USA team with my friend Bob Cozens. All were in the 75-79 age group except Tanaka, Ed Whitlock, age 80 and me at age 82 at anchor. This was definitely the most enjoyable of my races at Sacramento — we won in 5:41.63, 14 seconds ahead of the Americans and 16 seconds ahead of the Japanese. I recall the late legendary Ed Whitlock running a surprisingly fast 400m for our team —he also demolished his competitors in the 1500m and 5000m. We will miss him always. See the great photo attached of me, Olga and Ed as the Sacramento Worlds. Sadly Olga and Ed, two legendary inspirations for myself and countless others —are now only with us in spirit..

*Earl, Olga and Ed*

I notice in my 2011 training log: after the Sacramento Worlds I had several hurdle practices although there were no further meets. Now that is dedication. But I enjoy hurdling, just don't like the injuries that often come with it.

*With some regret I leave Sacramento;*
*Many had no medal for a momento*
*But mainly for the extra slow.*
*Your desert air nearly did me in—*
*On departure I was feelin' mighty slim,*
*And longin' for cool shores of Toronto.*

## BUDAPEST HUNGARY INDOOR WMA CHAMPIONSHIPS 2014

See Chapter 10 for the exciting details at age 85.

# 12

# MY HUNTSMAN WORLD SENIOR GAMES

## 2017 ADVENTURE

MY PARTICIPATION AT THE HUNTSMAN WORLD SENIOR GAMES DID not go smoothly as anticipated and as explained below. As you know there are factors that can slow you down in spite of good training preparation.

Firstly, my checked bag, filled to the brim, did not arrive with the flight. Then on the10 mile trip to St. George from the airport in my rented car I got lost—I blame it on the lack of good directional signs along the route. I had the GPS but was not familiar with it. However, 18 hours later my bag was delivered to my hotel at midnight. I thanked the United Airlines profusely making them feel good for some UA personnel going out of their way at a late hour.

The official track at a local high school revealed more problems and surprises. It was ancient and hard as a rock and with many cracks—running in the spikes sounded like a machine gun firing: with a "clack, clack,clack"… I learned after my 800m another two reasons why my time was slower than expected. The elevation was about 2800 feet above sea level —high enough to slow me about four or more seconds; something I learned from a similar experience at the indoor USA nationals a few years ago in Albuquerque with a similar elevation. The high temperature of 26 degrees C was not a big problem in view of the many scorching days training in Mississauga this summer. I finished well ahead of the 16 in the 800m race including ages 80 to 92— and 11 seconds ahead of two USA 80 year olds —but in my case with tired legs from the hard track and a sore throat from the very low humidity causing some exercise induced asthma for a few days. Based on my 12 time trials (600m to 700m at 800m race pace) for the past 2.5 months since the NCCWMA meet and the above three deleterious effects — I estimated these effects above could have slowed me about eight seconds. I have found nearly all my world records in the past have felt easy or at least not painful when I was well trained and ready. But not the case in this Huntsman 800m when I was well prepared—in fact one of my hardest races that I can recall.

The next day I ran the 400m in my running shoes to save my legs and feet as I felt I had nothing to prove or benefit after my 108.5 % age graded 400m race at the NCCWMA meet In August 2017. In the world rankings in 2017 I am number 1 in the 400m and will be number 2 in the 800m based on my Hartshorne time which was still age graded just above 100 %. I presume multi-world-record holder David Carr of Australia at age 85 who broke my 85-89 age group record will be ranked number 1 in 2017 in the 800m when ratified; he broke my 800m world record in July, 2017 in a small local meet in Australia.

It is possible that I may have reached a peak in my training prior to this meet as it was a long 3 months after my last meet at York U, a NCCWMA meet. My 12 time trials in 2.5 months was perhaps too ambitious, but there was only 800m training, no 400m training, and no intense cross training activity in between three running days a week—usually involving: a short long run, intervals, and the 800m time trial in a session.

Would I come to the Huntsman Games again? I think not—the friendly people and the beautiful new track next year do not make up for the elevation, dry air, the air fare expense for a distant Canadian, and the too late in the season schedule—not to mention the high overall expense. However, I will treasure my three gold medals including for the javelin where I was the best of the worst in my age category.

On my last day at St. George I visited the spectacular Snow Canyon (see photo) 20 minutes drive from town. But on the way back got lost twice on some poorly marked roundabouts…. I thought my problems were over, but just prior to departure at the airport it was announced that the plane to take me and about 30 others to Denver had been damaged prior to landing at the airport, by a hawk that flew into the plane's nose –causing many feathers in the electronics and radar. But 4.5 hours later I was on my way, a much longer route to Toronto via Salt Lake City and then Calgary to Toronto on an (ugh) red eye flight, arriving about 5am in Toronto..

In spite of the above problems I believe my training for the meet was very useful to help me retain my 800m speed for next year. I can build on this experience prior to my new age group 90-94 in 1.5 years.

One final word for the non-athletes and the athletes: It occurred to me while in St. George (my lost bag experience) to remember always to be grateful and recognize and point out to others their good deeds; this recognition not only makes you feel good but makes the recipient feel good and it will even rub off from them onto others. It has an expanding effect— I call it the "snowball effect", the title of my next poem.

# 13

# EXTRA CURRICULAR ACTIVITIES AFTER MARRIAGE

## KARAOKE

GARY LUBIN. MY UP-BEAT FRIEND GARY, NOW AT AGE 77 IN 2018, IS AN interesting character as some might say. He has two big obsessions; karaoke and coaching the high jump, and very proficient at both. For example, he has coached an Olympian high jumper and other world class high jumpers, and even coached me to two Canadian high jump records in my 85-89 age group after just two training sessions. If you are young or old and have long legs and look athletic he is very apt to recruit you as one of his high jump students. Mostly, he does this out of the goodness of his heart and the satisfaction of progress. His cottage in Mississauga near the Credit River is dedicated solely to Karaoke. And he thinks I am his older brother –although honoured, I am not even Jewish, but I *am* older by 12 years.

He is also very talented at the piano—playing others favourites faultlessly without music and at the same time often coming up with some original catchy or humorous accompanying words. He claims he learned the piano by watching his mother play, which is amazing. When I hear him play at some retirement home, etc., I think of the poem, "The Shooting of Dan

McGrough by Robert Service and the line: "Then he clutched the keys with his talon hands—my God, that man could play."

Gary introduced me to Karaoke which he has been doing enthusiastically at some pubs for over 30 years. So this has also become one of my favourite pastimes at home and away from home, now for about two years. Initially, I would often get off key, but now with perseverance have become reasonably proficient with enjoyment rather than nervous fear, and now attempting harder songs. After all like anything, proficiency comes with constant practise. Using Gary's hundreds of discs and his several old Karaoke players we would often sing about 15 to 30 songs in a session at his cottage near the Credit River in Mississauga. But we even sang about 35, mostly the Beatle's songs in a three hour session. I might add this can make one a bit thirsty.

Gary and I both bought a $300 portable machine that came with over 2000 songs (English, Philippian, and some gospel that could easily be downloaded or could be shown on a TV screen. This has been superseded by a better and bigger program called "Karafun" that can be downloaded from the computer onto my computer screen for $9.99 a month. This has enabled me to increase my repertoire considerably, by practising at home. I believe if I practised for just 15 or 20 happy minutes a day on a new song I would have over 300 new songs in a year.

Karaoke is good for happiness and moral— good for the memory— preventing depression and dementia— and also good for the lungs. I realize now that it is also beneficial for preserving a young voice and preventing the crackly voice of old age like the crackling of popcorn.

Here are some of Gary's favourite songs which have entertained hundreds of Karaoke friends and bar people:

My Way and New York (Frank Sinatra), Hallelujah (Lenard Cohen), No Girl No Cry and Yellow Bird with Caribbean accent (Bob Marley), Rich Man Poor Man with Jewish accent, Cabaret with English accent, Sometimes When We Touch (Dan Hill), Hallelujah ( Leonard Cohen), Always In My Heart (Willi Nelson),and countless others.

Here are some of my favourites as of March 2018 which I have sung at pubs without getting- the- hook:

Fernando (Abba), House of the Rising sun (the Animals), Against the Wind, (Bob Seger). McArthor Park (Glen Campbell), Phoenix (Glen Campbell), Lady (Kenny Rogers), Hello ( Lionel Richie), If Tomorrow Never

Comes (Garth Brooks), Four Strong Winds (Ian Tyson, or Neil Young), Look At Us ( Haggard), Still the Same (Bob Seger), Sunday Morning Coming Down (Chris Kristopherson), Love Me With All of Your Heart, and Spanish Eyes (Englebert Humperdink), Yesterday When I Was Young (Glen Campbell). Delilagh (om Jones), A Whiter Shade of Pale (Procol Harum), Sweet Caroline (Neil Diamond), You'll Never Find Another Love Like Mine (Lou Rawls) I have a Dream (Abba). Gypsy by Fleetwood Max (not yet), Sinking Like a Sunset by Tom Cochrane. My current favourite is Lady in Red by Chris De Burgh.

Sometimes for a song I like and by someone with the same pitch of voice—I try to imitate this professional singer, and practise it over and over.

Karaoke is a lot of fun and good for the voice, brain and morale. Give it a try. Or just sing in your bathroom or in the car. I guarantee you will experience an immediate uplift—even if you are off key occasionally. It just occurred to me—thinking of suicide: sing a couple of happy songs—I suspect you will reconsider.

# HIKING

My good friend, Daiva Slenys, for over two decades, is a tall attractive blond, and several decades much younger than me. When she is away from her paramedic duties— she is a Nature girl: frequently delving in all manner of sports, mainly outdoor sports—hiking, scuba diving and photographing underwater large turtles, etc. in the Carribean, canoeing in northern Ontario, running trail and mudder races—and swimming (her Facebook page is under the name Daiva Swimmer so this tells you she is also a strong swimmer. I met her at the local WMCA and I noticed she worked hard in the weight room on the free weights sometimes for over three hours. This list above is tiring me out just thinking about it. Daiva and I became acquainted in the swimming pool as she was frequently happily swimming her countless laps and I was constantly running madly in the deep end of the pool, pretending I was in an 800m or mile race, in the early days without a flotation belt. Eventually she joined me.

For many years we would hike in the beautiful spring or summer, the refreshing fall, even the frigid winter and mainly at Rattlesnake Point on the Niagara Escarpment at a good pace for 2.5 to 3 hours. Daiva being much younger would insist on carrying our backpack with our various articles. And with her being an experienced paramedic by profession —she was the ideal person to hike with in the event of some mishap to my injury prone body. I would also often hike at various different sites on the Niagara escarpment with my good friend and training partner Keith Rodrigues also mentioned in my memoirs elsewhere. Keith knows these various hiking sites in Southern Ontario very well, and acts as the official guide for large groups from the Mississauga WMCA. The three of us would also hike together. Sometimes I would require a nap to recover after. On one outing a cellphone was lost and on an other while hiking adjacent to some high cliffs and soaring vultures a terrific wind came up requiring a fast retreat to safer ground. See my poem below which tells what hiking is all about.

# We Love To Go A-Wandering

We love to go a-wandering on trails serene:
Where nature abounds all around;
Where cares take flight and float away...
In heady air to a happy sky.
The forest has many regal faces reminding of:
The spring: a new born baby fresh and eager for life;
The summer: a young princess dancing in garb of green;
The fall: a stately prince parading in multi-coloured robes;
The winter: a king sometimes harsh but sometimes sprightly
With ever flowing white beard.

Today though the fall has nearly died—the woods are still alive
Passing their energy to our band of three.
It's tempting to linger here and there—
At each sparkling stream or lookout supreme
As we marvel at each bend and rise of the trail,
And stand and stare—drinking in the wonder of it all...
But then, feet are eager to fly once more o'er the ground.
At days end—spent and reluctant we depart our forest friend.
Decades later when the trail becomes too rugged and long,
Our memories will linger there...and relive each step...
Those joyful hours of wandering and wondering...

In the beginning of my hiking adventures one bitter cold day in a large group when I was more appropriately dressed lightly for running instead of hiking— I became very chilled and miles from our cars. Fortunately, the experienced hikers lent some extra clothing. It was a learning experience. I also learned to: wear the proper footwear, and don't hike too late in the day and get lost in the dark as some female friends we knew. Also I found an energy gel pack taken would instantly give me a jet propelled boost while hiking, leaving my friends behind. But that was the old days.

These were happy days but unfortunately, my knapsack carrier and photographic model has now taken a paramedic position in Ottawa. But I'm not moving quite as fast as previous anyway. These hiking outings with nature helped a great deal with my running endurance and my morale, and even helps to ward off Alzheimers. I highly recommend it. Thank you Daiva and Keith.

# RUNNING/COACHING

The following is apart from the running training and competitive meets discussed elsewhere in this book.

After going to training camps twice in Florida and once in San Diego with my boys and others with the North York Track Club— I started running training again in 1986 at age 57 with the same club. Since then I have met and made many friends in Canada and abroad while participating in running competitions. For instance, I have three great young friends that I used to coach in Mississauga: Louise Soucy Fraser, Nanci Sweazey Patton and Mike Carter. We used to unwind frequently with a wine and cheese party between training sessions. Nanci is a versatile runner and hurdler but mainly a great race walker with several Canadian records and maybe even some past world record since she is that good, now living in Germany in a log bungalow with many modern features, heated floors, etc., which she designed. Louise was a strong middle distance runner and now a competitive rower who gets up early every morning to row at 5am with her club members. How competitive and inspirational is that? In addition to her French language teaching, she coaches with great success: running and other athletic teams at her school and has produced many musicals involving the students. These are two of the most clever, mentally tough and intelligent ladies including my daughter

Melanie that I know. (Melanie is very witty and a master of the repartee—she is in the wrong occupation, as she would make a good lawyer.) The other member of our foursome running group is ex-policeman, Michael, originally from Trinidad—20 years younger than me and a strong running training partner for over two decades. It also helps that he has a great sense of humour. He loves to talk and joke, but I have found during one of my harder workouts he saves his energy for running rather than talking, and this saves me from some verbal bombardment. Mike would make a good politician. Mike's wife Myrtle loved to attend the World Masters Athletic Championships and on several occasions found some excellent accommodation for myself and many of our friends at several World Masters championships, e.g., Brisbane, Gateshead, Puerto Rico, Riccione and Lahti.

# CURLING

During my working years at Atomic Energy Company Ltd in the winter I enjoyed the sport of competitive curling with my fellow workers, once a week. I enjoyed the camaraderie, the strategy of the game, the vigorous sweeping, the jokes and, drinks with friends after the game. And I joined the highly respected Dixie Curling Club after my divorce. I was so keen that I used to practise by myself once or twice a week. Unfortunately, my wife Kathi objected to my going off with my friends for the day to compete in a bonspiel, leaving her to "babysit." So she normally took revenge by having a "night out with the girls."

On one occasion our masters team won a big seniors competition with big prizes in Ontario, involving a lot of good teams. At the Dixie Curling Club many years ago—once a year the bar was open for a half hour with free drinks. You could imagine continuous stampedes to the bar during these 30 precious minutes. This foolhardy practice would not be tolerated now.

Eventually, I gave up the curling that I loved since it involved me playing right after my running training which resulted in having my supper at about 10:30 pm or later. It was either curling or running and I chose running.

# *14*

## WELCOME TO MY MODEST MANSION

WELCOME TO MY MODEST MANSION. WERE YOU NOT CHEERED UP BY sight of my burgundy garage doors, front door and the wide pink rock walkway?....On this tour I will be pleased to take you inside my modest mansion within which you will see many treasures that I had the good fortune to cross my path. This tour will help you to understand my personality and my mode of living. I will not bore you by describing every antique or artifact— only those with an interesting or colourful story.

Let us start in the hallway. Please direct your gaze to this Piccaso-like painting, actually an expressionist painting of a sexy green goddess with nude upper body by my late artist brother Maurice. You will see many of his colourful acrylic portraits gracing these walls, all of mostly of women —for some reason that baffles me since he was a homosexual. These paintings, over a hundred in this establishment, make me feel like a millionaire. But I digress. Also in the hallway you will notice a cabinet with 16 open compartments filled with of about 18 pairs of running shoes,running spike shoes and a large variety of orthotics. It appears someone in this house is a running fanatic.

Let us move upstairs to the master bedroom. First: off in this expansive room, the whole width of my house, you will notice one wall is completely occupied by old books accumulated starting in 1979, on poetry and miscellaneous topics.I am now in the process of reducing this mini library. Here is a fine antique oak desk I stumbled on at the Salvation Army. I'm sure you can appreciate the refinishing by yours truly. To me refinishing some old furniture is like taking a tired rundown horse and making a racehorse out of him or her. And here is a fine chest of drawers I spied one day languishing by a busy road, In view of its many possibilities and in spite of a few remedial defects I was able to hoist this onto the top of my car and speed home 20 miles away without mishap in the heavy 401 traffic. I was more daring 29 years ago, but I knew a good thing, like a female with good assets, when I saw it. Similarly, about 45 years ago I saw a discarded heavy desk during one of my runs which appeared to have many more years life. In those days I had more muscle and nerve— so it too wound upon top my car and soon after upstairs to another bedroom, all single handed I assure you. Using some physics principles I was able to maneuver it up the 14 stairs by myself. This spur of the moment mode of transportation involving no roof racks and only some rope and bungy cord and a prayer —is not recommended for the weak at heart or any healthy person for that matter. Now older and wiser I would not attempt it and shudder at the prospect.

In this adjoining bedroom see this large western oil painting of a cowboy on frantic horse at forefront chased by a thundering herd of mad steers... threatening to trample him. It is a copy but very exact I would remind you. Not sure if he will survive, but this chase has been going on now for over 60 years and he is still surviving. My dear mother loved this painting being raised on a farm out West.

Let us move downstairs to the living room and dining room. Here most people are immediately struck by over 700 medals hanging in chronical sequence in the wide doorway on both sides between these two rooms— and over the windows —and the multitude of plaques and trophies in the tall buffet. See the attached photo, showing my large anti aging book, *100 Years Young the Natural Way.* I don't know how I managed over 20 races (indoor, and outdoor) every year for the last the last 31years. No wonder I was frequently injured—but particularly of late.

Here you can appreciate four more of dear brother Maurice's colourful paintings and two of my large graphite sketches of Western scenes, by myself, actually very exact copies of a small Remington western scenes involving horses which I am fond of. One of these a stagecoach driven by six horses, some stumbling, and chased by some deadly unfriendly Indians on horseback. My dear daughter loves this sketch and insists it is hers one day. Mmm, I think so, if she keeps doing me favours. This charcoal sketch took me about 35 hours during a strike at my work (Atomic Energy Company Limited). In this room I draw your attention to the colourful chesterfield and chair, something I actually purchased new many decades ago. Note the peacock feathers and flower pattern on an orange background. I fell in love with it about 46 years ago and am still in love with them and they love my body. Last Christmas I was standing on the arm of the lounge chair putting a light on the top of my usual eight foot real fir tree. On getting down backwards I fell backwards and slid through a narrow space between a cabinet and a heavy end table— fortunately, a good landing and no concussion. From now on I use a ladder.

Around my chesterfield is a long table in front and two end tables, all in oak and covered with attractive tiles— these tables manufactured by yours truly with time on my hands after my divorce. On the table there are some bronze figurines or statues, one a heavy Remington purchased in Los Vegas of an unruly horse which has bucked off the rider laying on the ground underneath— and a heavy bronze replica of a boat used in Ireland for fishing with three fisherman in the boat. I was given this in Ireland at a lavish college sports banquet after giving a speech, with the inspiring Chariots of Fire music playing in the background and the crowd cheering. Maybe my best party ever. At this dress up affair banquet, I can assure you the Irish, my ancestors, know how celebrate in a big way. I gave my well accepted humorous/inspirational speech while my heart was having a Tachycardia episode. My sons say the bronze replica is the three of us fishing. Now nearby, notice a very comfortable cream lounge chair with huge arms which although elephant sized once again ended up on top of my a car which I noticed in driving by. I was happy to give it a new home. Although in perfect shape the owner told me she didn't have space for it and even offered me further new looking furniture, but I too was sadly running out of space, even wall space.

In the dining room you see a one of a kind elegant Danish teak table simplistic in style with an extendable leaf, About 60 year ago I purchased it for a measly $100. It is possible to fall in love with some furniture and like a beautiful woman it is always a pleasure to behold.

See here also large posters, mementos from two separate paid photo shoots. One poster is actual size from the back page of a newspaper advertisement showing me in the runners start position. The inscription says, "RESPECT. Your elders and for land's sake, get out of the way." Allianz Insurance. A monster version of this photo is in the lobby of Allianz Insurance in the USA. On the day of this photo I was the lone actor in a video jumping over hurdles; a production requiring many personnel and about six trucks, all at York University. I carried on after a hamstring injury from being held in a sprint starting position— too long. All for $2200. The other poster shows a facial shot of me with a tag on my forehead reading "Best Before 65", and below "Nobody has a shelf life." A message to stop discrimination against seniors..

Here in the kitchen is a fine circular wooden table with four matching chairs all like new which I purchased at a neighbourhood garage sale for a measly $30. You no doubt suspect that I love garage sales— although I have a good pension and am not a Scrooge-like person. All true! For example, at a local garage sale I once purchased two expensive tailor made suits in perfect condition for $25 each. I said to the lady, "Your husband must be the same size as me." She somberly replied, "Yes— he was." However, it didn't bother me. Gone are the single days when I would l pay $ 500 for a tailor made suit— and for new cars. Besides it is what is inside the suit that matters most.

In my family room I direct your warm gaze to a beautiful silk Persian rug of crème and burgundy colour. Over this is a long slim cocktail table in teak with a story to tell — a wedding gift from a friend Bill Casey about 50 years ago. I still love this table. One day some days before my wedding my future wife came up to my apartment and seeing the table for the first time said loudly," I don't like it!" The problem was that "Casey," as a joke before her arrival, was in the bathroom hearing this comment. I suspect it was one of my ex-wife's biggest embarrassments or faux pas. At my age 88 my good friend but slightly weird Casey like many of my past friends are but a fond memory.

You would probably notice in a tour of this home an abundance of nick knacks — a serious weakness or a frailty of the aged. I blame it on my local Value Village which has all of these hard to resist used bargains. But I say one man's lack of appreciation is another man's treasure. For instance, see several music boxes, for example, this music box a clown playing a violin to a tune of: "Where are the Clowns, Bring in the Clowns". As a lover of all kinds of music I can appreciate this gem. I have other weaknesses too— for book ends, old liquor bottles, and of course old poetry books. Just recently I was at my huge local Value Village. I admired, perhaps too much in retrospect, a large mirror in an expensive looking ornate metal frame for just $12, or actually $9, as it was seniors discount day. I said to myself (As Trump would say), I must have this, although I was running out of wall space. I walked away briefly to glance at some smaller items. About a minute later I returned to pick up the mirror. But I was shocked, double shocked, to see only an empty space where this gorgeous bargain mirror once resided. It was a hard bitter lesson: One should not admire and desire something too openly, as instantly it becomes valuable to others. And opportunity is as fleeing as a breath of air. Remember this you bachelors out there.

But, I will not bore you further. Come again in a few months I guarantee there will be further antiques, nick knacks, book ends, music boxes, etc., all treasures to admire. I tell you temptation is a curse. The ever present problem is what to discard to make room. But I am a beginning to see the error of my ways. Please come again.

# *15*

# HABITS-THEY MAKE YOU OR BREAK YOU

I INCLUDE A CHAPTER ON HABITS IN MY MEMOIRS AS ANY SUCCESS I have had is based on good habits. So I reveal some more of my secrets here.

## INTRODUCTION

*"Motivation is what gets you started."*
*"Habit is what keeps you going."* **Jim Rohn**
*"If you really want to do something, you'll find a way."*
*"If you don't you'll find an excuse."* **Jim Rohn**
*"First we make our habits, then our habits make us."* **Charles C. Noble**
*"Perfection and quality is not an act. It is a habit."*
*"We are what we repeatedly do."* **Aristotle**
*"Without habit and repetition our best qualities are not revealed."* **Anon**

# GENERAL

In a recent talent show on TV the audience were amazed at a contestant performing gymnastic tricks, sitting, standing or laying on a swaying unstable rope about eight feet above the ground between two solid posts–like a rope hammock I envisioned hundreds of bad falls in perfecting these complex balance maneuvers. **Such is the power of repetition and habit when the hard eventually becomes easy.** We become what we practice frequently.

Good and bad habits start at youth and are contagious, inborn, and easily inherited from your parents, For example, good habits in sports, music, and art, but unfortunately also bad habits are too easily picked up from parents, for example, unhealthy eating habits, obesity, smoking, and lack of exercise. And good and bad habits formed at youth can last a lifetime.

Your life is a bridge between Birth and Departure. Habits are like cables between Birth and Departure across the chasm of life. Or imagine— you are suspended on a lifeline, below is Demise. The good habits are the strong strands prolonging life, but the bad habits are the weak strands shortening life.

Habits will affect the way you carry your body. Our bodies stand erect, confident and strong— or bowed, slouched and weak, depending on ones good or bad habits.

*"Beliefs become thoughts, thoughts become your words, words become actions, actions become your habits, habits become your values, and values become your destiny."* **Gandhi**. In all due respects to Gandhi I believe "Beliefs and thoughts" are not sufficient motivation for most people. I say passion is required. Everyone should have a passion about something—happiness is working on your passion. My dear late artistic brother Maurice told me so, decades ago he was working on his passion —acrylic oil painting.

Here is the secret of success. Have a dream and a passion about something. Decide what actions have to be done to achieve your dream. This requires the correct knowledge. Next there has to be many repetitions of details; namely, diligent habits, to complete. At university, with good consistent study habits I was able to receive five scholarships and an Earl of Athlone Fellowship for two years study in England. At university I would review the lessons on the same afternoon or same night as the lecture and also on the following weekend, study at night until 10pm, and at exam time rise at 5 pm to study again. There were no wasted hours as I had to make time for training on the track team. I used a similar regimented procedure, to the above, in running training in breaking world records in running and hurdling. In writing my five books after I retired— I had the habit of writing for about three hours each day on one chapter at a time for as many weeks as it took. In this way the writing of a book was not formidable. Efficiency dropped off if excess writing hours per day were attempted.

But don't set out on a quest to be a virtuoso violinist unless you have the aptitude. Perfection —unless you are a freak of nature or prodigy—involves several thousand repetitions over a six to eight years period. This is a true fact. *"The soul grows into lovely habits as easily as ugly ones."* **Kate Wiggin.** But good habits require will power and more effort than bad habits which give in to impulse and temptation.

With repeated acts habits grow from rivulets initially, to streams, and finally to roaring rivers. Or initially from thin threads— into threads woven together to form ropes—then steel cables that secure us.

A habit is like a seed in the beginning, but with constant care and nurturing it becomes ingrained and automatic without thinking. In the beginning the nerve impulse of this repeated act travels along an unused rough jungle-like path, but with many repetitions the neural pathway becomes a well-worn and smooth highway with high walls. Habits form grooves in the neural pathways.

**What if you were to form a good new habit every month and get rid of a bad one? What a success story you would be. Nothing beats habit and experience.**

## GOOD HABITS

With any of the following characteristics and beliefs, good habits are formed—love, kindness, compassion, diligent focus, regularity and orderly, positive, tenacious, purposeful, flexible, punctual, determined, disciplined, wasting no time, industrious, resisting temptation, good thoughts, adaptable, and truthful. Success is knowing what to do to be successful and doing it every day, and being careful to provide recovery of the body and mind.

The road to success must involve some pain and discomfort. Habit and repetition enables you to bear the pain and fatigue.

Success is a mass of good habits— not a miss of good habits.

What is the ultimate supreme good habit? The supreme ultimate good habit is to have the habit of forming good habits. This is the secret of the successful. They have the desire, the knowledge and the skill necessary.

Successful habits = Success. Bad habits = dumb practice, and wasted energy.

## BAD HABITS

With any of the following characteristics and beliefs, bad habits are formed— angry, lazy, unforgiving, selfish, narcissistic, bad thoughts, pessimism, fear, procrastination, idleness, rude, cynical, sarcastic, untruthful and hating the world. What a nasty person! —not even a mother could love. Lord save us from these demons.

Bad habits can become indispensable. Bad habits are like an enormous flywheel: the repetition of bad habits adds to the momentum of the flywheel. Once started it is easy to keep going and the more repetition or momentum the harder to stop.

Whenever you repeat a bad habit it is harder to eliminate. It is easier to abandon in the beginning when they are like cobwebs rather than after too many repetitions when they are like steel cables.

Bad habits creep up on you. At first you don't realize they are taking hold of you. When you realize it—it is too late. Imagine you are in a race, feel exhausted, you slow down and stop. You have started a habit. You are trapped in a jail of your own choosing. It is important to fight the urge. Never give a habit the chance to get started. Prevention of a fire or a bad habit exceeds destruction of a fire or a bad habit.

How to break a bad habit. Act "as if." If you are frequently gloomy and sad, act as if you are happy. If you are lacking in confidence, act as if you are confident and walk energetically and without a slouch. It really works if you are fearful, lacking in energy, etc. Act the opposite. Also it helps if you have a substitute (a good habit) to replace the bad habit. For example, a cup of green tea instead of a glass of beer or wine.

The problem with most people: they are practising their bad habits every day. And they are lacking in will power, very comfortable and ensconced or stuck in their bad habits—with one timid foot in the good and one bold foot frequently in the bad.

Beware of feel good habits. Choose good for you habits. Too much fun, frivolity and comfort is a bad habit. It will bite you in the end (not the posterior). The remarkable Jack Leanne used to say, "People are working on dying not living." You are either growing or receding. Break out of your comfort zone and become comfortable with good habits. For example, improving at running is stepping out of the comfort zone repeatedly. Get rid of the mundane comfortable habit before it is too late.

Some have spiritual bad habits or spiritual weakness and do not realize it— for example, not helping others, not compassionate, or too self centered and selfish. This is often associated with a negative woe-is-me personality.

Beware of men who are looking for a good girl with many bad habits.

Impulse is a common bad habit involving lack of control. Once entrenched it is hard to resist and can happen too frequently.. It is the Devil tempting you. USA President John Kennedy was asked, why he frequently succumbed to the sexual temptations of females. He replied, "I can't help myself." Too often after working hundreds of hours to accumulate some savings— it is blown in a few hours. This may be worse than gambling since in gambling usually involves more thought.

But by delaying any action and weighing the pros and cons…there is time to come to your senses. For example, for a $100 expenditure consider for at least a day, for $1000 consider far a week, for $10,000 consider for a month. For $100,000 consider for a year or more.

One of the worst habits is a consistent bad attitude. Attitude is everything. If you don't like your circumstance change your dark attitude. Switch from the dark to turn on the bright. Grow a new attitude and a new you.

Don't fall in love with your bad habits. Fall in love with your good habits.

## RELATED THOUGHTS

Success starts in small details. Winning starts with a winning expectation.

> **Seneca** says: "*It is not because things are difficult that we do not dare. It is because we do not dare that they are difficult.*"

# CHANGE

To make a new habit there has to be will to change. Make the change if there are at least two good reasons to do so. Most people don't have the will to change, and they have their weak excuses to continue with their bad habits.

It is going to take willpower, time and effort and likely a change in attitude.

Recognition and admission are the first steps to change. Then comes willingness.

When crisis and difficulties transpire— adaptation is necessary. One has to be flexible. Then it is necessary to eliminate old habits and adapt new habits. Kill or replace a bad habit with a good habit.

Turn a disadvantage into an advantage, For example, if you are an injured athlete — can't run — do more weight training or become a better swimmer. Adapt and form new habits or improved habits for a period of time.

# MEDITERRANEAN, LOW INFLAMMATION, HEART HEALTHY DIET

It is essential to have good eating habits. The following is my recommended pyramid diet — **with most desirable foods at bottom and least desirable at top**— based on taking the best aspects from a wide variety of diets but mainly the Mediterranean diet, the anti-inflammation diet, and the low glycemic diet (low sugar rush). Twenty-five highly qualified researchers, doctors and dieticians ranked the Mediterranean diet best overall diet for 2018. The numbers below refer to the daily or weekly **servings** recommended. The following chart is worth a thousand words.

The anti- inflammation diet is important since low grade inflammation is at the root of most diseases, and particularly related to arthritis, diabetes, allergies, heart disease and even cancer. They all start with low grade inflammation. The best foods to prevent low grade inflammation are: fatty fish (salmon, mackerel, tuna and sardines) green leafy vegetables, fruit, fermented foods, onions and garlic, whole grains,fermented foods, herbs and spices.

**Fast Food NO** [1,2,3]

**Processed Food NO** [2]

**Starch with Protein at a meal NO** [6]

**White Products**: Bread, Rice, Flour **NO** [3,7]

**Butter, Bacon, Red Meat** 1 serving **WEEKLY or NO** [1]

**Potatoes, White Pasta MINIMAL or NO** [3]

**Sweets, Sugar, Chocolate. Fruit Juice MINIMAL** [3]

**Dried figs, dates, apricots, Greek yogurt PREFERABLE SWEETS**

**Wine MINIMAL**

**Low fat Dairy Products 2-3 DAILY** [1]

**Skinless Poultry, 1 to 2 WEEKLY**

**Eggs 2 WEEKLY for Men and 4 WEEKLY for women**[5]

**Oils**: Olive oil mainly, Canola or Grapeseed **1-2 tablespoons DAILY** [8]

**Supplements**: Multi Vitamin/Mineral, Magnesium, Vitamin E, Q10 coenzyme, etc. DAILY

**Water**: Distilled **8 glasses DAILY**

**Fats: Extra virgin oil, walnuts, avocados, seeds, ground flaxseed: 6 DAILY** [8]

**Whole Grains 5 DAILY** [4]

**Omega 3 Foods**: Salmon, Trout, Tuna or Sardines **3-4 WEEKLY** or Fish Oil **DAILY**

**Beans and Lentils 1-2 DAILY 4 and Nuts and Seeds 2 tablespoons DAILY** [8]

**Fruit 3-4 DAILY** [4]

**Vegetables 4-5 or more DAILY** [4]

**Leafy Dark Green Vegetables**: Kale, Spinach, Collards, Lettuce, etc. **2 DAILY** [4]

1. To reduce saturated fats
2. To reduce Trans fats
3. High Glycemic food
4. Low Glycemic food, high in fibre
5. To reduce prostate cancer risk in men and lower LDL cholesterol in women
6. Reduces digestion, & nutrient absorption
7. Low fibre, low vitamin B
8. Vitamins and minerals, healthy fats

# *16*

# INTERESTING CHARACTERS, AND AMAZING FRIENDS

NOTE: DEAR FRIENDS IF YOU DON'T MAKE THE DESCRIPTION LIST below it just means: you were either dear to my heart but just too normal, not weird enough, or too good hearted for words.

## UNCLE JACK

What makes life most interesting? Characters like Uncle Jack. Uncle Jack was married to my Aunt Bertha my mother's sister. Twice Bertha married Jack. It looked like maybe two mistakes as I thought she deserved better after divorcing my Uncle Wellwood—who was unhappy with Bertha being unable to conceive a daughter. But I grant you, Jack must have had some hidden admirable qualities. Jack was an ex-merchant mariner in World War 2, overweight due to atrociously poor diet, mainly canned goods and beer, and was a big man like Uncle Wellwood. Some of his escapades below will describe and reveal his character more than mere words.

Jack courted Bertha lavishly during their engagement. Later, Bertha found he had used her credit card to do so. Bertha was actually about 27 years older than Jack but successfully hid her age from Jack for decade's right up to the end. My Aunt Bertha looked several decades younger than her birth age, like my mother —but when Bertha was in hr early 90's and ill, I suspect Jack must have seen some document that threw her age into doubt. Bertha passed away at age 93 when Jack was in his mid-sixties. During one of our last visits to see Bertha in Detroit when I had taken my children Melanie, Tyler and Curtis with me —Jack asked me: "Earl, do you know anything about this —Bertha is suddenly looking many years older —can you explain this?" I said: "That's strange, sorry, I can't explain, I know nothing." But I knew.

Jack enjoyed carpentry in his spare time as he had lots of it being unemployed a fair amount. He made some bird houses and sent them to President Johnson as a gift. The American Security Services were suspicious and sent him a letter asking why there were no holes in the bird houses —they were completely sealed and absent of holes for the birds. He replied that he didn't know how big the birds were in Texas.

On another occasion he made a gift for my dear grandparents: He took a rowboat, added a roof which made it very tippy, added some front and rear lights, and covered it all with three or four different colours of paint. I suspect, knowing Jack, that he envisaged a boat fit to transport royalty. Then he towed it from Detroit, six hours away to Eagle Lake near Kingston Ontario to my grandparent's cottage— and proudly presented it as a gift. At the US/Canada border the custom officer after a thorough search, informed Jack that he owed $30 in customs duties. Jack was insulted stating, "What do you mean just $30. I spent three weeks working on this boat." This masterpiece of a boat found very limited use since it was unsafe —apt to tip over at a moment's notice—and was soon decommissioned and relegated to the flower bed sanctuary to Jack's chagrin.

On one visit to Detroit—myself, Melanie, Curtis, Tyler and Melanie's husband Alastair, we all went to a restaurant with Jack and Bertha. Jack had been drinking all afternoon, a frequent habit as evidenced by the girth of his stomach, and announced at the restaurant that he was going to be sick. I nervously escorted him to the washroom past many customers in the crowded restaurant Fortunately, to my relief he made it in time but he couldn't hold back in the parking lot to our dismay. Alastair was particularly and likewise affected.

In the hot summer months his solution for their hot apartment without air conditioning was to sit mostly naked in his Jockey shorts underwear in his big chair facing the open door leading to the busy hallway. I could imagine him sitting there with pot belly showing and happily sipping a cool beer. My daughter swears there was no underwear.

When Bertha was bed ridden I came with my children for one of our last visits. The whole apartment was highly unsanitary with a bad smell, so I spend quite a few hours cleaning it up particularly the bathroom and kitchen. In appreciation Bertha gave me $1000. She had done the same for brother Maurice on an earlier occasion. I took the cash although I was not lacking for money, but mainly because I knew this gave her a lot of pleasure. About a year later Jack mentioned that someone had stolen Bertha's money from under her mattress. I could imagine most likely where the money went.

Bertha was a real gem—we all loved her. One day she told me, "Earl your mother would have been very proud of you." My mother had died suddenly at age 69 from an angina heart problem, but Bertha lasted another 26 years even in spite of participating in Jack's atrocious canned food diet, but without the beer. I recall when Bertha and Uncle Wellwood would visit us on Christie Street in Toronto near Christie Pitts —Bertha and my mother were forever laughing. They were happy happy times They were much more than sisters. They were so overjoyed to see each other and reminisce about their years growing up on the farm and the characters they had encountered. In earlier years the visits by Uncle Wellwood and Aunt Bertha to Toronto, Uncle Wellwood, a brusque character, would take delight in doing his "wooden leg dance," while under the liquid influence. Ironically this was before he lost his lower leg due to gangrene. Then he could have done a most realistic one-legged dance, but no! it was no longer hilarious or even funny. This was the subject of one of my poems written 70 years later.

See the poem below which I wrote describing our last visit to see dear Aunt Bertha in a hospital for the elderly. I recall n the way out from our last visit, one of the elderly female patients was sneakily beckoning Tyler to come in to her room.

# "I'll Be Home for Christmas"

The imagined last words of dear Aunt Bertha, December 1999

"Ninety-five years filled with work, work, joy and loved ones;
Now there's only pain, tears and strangers;
Ninety-five, but it seems like forty-five.
I'll be leaving Detroit soon:
This boom box black and white city
of cars and broken dreams.
Seems like yesterday on the farm
        with sisters Lola, Alice, and Della;
The prairie got in my blood,
The endless sky over a sleeping giant with the golden flowing hair.
How we loved our mares and stallions:
Laxie, Goldie, Maxie and good old Jake."
—"I'm riding my pony Lucky in the sun once again:
Feeling free and fast as the wind;
Come Lola I'll race you back to the barn...
—Della and Alice come look at the fireworks
One-hundred miles away—that's Saskatoon Exhibition...
—Papa's been gone too long from town:
It's a blinding snow storm—
Mama keeps looking out the window,
but there's nothing to see;
When fear sets in the wind whistles and wails right inside the heart...
—It's forty below and we're stranded in our sleigh caboose
        the six of us;
Thank goodness for the hot rocks at our feet;
The horses are exhausted after plunging through the snow
        up to their bellies;
Now they can move no further...
—Its spring, glorious spring!
Look Mama three new born calves;
Papa will be pleased...

*—It's fall and I'm helping Mama in the kitchen*
*at threshing time;*
*We seem to be cooking and baking all day and night;*
*But look at the satisfaction on their hungry faces...*
*—But they're all gone now:*
*The animals, the threshing crew, Mama, Papa, and three dear sisters;*
*And I pray I'll be with them soon."*
*"My eyesight is bad too:*
*My strange helpers only a blur,*
*        moving in a fog;*
*They speak so soft and low to me,*
*Why can't I hear?*
*Feelin' weaker every day.*
*The high walls of this bed are a jail to me—*
*Like a children's crib.*
*I feel like a child again with diapers and all.*
*If only the Lord would take my in his arms*
*to erase this pain and tears.*
*Christmas is around the corner I think—*
*My last one for sure, but—*
*I'll be home for Christmas"*

Thank you Jack your antics kept us laughing for many years —and laughter is the spice of life. And God Bless you and dear Aunt Bertha.

## CHUCK SOCHOR

**I** went to many track meets for many years with my good American friend Chuck Sochor, also a good friend of the late Payton Jordan (see article below) and Louis Zamperini, the Olympian runner and war hero in the movie and book "The Unbroken."

I highly recommend the book by Laura Hillenbrand about Louis's ordeals during World War 2. Chuck was a pugilistic teenager, and later while still a teenage a lieutenant in the navy during World War 2. He was in a convoy of ships for the invasion of Iwa Jima. After the war he was a strict supervisor in the auto industry in Detroit.

Chuck and I travelled together while competing at the following WMA world master's championships; Carolina Puerto Rico 2003, Gateshead England 1999, Buffalo US 1995, Miyazaki Japan 1993, —and also two NCCWMA meets, many track and field meets in Toronto, several meets in Raleigh NC, and Eugene Oregon, a meet in Grand Rapids Michigan and another in Michigan, and not to mention many smaller meets. At the latter Michigan meet I recall suffering from dehydration: it was a torrid hot day after running the 800m the 200m was right after — when I finished I was dizzy and the green grass had all turned yellow but I returned to normal resting in the shade. There would have been more World championships but Chuck's dear wife Rose Marie was wheel- chair- bound requiring Chuck's constant care, including all household duties and shopping, etc. preventing him from leaving the large house on Lincoln Lake near Grand Rapids in Michigan for extended periods.

Chuck was proficient in many track and field events, sometimes competing in 10 events in a single day or a weekend including the steeplechase and hurdles. So I would say he was a true ironman. He had considerable speed, for example, at age 66 he ran the following impressive times: 100m 13.39, 200m 26.94, 400m 59.77, and at age 67 48.07 in the 300m hurdles. He should have been inducted into the US Masters Hall of Fame, but somehow slipped through the cracks. However, he has started up competing again at age 90, so perhaps, there is still hope to be selected for the US Masters Hall of Fame. While in his sixties he was able to train with young students at nearby Grand Valley Sate U. He was too fast for the women so had to train with the men and was even able to beat some of them. At world WMA championships I witnessed his participation in several gold winning sprint relays, and gold performances in the sprints, short hurdles in Puerto Rico and the long hurdles in Miyazaki. For hurdle practice Chuck used some home made hurdles and had many sessions on the gravel road in front of his house. That is impressive dedication..

On the long return flight from Japan his several Miyazaki medals proudly clanked about his neck. Chuck compared to me has an aggressive personality—I suppose from raising 10 children would require that. For example, if there was a long lineup he would find a way to get to the front. On a return trip from a masters track and field meet in Cancun Mexico to the US he was allowed by customs to retain without duty his six bottles of cheap brandy, after a private interview.

At most of the meets lasting more than a few days Chuck would bring ample food supplies from home. At a NCCWMA meet in Mexico there were many poor people congregating and sleeping on the cathedral steps. Chuck donated many of his canned goods to them and was mobbed by the crowd. At a previous NCCWMA meet in Mexica he complained rightly that this telephone bill was more expensive than his five day hotel room. In Miyazaki Japan in1993 we visited many temples and shrines in Tokyo for nearly a week after the best ever world championship— and while doing so he collected 10 kimonos as souvenirs for his 10 children.

Now at age 90 in 2017 with the passing of Rose Marie —Chuck has taken up running training again. Although his layoff for over a decade is a drawback, I firmly expect in view of his unusual strength for his age, his present and past active lifestyle and his past track and field experience— he will have renewed success. And I eagerly look forward to see my friend in action again.

## KEN COOKE

In the world of perfect friends and interesting characters my late good Aussie friend Ken Cooke would rate very highly. I know now that life had smiled on me to have him as a friend. I will describe below some of his escapades. I speak of Ken in my memoirs because he was one of the highlights in my life.

We became friends as I enjoyed his company and his kind and easy going affable personality. With his Australian accent and his swagger he was the true Australian. I stayed with Ken at his apartment for a year while I was renting my house, although initially it was to be one or two weeks. Later, he stayed for about the same length of time at my home, hence we became best friends, and never an argument at any time. He lived life to the hilt every day, but with a great thirst for alcohol –a bottle of sherry in an evening was possible without being intoxicated and still talking intelligently, for he was very knowledgeable in all areas. But no doubt his liver was suffering and was told so on many occasions by one of his two daughters, a doctor, from one of his three marriages. He was kind and maybe even too generous but could be tough if you crossed him, as I found out one playful day.

Ken was married three times and had two Australian daughters from his first marriage, one a doctor. While residing in Toronto he married an attractive Jamaican woman, but the marriage only lasted a few months when it was soon revealed she only wanted to be married to a Canadian to get Canadian citizenship. Ken had dual citizenship with Australia and Canada.

As an engineer at the same company, Atomic Energy Canada Ltd, (AECL) as me--he was an intelligent engineer, but unlike myself his heart wasn't in the work of designing nuclear reactors for production of electricity. So he didn't progress far in the company in spite of his high intelligence. He desired to be laid off after about 20 years for the benefits of what retirement offered. Finally, he got his wish with a retirement package. At the time he had a huge credit card debt of over $25,000—so a large portion of his retirement settlement went for this debt. Another large portion was for a two week holiday with his new found lady friend. She was not told of the destination—it turned out to be Hawaii. I suspect he was thinking of a honeymoon type of holiday–but she insisted on separate rooms, which ate heavily into his planned budget. After one week of luxurious meals and living they decided to go on a food reduced diet for the remaining week. On return they broke up shortly after.

When Ken left Mississauga to retire in Sydney Australia, he had a pretty young female friend of convenience shall we say, if you get my drift. He generously but not openly tried to set me up with her when he left after his retirement to live in Australia--but I had no interest in this kind of friend— and in any case I was faithful to my friend Shirley. He also left behind an old Buick car which went to the above friend. This vehicle had the bad habit of not starting at awkward times–starting involved getting on his overalls and going under the car and banging the starter with a hammer. Evidently this had happened on dates with women, but he treated it in a casual way. I'm not surprised as he always had a lot of female friends. (Now at age 87 I wish he was around to give some tips on meeting the opposite sex.)

When Ken returned to Australia to retire he had spent most of his retirement package and was near penniless except for his medium sized pension. But financial smiled on him shortly. His mother bequeathed him half her house, the other half going to his sister who was eager to sell the house. But Ken was living there and determined not sell. When potential buyers came to look at the interior it was in a cluttered condition (Ken was the master clutterman) –and also the house had more than the usual large cockroaches, a common problem in Australia I learned from experience. So the sale was put on hold. Then one day his close female friend who was dying from cancer of the brain, asked him, " Who do you think I should have in my will?" Ken giving his true opinion said, "What have your relatives done for you." Ken had been looking after his sick friend for over year with her eyesight going quickly. When his close friend died shortly after— she left him in her will the expensive apartment overlooking the Sydney Harbour, the famous Bridge and Opera House. (It is strange to me that such a magnificent modern structure should be called a House.) After selling this apartment he bought two cheaper ones –a smaller one for himself and an adjacent much larger one occupied by his new close female friend. Knowing Ken I would not be surprised if she was living rent free. I visited Ken's smaller apartment on a few days stay in Sydney on the occasion of competing at the World Masters Championships in Brisbane in 2009. Ken had a bad habit— he was an atrocious collector. The apartment was piled up inside, particularly with high stacks of daily newspapers. There was barely room to walk, only a narrow path to the kitchen, bathroom, and bedroom. This indicated most of his time was spent next door. When I visited Ken on my return from the Brisbane Worlds, he insisted on paying for my hotel and all meals. Also he said," I am taking you and my lady friend to the best restaurant in Sydney overlooking the Sydney Harbour. It was a memorable fabulous experience with cocktails, two bottle of wine, one for $250 ( the best I have ever tasted and one for $130 (over priced) with a total bill of about $700 Australian which is close to the same Canadian. His lady friend was doing all the ordering. When I sympathized about the size of the bill he said don't worry I won about $1000 in a slot machine last week.

Ken was one of the kindest and most generous persons you will ever meet. For example, on one occasion he delivered, without being requested a very heavy sewing machine from Sydney to Montreal Canada to a past lady friend-- she had left it behind when she moved to Canada. The story goes (maybe not true) that she was shocked to see him and was unappreciative of his major gesture. But in any case, it was a very noble charitable gesture. On another occasion he came from Australia to visit and perhaps cheer up a young engineer with cancer he had also worked with at AECL. He stayed at my home when he came to visit past friends. On one of these occasions he noticed I didn't have an air conditioning system, had it installed and paid for it. It has provided me with cool comfort now for over 24 years.

Ken had a disappointment after travelling from Australia to Mississauga purposely to see a sick past female friend. On this day I went with him and a mutual friend Madeleine to a local retirement home after making an appointment—and asked to see her- the three of us knew her very well as a past neighbour and party friend, Presently, she came out, looked at me, Madeleine and Ken and said bluntly, "I cant see you. I'm having company."—and then hurriedly left. It was Alzheimer's speaking, so Ken didn't return.

While I was married and living in the country Ken came to the rescue many times. One time It was the result of my losing my drivers licence for several months in the winter. My young brother Wellwood living in Calgary had come to Toronto on business. I visited him with the children at the Sheraton Hotel for a couple of hours next to the City Hall. It was Kathi's bar night out with girls so I had the children. After some cognac celebration with my brother–something I was not used to drinking- shortly after I left in the car one of the boys said he had to urinate urgently, so I stopped at a small quiet side street, aptly named Pearl street (my mother's second name), believe it or not. (Incidentally, while at high school I dated a girl on Earl street in Toronto.) But the police were on Pearl at the time as luck would have it—and I was unable to walk the line sufficiently well. Most people have trouble with this even when sober particularly the elderly. Without my licence I would be unable to attend curling once a week with Ken and others from AECL. Ken wouldn't have it—he drove me many times to curling and after the game to my house in the country— then returning to Mississauga, How many friends would do that? As luck would have it—my licence was returned to me after about three months, based on "my good driving record". Such good treatment would not happen these days, four decades later. It wa hard lesson.

Ken passed away at age 78. A true golden friend. Fifteen years later I wrote the following poem which would apply to many of my past and present friends:

# 𝔄 Special Friend

*In this brief lifetime*
*We are truly blessed*
*And fortunate beyond compare*
*If we have a special friend who:*
*Cultivates the friendship through the years;*
*Not allowing the weeds to grow;*
*Alleviates our worst fears;*
*Is there when needed without urging;*
*Gives without receiving;*
*Understands and asks not;*
*Says what you need to hear;*
*Forgives and tolerates our weaknesses;*
*And truly cares.*
*OWith such a friend you are rich indeed though poor.*
*I have found a treasure it's true*
*For such a one is you,*
*Dear friend!*

Now in retrospect I realize as in most or many friendships it's way too late to show and speak of my vast appreciation. Don't let it happen to you.

## CHRIS ERICKSON

I include my past lady friend, for two years. in my list of interesting characters since Chris had an unusual life story like the material that makes a good movie. I was fortunate to meet her at a Graduate dance attended mostly by single university grads. Chris was a an attractive white lady close to my age with colorful hair that could change frequently. She had recently migrated from South Africa when I met her.

I learned she and her husband named Earl, coincidently, had owned a popular spa in Johannesburg and were quite prosperous, for example, owning a couple of Rolls Royce cars. But her husband who had a WIFM policy, (What's In It For Me), was murdered during a robbery in in their home. Little did he realize what was in it for him when he encountered these robbers with their guns and machetes. This bad experience and the crime in South Africa prompted her to move to Canada. But the Government policy prevented her from taking her money out of South Africa. Without her permission I cannot carry on with her interesting story.

## ERNIE AND MARY ELLEN MILLS

Ernie my best and loyal friend for several decades, enjoyed his bachelorhood and seemed in no rush to get married— marrying at age 35 somewhat like myself at age 37. After all, there were three girls to every man in the Trident Club of over 700 members where Ernie and I in our 30's were both fortunate to preside as presidents for a year each in the prestigious Timothy Eaton Memorial Church on St Clair West, Toronto. Ernie obtained his Bachelor degree the hard way, by night school and had a huge collection of jazz records.

Ernie and I had some exciting times. And each year going for a week of skiing at Grey Rocks in the Quebec Laurention mountains— always in January at the coldest and cheapest time of the year. And also frequent trips to Lake Rosseau, Muskoka region in the summer for water skiing, tennis and dancing. Ernie was fearless on the skies. I would be too if I was that close to the ground. When we would ski in those big moguls Ernie would often disappear between these small mountains and I would think: "Has he fallen or what," but he was never late at the bottom. Although short in stature he made up for it with his big heart and his great sense of humour.. And he was always available in time of need.

You will never meet a more genuine, kind, honest, upstanding, helpful, generous, reliable, religious couple. They provided me with valuable advice on many occasions. And for many decades not years, after my divorce, I enjoyed their wonderful Christmas dinners at their home. That means they could have heard some of my stories several times over. When I grow up I want to be just like them. We have to count our blessings—I was blessed with the friendship and love of Ernie and Marie Ellen for over 45 years.

# JOHNNY BOWER

I have lot of respect for the late (December 26, 2017 at age 93 from pneumonia). Johnny Bower, the popular Maple leaf goalie of the 1960's and early 70's, 4 times Stanley Cup and 2 times Vezina trophy (goalie of the NHL year, and the goalie with the most wins ever (356). Named Johnny as John would not suit his warm- fun- loving personality I had the pleasure to meet him, also born in Saskatchewan, just twice. The first meeting when we were driving small cars in a fund raising charity sponsored by the Mississauga Sports Council. It was his habit to support many charities and act as a volunteer.. The second meeting more recently at a Mississauga Sports Council banquet: I introduced my two sons Tyler and Curtis, hockey players, to him and took their photo together. Then fifteen years after the above charity event —at a Mississauga Sports Council banquet after I presented an award to an athlete— he stood applauding (the only one of the 200 or so attending) in recognition to me as I left for my seat.

At age 14 he lied about his age to enter the Canadian army during the Second World War; this tells a lot about his character. Johnny had all the admirable qualities; a modest gentle warrior, who worked at his goalie craft for 11 years in the AHL—then started in the NHL with the Maple Leafs at a late age of 33 lasting to age 43. And loved by all— losing teeth and receiving many stiches to his maskless face from flying pucks —always with a great sense of humor through it all. Some people you can see right away the goodness in their heart. That was Johnny Bower— the soul of the Maple Leafs in those early days, modest, kind, and "one of a kind."

# GRANDAD

My grandad, Tom Hampton, on my mother's side, kind, and strong, was my hero and inspiration. I hope I have some of his genes.

Unfortunately, I only know a few stories about him. When he was 16 in Tichborne, Ontario, near Kingston city he built a two story house for his mother. A few years later in the early 1900's he decided to start a new pioneer life out West. He rode the boxcars to Alberta. On this winter trip his winter jacket was stolen while he slept one bitter cold night in a boxcar. He went from one boxcar to the next on the moving train looking for his jacket and eventually found it. I pity the thief for grandad was a tough hombre.

During his search for farmland he considered free land offered by the Government at the present site of Edmonton. Had he settled there he would have ended up a multi-millionaire due to the present land value. He decided against this location for some reason— perhaps the bad weather in this area. He decided after searching the free land packages on horseback to settle in Saskatchewan near the small town of Elstow. Initially, there were few roads. It was hard work clearing the land of the tall grass by fire and picking up endless rocks. It was a lonely life with the closest neighbours miles away. One had to be a Jack of all trades, a carpenter, a machinist, to repair the machinery, an animal doctor, and above all an expert on growing wheat and other grains. He married Flossie and built a two storey farm house and a two story barn. After he sold everything and moved to Ontario onto crown land, this grand red barn housed many small stores and was a popular shopping spot for miles around, but was eventually destroyed by fire. As the children grew they were more help and more land was purchased until they owned several hundreds of acres. Oh! the excitement of harvest time. Della and Alice helped in the kitchen while Lola and Bertha help outdoors. At a young age in those days, a 10 year old was doing adult work. Initially there were many calamities to contend with like frequent storms, hail, grasshopper storms and failed crops but sometimes diversity saved the day, e.g., one grain crop failed but another type flourished. It was sad day when they left it all behind< the farm and farm animals be had that had become pets. They had prospered where many had failed.

Grandad at one time had a married man and his wife as helpers, but the man was beating his wife. Grandad took the huge man and taught him an unforgettable physical lesson to stop this abuse. For grandad was also an artist of the pugilistic arts. He would often entertain guests and family reciting Robert Service poems like the Cremation of Sam McGee, The Parson's Son, and the Shooting of Dan McGrew and other Service poems. But, these recitations were always much improved after a few drinks of his favourite peach brandy. I recall he would go to Elstow for machine parts or other items and always return with a huge bag of peanuts. Hence, my love of peanuts. Grandad passed way at about age 85 a few weeks after a fall and developing Alzheimer's shortly after. I loved Grandma Flossie too, but my pioneer- of- the-West grandad remains forever my hero and inspiration. I still cherish the tattered little book of Robert Service poems, over a hundred years old, that he used to learn to recite so well these famous poems.

# PAYTON JORDAN

## PAYTON JORDAN ON SPRINT TRAINING

*Payton Jordan a late friend of mine if you do not know was a multi- world-record holder in the sprints, and also the track and field USA coach at the 1968 Olympics. See other details below. He graciously consented to write the foreword in my book, the Complete Guide to Running. I had several letters from him before he died from cancer I believe at about age 88.. Since I have a lot of sprinting friends I could not resist describing below his thoughts on sprinting technique.*

Note: **The sentences in (brackets and italics) are my own additional explanations, not Payton's.**

One of the best track and field coaches in history

Member of Track Coaches Hall of Fame

Head Coach at Stanford U from 1957 to 1979

1968 US Olympic T. and F. Coach in Mexico

Multi age group master world record holder in sprints

Payton wrote the glowing Foreword in my book, "The Complete Guide to Running." Payton was a good friend of long time friend Chuck Sochor and also good friend to Louis Zamperini, the II World War hero in the great book the Unbroken by Laura Hillenbrand. So I could not resist in including Peyton's sprint advice in my memoirs.

## WHAT MAKES A CHAMPION?

Commitment, goal setting, discipline, strong work ethic, appreciation and giving credit to others. (*I add it is a 24 hour job, thinking, believing and acting like a champion.*)

A sprinter must have flexibility, strength, good form, and fast reaction.

## FLEXIBILITY

Flexibility is absolutely essential for sprinting. (*Do the stretches in the warmup, but more in the cool down.*) (*I personally like the exercise in the shallow end of the pool by the wall, swinging the legs every which way. The buoyancy helps increase flexibility and at the same time builds some strength due to the water's resistance. Stretch every day. Yoga and Pilates also helps. In the sprint drills don't neglect swinging the legs.*)

## SPRINT TRAINING

Work on speed first then distance. Begin with short distances and work toward longer distances at the same speed. But always thinking of relaxation and good form. Over time increasing intensity and yet feeling the same comfort zone.(*This is also the Charlie Francis system.*) But for distance training—develop from stamina to speed, i.e., it is usual to train firstly for distance and with time proceed to faster speeds at the same distance.

Sprinters begin with short distance e.g., about 40m then 60m and later as speed develop to 150, 200, 300m, all at near full speed, thus developing stamina gradually. To increase sprinting stamina. some longer slower runs at 400m and even 600m are used. (*Note, I speak of meters here, but in Payton's days it was equivalent yards.*) To develop efficiency of the human body put it through repeated action under pressure duplicating in practice the actual race..Learn to turn on more and more steam without straining. Sprint against the clock or team mates. (*Always train and run within your present capabilities without straining.*)

(*It's not all about physical training. Do not neglect training of the mind— before and during a workout think of the benefits of the specific training on each training day— in this way more is achieved form the workout and this also helps to tolerate some uncomfortable sessions. Mental training can also increase confidence, eliminate fear, and improve energy.*)

## STRENGTH

In sprint training build strength with weights and running up hills and up steps. Physical strength is also developed by duplicating race conditions over many shorter distances at near race pace (*90 to 95% race pace*) and also at a longer than the actual race but at slower than race pace.

If you neglect to strengthen the abs and oblique's—you lose it all. The strength of abs and oblique's ensures efficient transfer of power to the legs. Also, there must be pronounced definition and bulk in the hip region. (*Hence strength exercises in this region are essential. A lot of injuries result from weak gluteus muscles.*)

Free weight training can be done at end of the running training (but not the day before training). (*Charlie Francis had his track athletes doing this as well.*)

Some of Payton's recommendations are free weight extensions and curls — leg lifts on an incline board— knee lifts with 3 to 5 pound weight on feet—arm turnover in front of a mirror with 5 pound weights in hands— and half squats with 50 to 75 % of body weight.

(*Squats are a favourite exercise as they work all parts of the body particularly when weights are carried. Feet are hip width apart, slightly turned out, chest up, back straight, knees are over toes. weight on heels and balls of feet, not on toes. Start without weight and progress to holding dumbbells to weights on the shoulders. To help explosiveness from blocks accelerate on way up.*)

## REACTION and RELAXATION

Reaction drills improve the speed of the nervous system.

Payton recommends fast feet in place running referred to as "eggshell running." Payton also recommends fast arms in good form in front of a mirror with or without light weights—(*a favourite of mine done at faster rpm than actual sprinting, so it is good for working on relaxation*). Shake loose muscles. Relaxation at full speed is essential. Learn to stay loose by relaxing during warmup and cooldown drills. The usual ABC drills should be done during warmup, and each warmup drill twice and 50m in length—concentrating on looseness in arms and legs.Shake the loose muscles. Also during the drills maintain the desired lean. A straight line drawn from the driving back leg through the navel (the centre of gravity) to the head should be about 80 to 85 degrees.

Lead with the chest, not from the waist. At pushoff: rise high on the toes. Hold thumb loosely against the first finger. Tension in hands will transfer to arms and shoulders. Think loose, fluid, relaxed. (*Tell yourself I am running with minimum energy.*)

One drill recommended by Payton and new to me is: alternate jog and quicksteps each repetition 4 to 6m. (*Re: the "goose stepping drill," Payton's name for this drill with the straight legs: In my book "The Complete Guide to Running," my German publisher, Meyer and Meyer, objected to me calling it "Gestapo" stepping. This word was the only word in the whole book that I had to change. All other words were golden to them.*)

(*To improve reaction my recommendation—use the stationary bike and cycle at a higher rpm than race pace, for short bursts, e.g., 110, or 120 rpm for 30 seconds, or 1 minute with a 2 minutes rest between. Other reaction drills are the ladder drills done fast. And also fast feet on the spot without moving forward. Work on these to improve the speed of the nervous system. Don't neglect speed during the base building part of the season. This applies to middle distance runners too. Work on speed or you lose it.*)

## FORM

The ABC drills help develop good form.

In training think of relaxing the jaw, face, neck, shoulders and hands. Look out for raised shoulders, strained neck, or tight hands. Learn total relaxation first at ¾ speed or less—then later at nearly full out speed. (*Tell yourself I am running economically with minimum energy.*)

(*When I was a young teenager I would run many repeated 100m at about 80 to 90% speed just concentrating on form and —relaxation. I recommend this to other runners.*)

Aim for effortless movement. Think of the track as a hot surface to be touched just briefly on the toes with a quick recovery.

Strive for a fluid free, loose and relaxed stride. (*Some head on photos show arms and legs and feet moving awkwardly sideways, indicating gross inefficiency in form.*) A forward lean aids forward momentum and helps to ensure a strong push from a straight leg at the back during pushoff—which ensures a good knee lift at the front..

The vigorous and extended push of each leg through the full range of motion—is called "power" driving. The aim is to feel free and easy while running at maximum speed. (*Straining, especially in the neck area, will slow you down.*)

Lean with the chest up and not from the waist and with a full extended push at the back. (The forward lean aids forward momentum and helps to ensure a strong pushoff from a straight leg at the back —which ensures a good knee lift at the front. I personally have a good lean forward, not too much and not too little —lacking in a lot of runners. A good lean looks good —you can see the power in the leg thrusts, like you can see the speed in flying hair. Excessive knee lift results in longer stride but slows you down.)

Hold the thumb lightly on the index finger. Loose hands relax the arms; do not exaggerate the backward thrust of the arms. (*I suspect Payton recommends this as a longer back thrust would result in a longer arm movement and hence reduced turnover, and a too long stride in front.*)

Lift the knees but not reaching so far as to be beyond the centre of gravity. Over striding will result in slower speeds. The height of the knees comes naturally from an aggressive stride and push off. The height of the knee at front should not be exaggerated. The whole stride should feel natural.

(*Running form will deteriorate, even drastically, with age and particularly past age 75 and 80—due to stiffening of joints, arthritis, and loss of flexibility in tendons and muscles. We should fight this if we intend to have a lengthy running career as I do…. Coach Earl suggests the following—keep up with fast movements like short fast interval training (HIIT) —do ABC drills in good relaxed form but somewhat quick—end each particular drill with a short burst of speed— concentrate on good form during the warmup and cooldown—stretch twice a day, particularly the legs, gluteus muscles, groin and hip flexors—do yoga and Pilates—do regular strength training twice per week—do regular balance exercises to compensate for declining balance—and glucosamine with chondroitin for the stiffening joints may also help delay this problem. But don't start on this too late or it will be to late The better you move —the better you become.*)

## THE BLOCKS AND THE START

Only a relaxed athlete will be able to respond with a minimum reaction time. Properly shake out the muscles before getting in the blocks. The first two spikes should be in contact with the track surface to keep from popping up. In the blocks block out the world by taking a few deep breaths from the diaphragm by inhaling and exhaling fully. On "set" take a deep controlled breath and held it until the gun sounds—exhale quickly and explode out. In this initial part of the race the athlete should focus on full and complete pushes with legs and aggressive pulls with elbows. (Keep lean for about 25 metres.)

## PAYTON'S QUOTES

Quality before quantity.

Under-train rather than over-train.

A man or woman becomes a champion by working harder than their competitors.

Great sprinters are not born —they have innate qualities and genes that must be refined.

## FIGHTING AGING

With age the lungs become less flexible and reduce oxygen absorption, the fuel for energy production. Breathe properly from the diaphragm, not from above the breast line. Exhalation is double of inhalation while sprinting. Proper posture is essential.

Flexibility, strength and reaction in the senior years decline each year but can be offset to a large extent by frequent flexibility, strength and reaction training.

# JOHN WRAGG

I would be remiss if I did not write about my "amazing machine"/Canadian friend, John Wragg. As of May 28, 2018 he has done the seemingly impossible—239 long distance ironman races completed all over the world. This is 226 km/race of 3.8km swimming, 180km cycling, and a 42.2 km marathon, or a grand total of 54,000km surpassing the 40, 000km around the circumference of the world. All this since 1988 or 30 years and sometimes about 17 astounding ironman races or more per year. All this requires superhuman endurance and boundless mental capacity and energy. In addition, he does marathons and cross- country skiing competitions worldwide.

Since 2008 he has continued racing with a hip replacement due to a collision with a truck while cycling north of Milton— although the specialists said he would not run again. But John's inner doctor said, "Must continue on." He says there are worse obsessions. It seems a lonely business, but he is hooked on it. At age 68 in 2018 he says he will keep going until he can't finish the race. Seems a long way off for John.

In 2017 he earned a spot in the prestigious world Ironman races in Kona Hawaii in 2018, by winning the men's 65-69 age category in Korea in 2017. This indicates he is still going strong and still very competitive even at the top of his age group.

John is one of the top three, all men, in the world to have competed in ironman races in all six continents of the world. In 2018 or 2019 his lovely wife Elizabeth Model is expected will be the fourth member of this prestigious group. In 2018 Elizabeth has an impressive 85 ironman races completed by end of May 2018, and 99 marathons by end of in 2017—in the single year 2017 alone she had completed 8 half ironman's (called ironman 70.3's for the total miles in this extreme event). Elizabeth shattered her tibia and fibula in a cross country skiing crash in 2015 but has persevered to regain her racing shape. John and Elizabeth are an inspiration for all athletes. John says 2013 was the pinnacle of their career together —and in that year finished an ironman race together.

There is no doubt, John with his world records and Elizabeth with her extreme exploits will be leaving their forever imprints in the athletic sands of time.

# ED WHITLOCK

The late Ed Whitlock and his many running feats and multi world records was and still is my biggest inspiration.

The onslaught of distance world records from 1500m to marathon started for Ed Whitlock after his wife Belinda suggested he take up running to get him out of the little house in Milton Ontario after his retirement at age 60 from his mining engineering career— which he had started at age 21 in Canada. Many years later, Ed was to say in his dry humor way: "My wife is saying I am spending too much time on my hobby." So I believe one of Ed's great assets apart from his superior genes and talent was his tolerant and understanding wife, Belinda.

The many hours of running time developed mainly from his iron clad habit to run daily laps most days around the nearby and appropriately named Evergreen cemetery for three or more hours. This was his simple training which he stuck to assiduously and which he rode to legendary success. A personal visit there convinced me of the features he must have liked, the serenity, lack of traffic and the many flat paths shaded by mature Maple trees. He preferred not to run with others at their speed or be hampered by followers at his preferred pace. Also, in this cemetery he had only to contend with a wind against him on one quarter of the loop and if there was a problem it was only a short distance to home. His graveyard daily runs are so famous that others have mixed me up with Ed and asked if I am still running in the graveyard.

Ed had a good running background in England as a youth in his springboard to fame. He engaged in cross county races and at one point even beat Gordon Pirie in a cross country race, and was able to run a 4:31 mile at high school. He resumed running at age 41 and was a world class masters runner at 800 and 1500 metres. The gold medal in the 1500m at the World Veterans Championships in Hanover Germany in 4:09.6 in 1979 at age 48, at the top of his age group, was a good indication of his exceptional speed and endurance—also, at age 48 running a marathon in 2:31.23. After a rest from running from 1979 until his retirement, he started to participate in many road races in the early 1990's. and started breaking Canadian and then world records.

On approaching age 70 he realized that no one over 70 had run under 3 hours in the marathon and thought it was a long overdue achievement, could be done, and he would make an effort to be that person. No doubt this ambitious dream provided the incentive for many boring three hour trips around the cemetery in fair and foul weather for several decades. On one of his earlier and yearly marathons at Scotiabank marathon I observed him within a mile from the finish running at a good pace, the crowd excitedly roaring and cheering him on— but with Ed at a noticeable large awkward lean to the right due to oxygen deprivation. The marathon and the triathlon take a lot out of the human body, so one must be super fit to attempt these events.

**Physical characteristics.** Ed had the ideal body to withstand the countless hours of training and racing with an efficient 110 pound frame and 5 foot 7 inch height, but looking much taller when running—with a resting heart rate in the low 50's— and by treadmill tests at age 70, a maximum heart rate of 168 bpm, and an oxygen uptake, VO2max of 52.8 ml per minute per kg of body weight. His VO2max was exceptionally high for his age.

When running with his long relaxed stride, light and fluid, Ed was poetry in motion. It was obvious it was an efficient stride. His habit of landing on his heel suited him but was somewhat unorthodox and which in a heavier runner could result in tired calves in the long run. Usually, he was able to finish with an impressive final kick over the final 200 or more meters. At one point in my career he was slower than me in the 1500 and mile and then later became faster than me. At one point we both had the mile record in the 75-79 age groups, Ed the outdoor record and me the indoor record —and both near identical times within a second, i.e., 5:41 and change. Ed, always helpful, on one occasion at York University when I had started too fast as usual and he had passed me in the finish he seriously suggested I should follow him in our next 1500m race.

**Running Equipment.** Ed raced in a special pair of very light Brookes running shoes. He was so enamored by them he had another four pair for training worn out at the heel, these running shoes and his singlets all from the early 1990's. I had a pair of these Brookes shoes myself and they were as comfortable as a slipper but with minimum support. But the lack of support no doubt caused strengthening of his feet since it duplicated barefoot running. If you can tolerate the lack of support Light shoes can be a big advantage. Ed tended to land on his heels on each stride. He told me he shaves the corner of the heel to make for a better landing spot.

**Relays with Ed.** Ed had considerable speed as well as endurance, and could run an impressive 200m or 400m in a relay. But, he avoided interval training in view of an Achilles problem that flared up at higher speeds. But

He was forever helpful and could be talked into a 4x200, a 4x400, or a 4x800 relay even when tired after competing one or more longer races. For example, at the World Masters Championships in Sacramento in 2011— Ed and I although 80 and 82 respectively, ran in the M75-79 4x400 relay—running in the following order: Ray Wardle, Ed, Roger Davies and me—Ed got us good lead and we won gold by over 14 seconds in 5:14.50 over the two strong teams, the Japanese and the United States—it was an euphoric experience for me and our team.

See below also: two world records with Ed Whitlock. Both world records were in 2013,in age group 80-89 with Ray Wardle, Bill Thompson, Ed Whitlock and me, handing off in that order. Ray and Bill (the organizer) worked hard to prepare themselves for these relays.

The 4x800 at Canadian Outdoor Championships, Varsity Stadium, July 6, 2013, lowering the old record by the Aussies in 16: 01, our new record 14:24. Ed ran under 3 minutes. I ran a few seconds over 3 minutes as I ran with a groin problem and did not race the next day. Someone took a famous (some said) video of Ed handing off to me.

The 4x400, at Canadian Masters Indoor Championships, York University, March 16, 2013 in 6:06.28:. Old record was 6:34. This relay record is still existing in the World Masters Athletics indoor world record list as of April 1, 2018.

The most recent and last relay I had with Ed was at the Canadian Outdoor Championships at York University in 2016. Ed had broken the world record in the 10K the day before and the next day ran the 1500m and then the 800 but still agreed to run a 4x400m relay. He said to me, before this relay: "We must be crazy to do this." But as usual he was forever helpful. For example, before the 800 which we had both entered he told me he was tired, but would pace me If I wanted to do something special but I declined as I had the age group record and was not up to it, so he just tagged along. In an interview a month later he said he was finished in this 800m race after 200m —most likely since I went out fast the first lap and he finished a respectable six seconds behind. I told him after the race I was lucky he didn't feel fresh.

**Ed's records.** A complete list of all his records would take a volume to describe So only a summary is described here. The World Masters Athletics lists 18 world track records in age groups 65-69, 70-74, 80-84 and 85-89 in distances from 1500m, mile, 3000m, 5000m, and 10,000m in indoor and outdoor races. And world marathon records in age groups 70-74, 75-79, 80-84, and 85-89. In addition Ed's age group records there are even more specific age records and Canadian records. His latest marathon world record was also at the Scotiabank Waterfront Marathon in Toronto breaking the old record by a huge 28 minutes in running 3:56.33—well below his target of under 4 hours. Nevertheless he said he was disappointed in his time since he had not as much preparation as he would have liked. I estimated he had declined 4% per year between his world record marathons at age 80 to 85 whereas he felt his aim was to run no more than one percent per 1% slower per year which is the norm for most mere mortal world class athletes up to age 65 but increasingly larger every year after. Ed admitted to me that some years there can be a big drop in performance as I have personally noticed. In my opinion nearly all of his records will not be broken for many decades and some not in this century. Hence I believe he will most likely be the male master athlete of the 21 century.

### Ed Whitlock's quotes:

*Our performances do leak away as we get older. But we don't have to slow down as much as we think. If we keep active we can accomplish a lot.*

*People underestimate what old people can accomplish. Old people are the worst in that respect. They let themselves be intimidated by age.*

*I don't feel that different to when I was young, actually. (at age 76)*

*I train to race well, I train to race. I don't train for my health and enjoyment. I have to put in a lot of miles if I want to run well. I don't have to work on my speed for good performance, all I need is to do is work on my endurance.*

*On training: It's mainly a drudge for me. I wouldn't say I dislike it, But it's not a particularly enjoyable experience. It's just something I do to run well. (This indicates a great deal of perseverance and dedication to achieve a goal.)*

*I think the way I train has some validity—simple is not necessarily stupid.*

I asked him one day, what to you think about during these marathons and long distance races—his snswer: *"When is it going to end?"*

**Preparation** for 2014 world record marathon at age 73. His training apart from frequent distance races involved running long and slow for three hours most days of the week exclusively in a 300 meter paved circuit in his scenic Evergreen Cemetery in Milton, a short distance from his home, (In three hours this is a tremendous number of corners to turn). He claimed several advantages for his circuit including "no traffic problems and the drivers are a docile lot." For this preparation to be the first over 70 years to run a marathon under 3 hours he had 50 training sessions of 3 hour duration in an 11 week span. And at one period running 13 days in succession for 3 hours—this is staggering even to contemplate. This indicated the energy and heart of a much younger man of perhaps about age 30. He was adapting his body to his target marathon time, and running these sessions without liquid intake—to save time— unlike most marathon runners who have water and gels to boost energy. It was a case of running for time not distance or pace. But his pace did improve from about 9 minutes per mile initially to just over 8 minutes per mile about 6 weeks before the marathon. On other days in the 11 week buildup he ran shorter long runs or took a day off. In addition he ran 15 races of 5K, 10K, and 15K distances in the six months leading up to the marathon. He was convinced this "simple" training regime at age 73 was responsible for his successful marathon. He stated: "doing the odd long run would not do it for me." What amazing dedication and perseverance to achieve his ambitious dream goal.

**Training philosophy.** Ed believed more is better—the more training you do, the longer you train, and the higher the intensity the better you will race. To compensate for Father Time he believed more mileage was the answer. Basically, he trained the same all year round to be always ready to race—contrary to most athletes who have a competitive season and an easier recovery base building season. But for him certain races had more importance and training trails off after such an event.

There were many normal athlete activities missing in his unorthodox training. For instance, there was no coach, no training partners, no timing, no gismo watch, no doctors usually, no stretching, no weight training, no massage, no supplements, no special diet, no mental training, no liquids while training or racing,. and no hill or interval training to save his Achilles—an injury from his youth. When injured with his arthritic knees, or other problem—no chiropractor or physiotherapy, just rest and days or weeks off. Basically, instead of spending the time on many of the usual supplementary activities of the average runner he felt it "better to spend the time running," and in good humour stated, " I am already wasting too much time on my hobby." He used frequent shorter distance races to develop speed and on occasion a Fartleck session a day or two before a race. All in all he would not recommend his training regime to other distance runners—but believed as I firmly do that one must find what works best for each individual. Besides not everyone has the light frame and heart and lungs of Ed, and the super daily determination and perseverance for decades on end. Ed Whitlock, a worldwide inspiration for all future and present runners, young and old, has undoubtedly found his best way.

Ed's training philosophy was simplicity itself —run just past the edge of comfort for three or four hours at a time for three or four times a week—a total of 100 miles or more per week. At age 85 it went from three hours at age 80 to four hours at a time at age 85 — since at 85 his target marathon time was to run under 4 hours.

March 13, 2017 was a very sad day for me and millions of athletes around the world—the day the legend/marvel Ed Whitlock, always the gracious and humble gentleman died of prostate cancer.

Ed would get my vote for the male master of this century. Like Emil Zatopeck and other legends Ed's remarkable achievements will live on and continue to inspire as a titan of the track, long distance running, and the marathon. His life's race well run, the world conquered, dreams all accomplished now comes rest.

A few months after Ed's passing in March 2017 a super large (over a full page) article by Bruce Grierson author of "What Makes Olga Run" appeared in the Globe and Mail, with seven coloured photos. It compared in detail the training and lifestyle of Ed and myself—two very focused- on- our- goals athletes. Of course, I was happy and humbled to be compared with the legendary Ed Whitlock. A very interesting article since my athletic training was more normal and Ed's quite unorthodox (see details in my article above) — such as his rare visits to a doctor, which unfortunately may have shortened his life. Yet his simple methods produced truly amazing legendary results. We will miss you forever.

# OLGA KOTELKO

Olga Kotelko a friend of mine had many world records in her 80's and 90's before she passed away from a brain hemorrhage at age 95. Ironically, tests on her brain revealed a person decades younger.

The following information is about the legendary Olga gleaned from the great book " What Makes Olga Run" by Bruce Grierson, and my own relationship with her.

## SYNOPSIS OF BOOK "WHAT MAKES OLGA RUN"

### Introduction

The following is a brief synopsis of the best selling book "What Makes Olga Run" by Bruce Grierson. For these who don't know about Olga—she was simply a 95 year old, acting decades younger, super Canadian athlete, enjoying life to the full while breaking all the world records in 11 different track and field events.

"Understanding what makes Olga go could yield practical benefits not just for the 'old old ' but for the younger old, who could perhaps better slow the rate of muscular and aerobic decline," Grierson. This book goes into very interesting detail about what makes Olga tick or excel so successfully at age 95 and earlier. And what works for Olga can work for some others too depending on their background and their genes. The book has many tips and useful methods to aid in living a longer higher quality life.

The words below in (italics within brackets) are my own thoughts and knowledge of material in the book. Words within "quote marks" are exact quotes from the book. Sentences without brackets are paraphrased from Grierson's book for the sake of brevity.

**Super Seniors.** Only 2% of seniors (called Super Seniors) above age 85 have escaped the "Big Five" killers: cancer, cardiovascular disease, diabetes, Alzheimer's disease, and pulmonary (lung) disease. Parents of Super Seniors live 15 years longer than average.

**The Genes.** (The genome describes all the genetic material [cells contain chromosomes contain DNA molecules contain genes] in one organism.) Scientists claim a DNA sample can predict if a person will live to age 100, with 60% accuracy. (*But, it is also well established that old age is determined 75% by lifestyle and only 25% by the genes. More on this later*). "Everything significant that happens to us potentially alters gene expression."

The superstar gene, ACTN3 promotes either muscular power or muscular endurance. You get two copies of ACTN3 of the fast or slow version or one copy of either one. ( If you have the fast ACTN3 copy (such as Olga) then presumably you have predominately fast twitch muscles. And if you have the slow ACTN3 copy then you likely have mainly slow twitch muscles.) (*A neighbour told me he didn't have the genes to exercise; but I believe his muscles should be more suited for either fast or slow activities or a mixture.*)

Some people carry a gene that all but prevents Alzheimer's, or heart disease, etc. (Therefore DNA testing can foretell your potential future disease. Then you can take action to prevent. But some like Olga would prefer not to know.)

Chromosomes have protein cap at the ends protecting the DNA; they are called telomeres. Every time a cell divides the associated telomere becomes shorter. After many cell divisions the telomeres are too short to do their job and genetic damage results. Short telomeres indicate shorter life. The longer the telomeres, the more robust and stress resistant their owner. For example, chronic stress can result in short telomeres indicating cells looking 10 or more years older. Telomere measurement "tells something about what's going on in our body and our life." Researchers are working on developing a drug to spur production of the enzyme that protects and restores telomeres. (*This is a long way off. In the meantime it is up to each of us to live an active healthy lifestyle which will help prevent or delay onset of disease and make for longer telomeres and longer higher quality life.*)

Many health problems of the present day are due a "mismatch" between our genes and our environment. "We're maladapted to our genetic instructions, leading to abnormal gene instructions, which in turn frequently manifests itself as clinically over disease." Frank Booth, U of Missouri physiologist. In short we don't have the daily routine of arduous exercise to stay alive and cope with any conceivable threat of the Paleolithic man or woman. The key to robust health is to try to live in a way that shrinks the mismatch. Crossfit training is the ideal way to do this making you "harder to kill." Crossfit involves: "more work in less time"; no fancy fitness club machines, and mainly working against your own body weight; highly varied workouts to surprise the body; and workouts applied gradually over time. Sheppy the cross fit trainer states that his stuff builds Testosterone, Human Growth Hormone and Insulin–like growth factor. Olga's early and late life has been way more active than most and "more behaviorally Paleo than anybody," explaining another reason for her success at an older age.

**Olga's Birthplace.** One very interesting fact about Olga is she was born and raised in tiny Vonda Saskatchewan, population 300. (*Likewise for me.*) The book says there is a Saskatchewan effect, from the severe winter effect which toughens the body and mind and spirit. Hardship builds character. Toughness strengthens the immune system. Also there are a lot of successful executives also coming from Saskatchewan.

**Biological age** rather than chronological age matters most. In India and Southeast Asia, physical flexibility is often considered a more accurate measure of age than years. Angela Brooks-Wilson says your real age is "what you still can do."

Few of us unfortunately — let's face it— share the urgent desire to live for 100 years. But more than dying, boomers fear losing their marbles and becoming a burden. (*About 50% of those over 85 will have some form of dementia or Alzheimer's. But there are ways to retard the onset or prevent these problems, with mental and physical exercise, cleaner arteries and a healthy diet. See my book "100 Years Young the Natural Way" for details.*)

**The Brain and Neuroplasticity.** Olga's book describes the role of Olga's brain in her very successful athletic career in her nineties. Neuroplasticity defines the changes in neural pathways which are due to changes in behavior, environment and neural processes. The old thinking used to be that the brain was an organ that lost neural pathways and connections each year and became less plastic, or it was a case of use it or lose it. The brain shrinks over time, signals are sent more slowly, and memory declines; but new research indicates that experience like exercise can make favourable changes in the brain physical structure and functionality. The brain can retrofit itself growing new neural connections and improving existing ones depending on experiences and exposure. But daily routine prevents this growth. Doing tasks differently such as using the opposite hand helps new growth. And it is well known that what helps the body also helps the brain and vice versa.

Exercise delays or halts brain damage improving cognition. In particular the hippocampus can grow with exercise. The hippocampus is responsible for emotions, short and long term memory, and spatial navigation; for example, London taxi drivers have a larger than normal hippocampus.) A research study by Kirk Erikson, post doc. student of Dr. Kramer, showed after 6 months and 12 months of aerobic exercise that: "There was as much growth in the second six months as in the first."

"For building cognition Sudoku (and other brain teasers) is a shovel and exercise is a bulldozer in comparison)." "Studies linking puzzles to longevity are mostly short-term."

In a research study in 2006 Kramer put 60 to 80 year old couch potatoes on a consistent walking exercise program for six months. Their brains grew substantially: the hippocampus, the frontal and temporal lobes, with more neurons and connecting pathways. There were many benefits: improved reasoning, processing speed, learning, balance, and memory.

Besides growing the hippocampus, exercise is a stress reliever and treats depression. The long term calming effect can be seen in older master athletes. "There is an almost Buddhist serenity about many older master athletes." "Some researchers believe the more skillful, complex movements are truly a recipe for a superpower brain boost. For example, Olga's 11 track and field events which at the same time are explosive anaerobic movements.

**Longevity.** Bruce Grierson states that exercise isn't the greatest correlate of longevity. It is "means" —to be born in a comfortable, well-educated family in a developed county. Exercise is number two mattering more than diet or even genes. (*In my book 100 Years Young the Natural Way, physical exercise is number one, diet number two, mental exercise number three, the right kind of daily waste removal number four, and spirituality number five.*

*Means are important but I prefer to concentrate on things where we have control. Genes are not that important since they have only a 25% effect on longevity compared to 75% effect for healthy lifestyle.)* Grierson points out that exercise can reverse the effect of a genetic bad hand, for example a gene that predisposes you to obesity. When you add exercise to *anything* —from meditation to a healthier diet—you get "synergy effects," (where 1 +1 = 3).

Olga had a lot of traits attributed to the nuns of Notre Dame; many were centenarians or extraordinarily long lived, spry and sharp, with dementia almost entirely absent. They do brain teasers daily, almost all college grads, with solid diet and sleep, have daily exercise and with no daily stress.

Some people are not affected or less than others since they have what Columbia researcher Yaakov Stern has called "cognitive reserve." By living a healthy lifestyle with consistent exercise and social interaction— cognitive reserve is built up over a lifetime, like a "psychological retirement income." (With this cognitive reserve there is a buffer against mental problems.)

**Physical Exercise.** Women benefit more from exercise than men; "the more you work out the sharper you get mentally—is greater for women than men." Women have less muscle but it is better muscle —more resistant to breakdown; Olga is testimony to that. One reason is estrogen seems to promote muscle repair and maintenance. Exercise grows age-defying stem cells in everyone, but a study found the response was more pronounced in older women. Ninety percent of centenarians are women by holding off life threatening illness about a decade longer than men. (*Therefore it appears that Olga was too kind to suggest in her book that I would live to 121 and her to 120. If my quality of life is good this old age would be fine by me. But there might be a guilty conscience in still receiving my old age pension. Longer life means more opportunity to sample different fine wines, or even break more world records, or to take advantage of new medical discoveries, or leave an imprint. So it is important to have a goal and strive for longevity and quality of life.*)

The type of exercise matters and intensity matters the most. The hippo-campus growth is quantitatively related to intensity of activity. And intensity concentrates the physiological benefits of exercise. (In my two running books and longevity book I stress the advantages of anaerobic workouts such as short fast repeats. In fact Olga's book acknowledges that I am fully committed to the idea of intensity. This has enabled me to continue to break world records after I gave up on long slow aerobic running. And I am convinced, as many others, that intensity builds and retains fast twitch muscles, builds human growth hormone; and beats aerobic exercise in the longevity race.) According to Marin Gibala's studies at McMaster U, we can get by on even seven minutes of exercise a week if that exercise is intense enough. (*The popular Tabata exercise (20 sec intense 10 sec rest repeated 8 times, in four minutes, builds more aerobic and anaerobic capacity in 4 minutes than an hour of aerobic endurance exercise. See my longevity book,"100 Years Young the Natural Way." However, the true Tabata intensity is way more intense than most athletes think.*)

"Part of the challenge is the mind-set that we need to slow down as we get older," Scott Trappe, director of Human Performance Lab at Ball State U. Trappe states: seniors can work out less frequently as long as it's intense, "at least 80% of your max." Olga with her 11 different events was doing it the right way, i.e., heavy demands for a short time. But light activity is still preferable to no activity. But there is a limit to the intensity, (*e.g., injury, and possible burnout.*) Olga never pushed herself aerobically for long stretches, she was not an extreme athlete. The author recognizes that there could be a lot more Olga-like specimens, if circumstances lined up for them as they did for Olga. (*Olga started with baseball and a strong mentality and good genes.*)

"There is greater risk of atrial fibrillation, AFib, in people who have done long-duration or high- intensity exercise for a long time." (*Now I realize where my Tachycardia (similar to AFib) is likely to have come from. Maybe this is the price I have paid for my world records.*)

This book about Olga makes a good point about exercise: To be really 'fit' "requires stamina, strength, flexibility, power, speed, coordination, agility balance, and respiratory endurance." Two million years ago this kind of fitness, would have kept us alive to hunt fish and schlep (make love) another day. (*The fitness list is similar to that for a successful hurdler or a 400m runner. In my speeches I often make the point that there is usually some attention to aerobic exercise but strength, flexibility, balance and mental training are often neglected entirely, leading to a shorter, lower quality life.*)

**"Sitting** like a lump for long stretches is a travesty." (*Recent research has shown that sitting for three hours each day at a stretch can shorten your life* *by two years.)* (*To prevent this decline it is important to get up frequently.*) Standing up a lot is "the single most important habit we can acquire." " But standing for two hours has been likened to going for a two –mile run." It is important to get up and move regularly all day. Ideally you want to exercise and move around, which is what Olga did.

**McGill U Research Study,** (*see the Appendix for details of the tests on my body compared to the sedentary of the same age. At Mc Gill U, world champions over 75 like Olga (and myself, Ed Whitlock, Christa Bortignon, Jeanne and Bill Daprano, and Bob Lida, were thoroughly tested over a period of a week ÷for strength, endurance, max. heart rate, flexibility, memory, muscles, bone, and balance ÷ to learn why these champions aged much slower than the sedentary of the same age, and why muscle degenerates with age, etc. Tests at other research centers have shown that blood transfusions into old mice from young mice caused the old mice to perform better on memory tests. The blood serum is full of factors—circulating proteins, growth factors and immune system boosters—that age tends to deplete. Similar tests at McGill U from biopsy tests (ouch) will be done mixing couch potato blood and stem cells with champion's blood and stem cells. In my case the biopsy took an inordinate long time to heal. In the end to speed healing I had a blood plasma injection into the area—the "hole" as Dr. Galea described it. With a biopsy there is danger of hitting a nerve as happened to one of my colleagues.*)

Olga was quite a novelty at the McGill Research Study in view of her age, many world records and her toughness. She was tested on two separate occasions a year apart.

**Diet**. Here are some of Olga's diet highlights: loved rare meat and dairy foods particularly fermented food for the probiotic bacteria, had her own garden and ate a rainbow of colored vegetables and greens, drank a lot of water, took a multivitamin in winter and a daily aspirin, avoided refined grains and other high glycemic foods, ate minimum processed food, and had small meals four or five time a day, had steelcut oatmeal for breakfast (as I do most mornings)—but had a weakness for tapioca pudding. The book reminds us that "it is not just what you eat but what you *have* eaten in the past. Children's diets (for example, Olga's life on the farm) may have an outsize effect on future health."

**Routines.** The Dalai Lama was once asked the secret of happiness and he replied without pausing: "Routines." But growth comes when we *break* routine. (For example, to get out of a plateau rut, a runner has to make a 'change' such as more speed or less rest or more or less volume.) David Agus, personal-genomics pioneer, sees routine as key, a largely unheralded dimension of health and longevity, and "irregularity is a big source of physiological stress."

Olga had her routines such as thrice –weekly aquafit, two or three times per week for track and field training, morning oatmeal, and clockwork churchgoing. Then there was her "OK" routine. When she wakes in the night three times a week and goes into her "OK" routine which was up to about 90 minutes of self-massage from head, face, to foot even involving the fingers with some rubber balls and a bottle to roll her back on. "She considers her OK technique a key piece, maybe *the* key piece, of the puzzle of her youthfulness." Some therapists now think the name of the game is to get those muscle cells of the fascia (which surround every muscle and organ) to let go. "There are foam rollers made for that express purpose." (One of my routines is to use the big roller after indoor workouts or most nights before bed.)

(*While Olga had her OK routine at night I have the following nightly routine when healthy: Before retiring I usually do about 30 squats with the big fitness ball between me and the wall,, 12 one arm rows with a 30 pound dumbbell. and often about 24 to 30 pushups, plus about 7 to 10 minutes massaging the legs and back and glutes using the big roller.*)

(*And also for myself before getting out of bed in the morning I do a series of exercises mainly while lying mainly on my back.. Firstly about 10 repeats, with my feet, bending and rotating them in all directions imaginable until they are slightly tired. These help to prevent injuries to the feet. Next I vibrate my gluteus muscles. Then vibrate the left and right legs. Next do 50 pelvic tilts to strengthen the abs and wake up the intestines. Stretch the hamstrings, and quads —and then the abductors and adductors by swinging each straight leg horizontally from extreme left and extreme right side. Then some Pilates exercises still on my back— a series of vertical and horizontal leg circles repeats, clockwise and counter clockwise to exercise the hip joint and associated muscles including IT band, hips and buttocks. I used to use a rubber band while lying on my back in bed to gently stretch the quads, hamstrings adductors, and gluteus*) muscles. *Then 10 deep breaths, diaphragm breathing. Then I am tempted to go back to sleep. But no way.*)

**Personality Traits Affect Longevity**. Research on the long-lived elderly have determined they have the following five traits of personality or temperament. These five traits listed in the Neo Five-Factor Inventory are openness, conscientiousness, extroversion, agreeableness, and neuroticism.

**Openness** describes a person curious, broadminded, less bound to tradition, not threatened by the new, unprejudiced, etc. **Conscientiousness** describe a person goal oriented, determined in the face of difficulty, reliable, etc. **Extroversion**, an extrovert as opposed to an introvert, and who are more apt to retain and search for social contacts which prolongs life. **Agreeableness,** describes persons with lots of friends and few enemies, open hearted, generous with praise and affection, diplomatic, good sense of humor, basically a nice person, etc. **Neuroticism** is the only negative quality of the five traits in the Neo list; so this is to be avoided. Neurotics make life complicated for themselves, by worrying unnecessarily, more sensitive to potential trouble, more apt to be stressed out, etc. For example, healthy baboons, the least neurotic ones of a tribe lived 10% longer than the neurotic ones. (*My anti-aging book describes two major characteristics of centenarians: (1) the ability to avoid stress, making light of problems; and (2) maintaining social contacts. "One of the most rock–solid findings in gerontology is that strong social ties boost your likelihood of surviving, over a given time period, by 50%— the effect is larger than the impact of exercise."*)

Olga's book mentions other favourable anti-aging traits in addition the above five; for example; "the capacity for intimate relationships, reaching out intimately, persistence and orderliness." Olga's book describes optimism as a contentious personality trait since some studies concluded an optimistic attitude hindered long life and others concluded it lengthened life. (*My firm belief and others is that optimism lengthens life: a huge nurse's study in the US concluded an optimistic attitude lengthened life by an average of 7.5 years. A negative person is usually stressed out worrying about things that they have no control over; nearly everything is gloom and doom; this is bound to shorten life.*)

**Summary.** To sum up the big question " What Makes Olga Run. " It's the camaraderie. It's not the travel, the prizes, or the fame. " (*But who wouldn't* *love all that attention and success, and a feeling of being blessed—I admit to it and so did Ed Whitlock. I encourage you to have your own copy of Bruce Grierson's best-selling book, to see much more interesting, instructive material, even some kind references to Earl Fee.)*

# JEANNE DAPRANO

### USATF Masters Athlete For 2012

Jeanne Daprano of Georgia, was named USATF Masters Athlete of the Year 2012 and as of 2017 she has a total six indoor and outdoor world (WMA) records in the 70—74 and 75-79 age groups (One in the 400m and five in the 800m and mile). The schedule below shows her impressive workouts leading up to her world outdoor record in the mile in 6:58.44 in July 2012 in Pasadena CA. This record broke the listed record by a whopping 49 seconds. This would be equivalent to a 4:00 open women's mile or well below the current women's open record in 4:12.56. All quite amazing! I have a lot of respect for Jeanne and her accomplishments

I include Jeanne in my memoirs as her workouts are somewhat similar to mine, e.g., no long slow running and mainly intense interval training, and including rowing, running in the pool and cycling.. Christa Bortignon, Canadian, age 80 in 2017 is another famous female friend with many world WMA records in track and also field events.

## Jeanne's Workouts Prior to Her Mile World Record in 75-79 Age Group

The following are Jeanne's workouts in the 2.5 weeks before:

- **Wednesday**: 6x800m on rowing machine. 5 min. between each.
- **Thursday**: 3 x 1 mile on track, sprint 50m walk 50m. 5 minute rest between mile repeats.
- **Friday:** one hour stationary bike, 1 hour Pilates.
- **Saturday** core exercises, approximately 50 min.
- **Sunday**: 3x 1 mile on track, sprint 75m walk 75m, 5 min. rest between each mile.

- **Monday**: 30 min. on stationary bike, 30 min. Pilates.
- **Tuesday**: core exercises.
- **Wednesday**: 1600m on rowing machine, 30 min. machine Pilates.
- **Thursday**: core exercises.
- **Friday**: one hour on stationary bike.
- **Saturday**: one mile on track (sprint 30m walk 10m).
- **Sunday**: rest.
- **Monday**: core exercises.
- **Tuesday**: 900 m on track (sprint 40m walk 10m).
- **Wednesday**: core exercises.
- **Thursday**: Travel to Los Angeles. Jog a few laps on track, walk and stretch.
- **Friday**: rest.
- **Saturday**: 6:58.44 mile.

Note: the "sprint" mentioned above must be less than all out speed in order to complete the mile.

Jeanne's workouts involve no more than 0 miles of running a week, including warm-up miles, but with cross training: cycling, running in the pool, and rowing for endurance— and some unique novel short intervals on the track (two a week) for speed and endurance as seen below. For strength training (she calls it "core strengthening") she does 50 minutes of squat jumps, deadlifts, wall sits, planks, ketttlebells, lunges, and other flexibility and resistance exercises all supervised by her trainer.

My workouts are similar in some ways to Jeanne's. For the past 12 years or more I have stopped the long slow running and substitute rowing, swimming, running in the pool, some cycling, and power walking and hiking on recovery or non-running days. I was forced to do this due to a circulation problem in my left calf. But I have no problem training intensely at short distances. Fortunately, with the above cross training and lots of short fast intervals at near race pace (longer and fewer intervals than Jeanne's 30m, 40m, 50m, or 75m repeats) has enabled me to still break world records. I described my aerobic/anaerobic training in an article in National Masters News in 2011, and in my book "*100 Years Young the Natural Way*" published in 2011.

I see from the Masters Age records in 2006 a 75 year old female has nearly similar running times in the 400m and 800m as an 85 year old male. Hence, I conclude my training should be roughly similar or as hard as that of a 10 years younger female world record holder. Since Jeanne is just 7 or 8 years younger than me, I conclude, my race times in the 400m and 800m be somewhat similar to hers. Below is a comparison of our typical workouts.

1. Rowing: Jeanne does 6x800 and 1600m compared to my 2000m normally. although one day I did manage a reasonably hard 6000m. I was not surprised to hear she has some age group world record in rowing.
2. Cycling and Elliptical machine : She cycles one hour compared to my 15 minutes each on cycle and elliptical.
3. Pool running : She wears cuffs and ankles and wrists to make work harder. I wear a support belt or no belt and simulate 800 races with equal time and perceived effort. Also I swim for 20 minutes using a pool buoy float between the legs on some recovery days between track sessions.
4. Interval training on the track. Twice a week she usually does her sets of sprints for a mile, usually 25m to 75m repeats with equal length walk or shorter for recovery, and is able to do 3 miles of these with 5min. rest between each mile. I do not know how fast are her "sprints" as she calls them, but in any case these are quite hard workouts in my opinion. I like her workout for the indoors since it can involve no fast running on the curves..I am able to do one mile only if I keep the fast repeats to around my 600m race pace. One day I was going slightly faster at a pace between 400 and 600m race pace and was able to do only 1200m. So the "sprint" speed is all important, and varies with each individual. If sprint repeats are about 95% maximum speed or faster— sprint coaches usually recommend a maximum total of 600m. I do intense interval training three times per week; repeats usually between 150m to 400m, near race pace for the 400m or 800m; a maximum of 900m and 1600m for 400m and 800m training respectively. Within six weeks of a major race I do a time trial once a week. One hard indoor workout is: 3 sets of (run 350m at about 600m race pace, walk 50m, run 150m same pace or faster), rest 5 minutes between sets. See many other of my workouts in Chapter 9 of this book.

5. Strength training, Jeanne has her core strengthening for 50 minutes with her trainer once a week. I do weight training once or twice a week for upper and lower body, 2 sets and 12 repeats on 18 or 20 machines.

I attended a research study last year at McGill U Montreal (See Appendix) to compare elite (top retired Olympians and also world record holder athletes, with sedentary persons—all above age 75. This involved very complete testing of all important parts of an athletic body. My friends Jeanne and Bill Daprano were there at the same time as me being tested during the week. I was impressed with the intensity that Jeanne exhibited in all the tests— the same serious game face that she exerts in her training and races. For instance, in the VO2max cycle test she was the only one in our group who volunteered to do the test with an experimental tube through her nose and throat, and still produced impressive VO2max results. I and the others were having nothing to do with that nose/throat tube during *my* test which was captured on video.

Jeanne is an inspiration with her many world records, and with many of these records age graded above 100%. Her impressive workouts indicate great dedication and drive. And she is not letting age slow her down. She is a vegetarian with an impressive diet and a good example of what it takes to be a world class champion and as such is an inspiration to myself and countless others.

# *17*

# MY BOOKS

## MY SELF PUBLISHED BOOK

MY FIRST BOOK, *HOW TO BE A CHAMPION FROM 9 TO 90,* WAS SELF-PUB-lished in 2001 after many rejections from publishers and literary agents In spite of my 30 world masters records at the time (specific age and age group records) broken in the previous 15 years. An agent is reluctant to take you on as a client unless they feel your book is going to be a best seller —as they receive about 15% of the royalties of the author. And publishers usually won't look at your manuscript unless you are an established author, or recommended by an agent. Perhaps I might have had acceptance from one of the smaller publishers, but I did not pursue these publishers.

Before I had the plan to write a book on running training I started to gather information on running training as I was intrigued how the correct mental and physical training and recovery could produce winning results. For many years after training at York U I would go to the York U library and collect running information from good articles written by good coaches. I amassed a lot of detailed information —and I was learning from the workouts with my coach David Welch and observing other running coaches.

After breaking a few world records in running at masters meets I thought that I had enough credibility to write a book.

I worked on and off on the book for about five years. The writing came easy as I was used to writing detailed technical reports in the nuclear engineering business where every word was important. I eventually, had 24 detailed chapters on all the important aspects on running and on body, mind, spirit training — backed up with 5 to 30 references in each chapter. I learned that I could direct quote a sentence or two without asking permission as long as I referenced the quote. And it was legitimate to discuss another person's idea in my own fewer words if the reference was provided. Sometimes, I even had to pay for a lengthy quote. But later, I noticed a lot of authors were not as careful about referencing.

I tried to wrote clearly, concisely and comprehensively. And used a lot of headings and sub headings to eliminate long paragraphs. For example, Dr. Weil, a highly respected popular author— in his books has rare headings if any resulting in very lengthy paragraphs, making for tiring reading and lack of clarity. The workouts in my book were actual tried and proven workouts based on race times rather than actual times— this way the workouts could be used by runners of all capabilities and from young to old.

Just prior to printing my self published book the printing company fortunately found a spelling error in the header on each page— the word Champion was misspelled. Twenty five hundred books were printed for $18,000. Somehow, the outer margin was smaller than I wanted— I believe a mistake by the company who set up my book. Two skids of books 6 feet high filled up 25% of my 2 car garage. I began a marketing program contacting many Canadian Libraries, and paying for expensive ads that never produced results. I found word of mouth of happy customers was the best marketing. My best customer was National Masters News in the United States. In exchange I wrote several free articles for the monthly National Masters News. I shipped hundreds of books to them; they liked my book and advertised it for free. Eventually, after a lot of sales at track meets and shipping and trips to the post office I sold over 2300 copies which is excellent for a self- published book with about $15,000 net profit. But if my time was factored in, i.e., over 2500 hours of writing and research plus shipping the books— my hourly rate would be less than $5 an hour. So I wouldn't self publish again. However, the information I learned helped me break many world records later on.

The second chapter of my book titled Physiological Principles delves into effects of training on the body involving such topics as: the energy systems, muscle fibre, respiratory system, anaerobic threshold, VO2max, the heart and heart rate, blood volume, lactic acid, etc. These topics can be complex but I discuss them in a simple manner. Dr. Costill a world wide recognized American sports researcher reviewed this chapter for me and said, "You have done your homework." After selling a book to a female runner at a track meet one day— she returned it about 15 minutes later, finding this chapter too complex for her. She was the one and only unhappy customer.

In the end it was many long hours but enjoyable writing hours. I am a rather slow typist but the thinking process was not rapid so there was no need to be a rapid typist. A few years later as mentioned below this self published book was the basis for my book in color, "The Complete Guide To Running" by Meyer and Meyer, a very reputable publisher of sports books in Germany. I had made contact with Meyer and Meyer at a huge book Fair in Frankfort

# MY 2ND BOOK: THE COMPLETE GUIDE TO RUNNING

To promote my self published book, "How to Be A Champion from 9 to 90", I attended the Frankfort Book Fair in Germany in 2003 at great expense, about $7000 including air flight, accommodation, an exhibit booth, and shipping 48 of my self published book for the booth. Due to the huge crowds at this popular book fair, hotel prices were jacked up by a factor of two or three. The room for about 200 euros per night was so tiny that there was only walking room between the single bed and the couch.

My booth had a large banner which said:

**FEETNESS** company name

## How To Be A Champion From 9 to 90,
## Body, Mind Spirit Training

My book was nearly accepted by an Italian sports book publisher, a double shame for he had a most beautiful daughter with him. Also, I could have accepted a publisher from India but I felt an uneasy feeling about the honesty of this particular publisher. I found it impossible to get an appointment with any literary agent. And I never made use of 90% of the books I brought with me from Canada. However, I made contact with a reputable German publisher of sports books, Meyer and Meyer (M and M). A few months later the Meyer and Meyer president, Hans Meyer, came to Toronto, I believe especially to sign me on, as M and M have no business in Toronto. As a new author eager to get his book published it was not a good deal for me. M and M would have the copyright which is difficult to retain for a new unestablished author, and I would receive 6% of *net profit*. If it was 6% of retail *book price* that would an understandable deal for an author. I found later my royalties amounted to about 70 cents Canadian per book sold. The publisher accepted every word I wrote. It could have been a nightmare if an editor started meddling with each sentence and paragraph. I had to change one word only—I had described a warmup exercise, one of the ABC drills, as the "Gestapo" march; I changed it to "a military type of fast march with locked knees."

The book was published in 2005, actually an update version of my self published book, but with some chapters removed e.g., the Hurdling chapter removed and some chapters added such as Plyometrics, plus many detailed changes. It is a beautiful book with many colored photos many of which I supplied, color coded chapters, tables and titles in color print, and high quality paper in 22 chapters and 260 pages. The book is available in North America, Australia, Europe and recently in 2016 in China. Many have told me it is the best book on running training. A 2nd edition was published in 2007. Since 2005 over 4000 copies have been sold by myself and mostly by Meyer and Meyer. I don't know about sales in China. But I am happy that my book is being sold worldwide.

# MY 3ᴿᴰ BOOK: 100 YEARS YOUNG THE NATURAL WAY

I have always had a great interest in the subject of longevity and have collected a lot of information including about 15 books on the subject. Since I love to write I thought: there could not be a more useful book to write than one on anti-aging. In researching details for the book I would learn even more on this helpful subject and would have the enthusiasm to complete the book.

Most books on longevity are written by doctors of medicine—but normally they know little about diet, and exercise, two of the major factors affecting longevity. So I reasoned that a non-doctor author could compete and write an equally useful book. My particular diet and intense consistent exercise have helped me break nearly 60 master's world records in the past 32 years.

Is it essential to be a doctor author? I have a chapter in my book on Inflammation, the basis of most disease. When I finished my book I compared my chapter on inflammation with a chapter on inflammation by a well known Canadian doctor. My chapter was in no way inferior or less in detail than the doctor's chapter.

My plan was to write for two or three hours most days to produce about 600 words daily. After I started I could not stop writing for three years and the book evolved into three parts Body, Mind and Spirit, a rather large book of 37 chapters and 646 pages. Most books on longevity speak only of the body aspects. This book took about 2500 hours in three years mainly to do the research, typing and set up the font and select an impressive suggestive cover photo (a hand holding a hour glass), and select three photos one, for each of the three main topics. The contents below shows the book chapters.

## CONTENTS

### Part 1: THE BODY

Chapter 1 TWENTY-FIVE MAIN STEPS TO LONGEVITY
Chapter 2 LOW GLYCEMIC DIET
Chapter 3 PHYTONUTRIENTS
Chapter 4 FATS GOOD AND BAD
Chapter 5 SUPPLEMENTS

## Part 2: THE MIND

## Part 3: THE SPIRIT

After writing all these chapters particularly the technical ones, I felt like I could write a long treatise or chapter on anything, for example, maybe even: "The Love Life of the Tse Tse Fly." The book was published by Trafford Publishers in the USA in 2011, a print on demand publisher. And the book is available on Amazon Books and from the Trafford library. I provided the files to the publisher after setting up the font on headings and paragraphs and also inner and outer margins on the pages. So it was set up as I wanted based on experience from my previous two books.

If I were to write an up- to- date 2nd edition anti-aging book it would be much shorter with less chapters, more on diet, less on supplements, with a chapter on the genes and the microbiome (i.e., the great importance of bacteria in the intestines on health), a chapter on Statin Drugs, and a chapter on Meditation and Mindfulness).

## MY POETRY BOOK: THE WONDER OF IT ALL

When I retired in 1992 at age 63 after 34 year with the Atomic Energy Canada Ltd, I started doing two workouts a day on most days, e.g., a cross training workout—usually running or swimming in the pool- before or after a running workout. But to fill in the day usefully and enjoyably I started to write some understandable poems.

Some say— poetry is prose gone mad. And one should not go overboard in going around thinking everything is pretty. On this dubious subject I have found the following humorous quotations in Ned Sherrin's book, "*Humorous Quotations.*"

> *Writing a book of poetry is like dropping rose petal down the Grand Canyon and waiting for the echo.* **Don Marquis**

> *Poetry is sissy stuff that rhymes.. Weedy people sa la and fie and swoon when they see a bunch of daffodils.* **Geoffrey Willans**

> *Dr. Donnes verses are like the peace of God, they pass all understanding.* **James**

> *Life's a curse. Love's a blight, God's a blaggard, cherry blossom is quite nice.* **Tom Stoppard**

*While pensive poets painful vigils keep. Sleepless themselves, to give their readers sleep.* **Alexander Pope**

Anyway, I am away past waiting for my poems to produce an echo of any sort. I just enjoy what I am doing. To write a poem, I have to wait for inspiration to hit me, for example, when I come upon a very interesting situation or episode or an interesting title. I can't tell myself I'm going to write a poem today unless there is that initial spark there. After about three years I had about 150 poems on different subjects. I never occurred to me initially that I would write a book containing all my poems. This occurred to me after writing the above three books. I chose the title :"**The Wonder Of It All**", since I am in awe of this Earth and Universe we live in. Since my poems were on a wide variety of subjects I chose sub titles: Live, Love, Laugh, Pathos, and Spirit. Some have asked me : What is Pathos (sadness)?, I explain: since it is not a common word.

Since poetry is not a popular seller, I did not attempt to get a regular book publisher, but decided on a print- on- demand publilsher—Trafford Publishing in my case—where you pay to have the book set up and published from your files. This type of publisher sets up your book at Amazon Books on the internet for sale, and you receive 10 or 20% of retail royalties per book which is much more than about 75 cents Canadian per book in royalties from a regular book publisher like Mc Graw Hill or Meyer and Meyer. Also the print- on- demand publisher sells books from their line of published books as well. My publisher Trafford, was the same as for my anti-aging book, and based in the USA. This turned out to be a disadvantage since when I ordered books for my own personal sale at a Trafford author discount of about 35% I had to pay in American dollars. Hence in view of the exchange rate,. e.g., in 2016 to 2018 at about 75 cent American to the Canadian dollars —this meant I had to boost my Canadian retail price by about 30%— making my book expensive in Canadian dollars. So l stopped selling books personally and left it up to Amazon to sell my books. For this memoir book my publisher is Tellwell, conveniently based in Toronto. One disadvantage of a print- on- demand publisher is that if you have included a lot of colored photos the printing of a limited number of copies at a time makes the printing process very expensive. My print on demand colored poetry book, published in 2013, a beautiful book by the way, sells for over

60 dollars Canadian not counting shipping—way too expensive for most people. The book is available on Amazon Books on the internet or from the Trafford library in paper form —or digital form at about ¼ price of the coloured paper book. Since the colored poetry book is too expensive in view of the large number of coloured photos a black and white paper version was published a year after the coloured book.

My poems are a down to earth variety, some rhyming and some free verse, and easily understood, not attempting to be too clever so the meaning sometimes gets lost or is a mystery or a challenge to interpret.

On the subject of gratitude the following short poems of mine cover the aspects of helping others, with compassion to our fellow man, and exhibiting humility goodness, and gratitude. Since yoga is a mind, spirit, meditative experience my yoga teacher Courtney used to read some of these shorter poems in her soothing voice to her large classes at the end during the final meditative darkened room period. I was honored and grateful. A poem can get right to the point and arise emotions compared to a lengthy prose explanation.

# Let Us

Let us not be selfish, but be selfless,
Since togetherness exceeds helplessness.
Let us be happy with what we have got
And what we have not.
Let us carry hope on wings of charity
To the helpless and needy.
Let us do good all times, in all ways,
To everyone, in all places.
Let us smile and not take ourselves seriously;
For in the end our faces tell the true story.
Let us not forget to say, "Please," "Thank you!"
Or "I love you," often long overdue.
Let us be truly grateful and instead:
Not taking blessings for granted.
And let us enact gratitude,
With good deeds, or your golden wings

God will surely preclude.

# 𝔄 Helping Hand

May they recall you as a giver and a helper
And for your gracious heart and honorable deeds.
May you appreciate and replicate life's small treasures:
Some kind words, a courteous act, a warm smile.
Laughter, a loving gesture, and a helping hand.
And if ever, you're lacking in humility and gratitude—
May you lay on your back and peer up into the stars,
The surreal stars in the vast universe, in all its splendour.
May you remember always— the six magic words,
To open all doors:
"Please," "Thank you," and "I love you."
And may they remember you forever.

The following shows a typical poem in each of five main sections: Live, Love, Laugh, Pathos, and Spirit in my poetry book:

## A typical Poem In the Live section:

# 𝔄 Smile Pass It On

*It costs you nought, achieves much, and cannot be bought;*
*At home, at work, with friends, it is widely sought.*
*It cures a tired soul, mends a discouraged mind;*
*You are rich when in each hour a smile you find.*

*When its magic beams—the world is brighter by far;*
*With it there is no beguile or need to spar;*
*It warms the heart, and melts away fear and distrust;*
*You must agree to show true love it is a must.*

*A life of smiles is full and you're sure to win*

*When your face tells a tale of a sweet soul within.*
*But a bitter life full of snarls and scowls,*
*Gives a countenance of wrinkles and clenched jowls.*

*When a friend has lost their luck or lost a dear one,*
*Your downcast look will send them on the run.*
*But your smile can send them to a calm sun-kissed beach*
*And then carefree tranquil days seem within reach.*

*Now when you meet a stranger who is down and out,*
*Don't ignore or give him another nasty clout.*
*A smile may lift him to struggle on awhile;*
*With renewed hope he goes the extra mile.*

*One warm smile can grow and multiply if passed on,*
*From friend to friend, friend to stranger, hither and yon;*
*Don't miss an opportunity from dawn to dawn.*
*A happier world there will be—pass it on!*

## A typical poem In the LOVE section:

#  Mothers Love

*There are some bright stars in Heaven;*
*Though long gone their light will shine*
*To Earth for ever and amen;*
*These are the mothers of yours and mine.*

*A mother's love is warmer than a fire*
*After winter's bitter sting;*
*Soft and tender as an angel's choir*
*And as comforting as an angel's wing;*

*The best friend that God ever gave;*
*Only they could show such patience,*
*And faith while harsh words they would save,*

*In hopes of better deeds sometime hence.*

*Now their warm words are here no more,*
*But in our memory they speak still,*
*Like sparkling waves on a sun baked shore*
*They return, return, to stir our will.*

*Their lessons and stories are not forgot*
*In our journey through smiles and tears.*
*The truth, honour, and virtue they taught*
*Are with us to conquer our fears.*

*In yester year when we were frail,*
*They picked us up fall after fall.*
*And now when we stumble and fail,*
*Though gone, they are there after all.*

*Their first great sacrifice of many*
*Was to enter at our birth,*
*The black cloak of death valley;*
*Thereafter all sacrifice was mirth.*

*We wish to tell her all that she has been;*
*Her beauty, sacrifice, and tenderness.*
*Too late now to render conscience serene,*
*But never too late to recall her fond caress.*

*Yes, a mother's love is a perfect love*
*That goes on for evermore.*
*Someday—we'll meet again up above,*
*"Else what's a heaven for?"*

**A typical poem in the LAUGH section**

# The Party

*It was a party to end all parties,*
*Back in forty-nine in dear old Ireland,*
*A birthday bash for Uncle Ned to please;*
*Twenty of us happy and a four-piece band,*
*O'Reilly on the banjo, Mike on the flute*
*Sonny on the fiddle, and Sal on the uke.*
*We filled cousin Clancy's cottage to the brim*
*With smoke and laughter and plenty of vim;*
*Outside the soft, silent rain was a falling—*
*A white column of smoke slowly a rising*
*To the stars above the silver ground,*
*And the revelry could be heard for miles around.*
*The evening wore on past the moonlit night—*
*And the chilly morn recalled quite a sight:*
*The jugs were near empty; all feet sore*
*From jigging, and the band could play no more;*
*Two jugs of whiskey sadly smashed, one broken toe;*
*Twenty fuzzy heads coming in the morrow;*
*Clancy caught his girl kissing a beau;*
*Two strings busted on the old banjo;*
*Uncle Ned on his peg leg—out danced them all,*
*Then! finally collapsed like a domino.*
*Now when the fire died, they feared the end of the ball;*
*Without peat it was bound for defeat, so it was agreed:*
*Only one solution or we must retire:*
*Throw! Uncle Ned's wooden leg on the fire.*

## Another typical poem in the LAUGH section

# Old Suckers Never Stop

*"Just look at that old sucker go!"*

*marvelled the students as I propelled*
*my near sixty-five year old bones across the finish line*
*on the desert dry indoor track at York U.*

*I had just used up three-hundred metres of my life*
*in a stressful forty-four seconds,*
*even beating one of these teenagers who had not yet*
*discovered the secret of Dedication.*

*But surprisingly to those that marvelled:*
*there was no collapse— like a house made of cards;*
*the Red Cross did not rush up with oxygen;*
*and somehow the stretcher bearers were not required.*
*Then they saw some twenty pounds of lard*
*was missing from my bones,*
*and a look of steely Confidence in the eye was there,*
*born from thousands of hours of playing with my pals:*
*Speedy, Mighty, Hearty, and Persy (for Perseverance).*
*I plan to continue to "go like an old sucker"*
*until The Ultimate Meet Director stops me in my tracks,*
*after about ten times more around the globe— I reckon.*

## A typical poem in the PATHOS section

# he Fallen

*Too brief they loved*
*And were beloved;*
*They sampled the world;*
*Too fast life unfurled;*
*Too quick life blossomed;*
*Too short music strummed;*
*Too brief hearts drummed.*
*They joined the fray;*
*Some enrolled for play;*
*Some for golden glory;*

*Some for love of country;*
*Some for adventure;*
*And some were not too sure.*
*But all bent on peace*
*And the Hun to fleece.*
*Then blood spilt, bodies rent,*
*Souls to heaven sent.*
*We will remember them*
*Along with Bethlehem;*
*Though many decades later*
*Still our emotions stir*
*For those who carried the torch,*
*Those who fell at the ramparts*
*And the survivors that march...*
*Onwards ever in our hearts*

## Typical poems in the SPIRIT section

# Runners Prayer

*Fear give me your fury;*
*Let me taste your torment.*
*Pain give me your worst;*
*Let me feel your fire.*
*Unleash these wild steeds*
*Of Fear and Pain,*
*So they may be trained and harnessed*
*To obey my commands.*
*Let me test my mettle*
*In the flame of training,*
*In the heat of battle,*
*In the cauldron of competition,*
*And the furnace of the fray,*
*So I may forge my body, mind, and spirit*
*Like a sword in the glowing coals,*
*So they may be harder than steel,*

*Brilliant, and fearsome.*
*Then, ever ready for my friendly foes.*
*This is my prayer oh Lord.*

# Dig Deep

*Dig deep, dig deep*
*While sluggards sleep,*
*Relentless toward your dream*
*Though far away it may seem.*
*There's a promise to keep*
*And a glory to reap;*
*Fame will come in the end*
*If you'll not break or bend;*
*Your goal is not for the meek*
*Your path is not for the weak.*
*Dig deep, dig deep*
*While sluggards sleep.*

# *18*

# QUOTATIONS

## EARL FEE QUOTATIONS

### HOPE (from my poem *Wings of Hope*)

> Carry your wings of hope high in the sky,
> Never let them wither and die.
> Hope is a many splendiferous thing—
> With Belief, Patience and Dreams on the wing—
> Soaring the soul and making the heart strings to sing.

- Lose hope and you lose courage and a bright future.
- Hope —I pass my magic to all who believe: "I will."
  I come on the wings of Promise
  For brighter times and a happy quest
  And offer solace to a sorry breast
  While Fear and Despair I dismiss.
  I am Patience. Belief, Perseverance, Enthusiasm,
  And Promise all in one, to withstand the fickle winds of Fate.
  I am the armour, the magical cloak

Protecting against life's vicissitudes—
Making dreams come true.
I am the pillar of Purpose,
The mother of Resolve,
The sunrise of Optimism,
The constant rainbow of Promise,
And the belief in a silver lining after the storm.

## TIME (From my poem *Time Waits For No Man)*

I hope in your life you can see the waste of Time and not too late.
I hope in the end you can say: I'm satisfied —there was minor and not major waste.
I hope you can be proud of yourself and not moan about your sad state.
I hope you have the courage when knocked down —to arise in haste.
And I hope you love yourself—if you do you can be satisfied of your fate.

- When you realize time is the greatest treasure or gift—you become instantly as rich as any man.
- Time is the most precious treasure next only to loved ones ad health.
- Wasted time —we should regret it. But it will be felt moreso at your departure from Earth.
- Wasted time is too much emphasis on material things, and bodily excesses, and not enough on the mind and spirit.
- Useful time or useless time—it makes you or breaks you. (There is a sundial monument near my future gravesite in Mount Pleasant Cemetery with an inspirational poem about the useful and the useless in life. (Good name for a cemetery by the way, for it is very pleasant.)
- Spend your time as a miser spends his money.
- To spend your lifetime with a loved one is like living two lifetimes— since the joy doubles, but also the problems..
- The ravages of time occur to all —we are all getting older together, but the wise man knows how to reduce the ravages with better use of time.

- Two twins die: the one wasted his time, lived a selfish life, left nothing meaningful behind, and not remembered as a helpful person, hence soon forgotten—but the other twin treated each hour and day as golden time, and left behind a long lasting useful legacy, and was long remembered and celebrated for his useful healthy deeds as an unselfish helper.
- Life is great—new adventures and new mysteries await us all around each corner of time.

## HAPPINESS (From my poem *Happiness*)

> To be happy reduce your desires.
> Be content with what you have got.
> Wish not for the gold you sought,
> And for the way things were—pine not.
> Then you stoke the happiness fires.

- Doing the thing you love to do, doing it the right way, seeing improvement month after month, getting closer and closer to the best you can be—that's happiness. (Some philosophy from my late brother Maurice, the artist and ballroom dance instructor.)
- To be happy act happy. To be confident act confident. To be energetic act energetic. To defeat fear act fearless. It really works. Now walk tall, head up, shoulders back. Now you are a champion.
- Happiness comes from a simple life, and simple tastes, peace of mind, contentment and selflessness.
- You will never be happier than during the journey to fulfil your passionate dream.
- Enemies of happiness: pain—worry, taking on other's worries, phobias, false beliefs, boredom, inactivity, selfishness, discontentment, and negative thinking.
- A happy man lives longer, he spreads the joy to others and it multiplies like a rolling snowball...
- A happy countenance is an immediate beautifier—and shows a happy soul within.
- Happy thoughts turn into joyful works and kind helpful actions.

- Alcohol is not required to be happy, like running shoes are not required to run, but it sure helps. (Anon)
- For happiness, emphasize doing, rather than regretting and not doing.
- You make your own fun and happiness—don't depend on others for these.
- Too often after determined searching for happiness far and wide, the searcher returns home and finds happiness within—like the missing eye glasses on their very nose.

## ATTITUDE from my poem *Attitude*

- With the right attitude your light will shine—and others will see this and you will enlighten others.
- Your attitude will either balloon or shrink your situation, or make it disappear.
- When the decision is right it will feel right—so beware of the unsure nervous decision. This sets your attitude in the correct direction. So listen to your feelings.
- You don't need a psychiatrist to solve your problem: after careful thought just change your attitude.
- A change in attitude can solve many problems.
- Switch off the dark to turn on the bright.
- Gratitude is the greatest and most desirable attitude.
- A grateful person maximizes the favourable and minimizes the unfavourable.
- We become our thoughts and attitude.
- A poor attitude is revealed by a poor posture.

## ATHLETICS (From my book *How to Be A Champion from 9 to 90)*

- Possible = Impossible +Talent + Believing + Perseverance + Sacrifice + Correct Preparation, + Patience. Omit one ingredient and Possible = Failure
- One can walk tall and proud, even in defeat, after giving your all.

- Many wish to be a champion, but few have the perseverance and the necessary knowledge, and fewer are blessed with the right body, mind and spirit.
- Some say: I do not have the time necessary to be a champion, but we can always find the time where there is a burning passion or desire.
- Patiently weave and wear the habit of a champion every day, and you will one day be covered in success and wear the crown of glory.
- If you believe you can win, you can win, Faith is necessary, but also the hard work.
- Recognition is the spur to goad one on. A hole in one is useless without recognition by others. There is inner success and satisfaction but true success is to be esteemed by your fellow man.
- Train to eliminate, endure and conquer pain. And you race as you train.
- Never give up, but don't be a bloody fool —sometimes it's better to stop and say I'll be back another day.
- Persistent preparation breeds confidence, and defeats fear.
- Success is not always winning the gold, or coming out on top. It is setting your goal and reaching it, or achieving a personal best. Also, having failed after giving your utmost with sacrifice along the way is not failure but a learning experience.
- Train hard, have faith in yourself, establish the habits of greatness, and the big surprise will come.
- Believing is achieving. Until you believe you will run faster you will not make the attempt.
- Eighty percent of the road to success is a burning dream, a desire on fire, firmly believing you can do it, having a plan and making the first step. The other 20 percent is the dedication and hard work.
- On the road to success there will be blind alleys, and setbacks even with good planning—such as the loss of a complete large chapter in writing a book. Accept these without discouragement since it's all part of the necessary journey. Consider these drawbacks as a kind of progress. Before success you have to pay your dues.
- Everything has a price for your deeds or your dreams—or there is no pleasure without pain.

# MY FAVOURITE QUOTATIONS by Others For All Athletes

**Note my comments are in [brackets]**

Here are some great quotations applicable to all athletes from the book: by *Michael Lynberg,* "**Winning**!" Doubleday, Broadway, NY, 1993. The book has nearly 300 quotes but the following 24 are my favourites.

> *Be quick, but never hurry.* **John Wooden** [Relaxation is the key to speed]

> *The mark of a great player is in the ability to come back. The great champions have all come back from defeat.* **Sam Snead** [Injury is a form of defeat too]

> *Achievement is difficult. It requires enormous effort. Those who can work through the struggle are the ones who are going to be successful.* **Jackie Joyner Kersee**

> *You've got to love what you are doing. If you love it, you can overcome any handicap or the soreness or all of the aches and pains and continue to play for a long, long time.* **Gordie Howe.** [100 years here I come.]

> *The man who can drive himself further when the effort gets painful is the man who will win.* **Roger Bannister.** [Train hard to tolerate and accustom to the pain.]

> *You are never playing an opponent. You are playing yourself, your highest standards, and when you reach your limits, that is real joy.* **Arthur Ashe.** [To get rid of some nerves before a race forget about your rivals, aim for a personal best]

> *You play the way you practice.* **Pop Warner.** [Simulate and mimic your race during cross training. For example If your 1500m race is five minutes. Run in the water at same perceived effort for five minutes.]

*Every day you waste is one you can never make up.* **George Allen**. [The most successful people make the most efficient use of their time on earth. This means having a plan and sticking to it. My greatest dread is dying and looking back on a life of wasted time and wasted years. ]

*Talent is God–given, be humble; fame is man-given, be thankful; conceit is self- given, be careful.* Anonymous (often quoted by **John Wooten)**. [There is no greatness without humility.]

*You have got to want to be the best before you can even begin to reach for that goal, and you have to be prepared to sacrifice a lot to get there. If I work on a certain move constantly, then, finally, it doesn't seem risky to me. The move says dangerous and looks dangerous to my foes, but not to me. Hard work has made it easy, That is my secret. That is why I win.* **Billie Jean King.** [Nothing comes easy, until it does (Anon}.]

*If you're going to be a champion, you must be willing to pay a greater price than your opponent.* **Bud Wilkinson.**

*Working hard becomes a habit, a serious kind of fun. You get self-satisfaction from pushing yourself to the limit, knowing that all the effort is going to pay off.* **Mary Lou Retton.**

*Have fun in the workouts and you will improve.* **Derek Turnbull** [The late legendary New Zealand sheep farmer —my nomination for the greatest master athlete of the 20th century.: [56 world records later, this comment rings true in my case. This comment to me was just a couple of years after I started up after a 30 year layoff from running.]

*It is not always the strongest man who wins the fight, or the fastest man who wins the race, or the best team that wins the game. In most cases it is the one who wants it the most, the one who has gone out and prepared [and prepared], and who has paid the price.* **Tommy Lasorda**

*Failure is not fatal, but failure to change might be.* **John Wooden** [Make sure to learn the lesson from the failure.]

*You have to be a dedicated person. You have to want to do it more than anything else. You have to want to be number one. Then you have to have the ability.* **Mario Andretti.** [So true. Many are saying if you believe you can do it then you can do it, but they are not considering that the necessary skill is also essential.]

*I always have good finishes. You go as hard as you can until the end. You can always rest when it's over.* **Janet Evans** [With about 100 or 150 metres from the finish the middle distance race begins.]

*I believe if you are bored with life, your problem is that you don't have a lot of goals. You must have goals and dreams if you are ever going to achieve anything in this world.* **George Halas**

*Breakthroughs occur. If you have a positive attitude and constantly strive to give your best effort, eventually you will overcome your immediate problems and find you are ready for greater challenges.* **Pat Riley.** [You will remain on a plateau if you continue with the same training. To rise out of the plateau in running training you have to increase the speed, or the volume. and/or shorten the rest between intervals.]

*Failure to prepare is preparing to fail.* **John Wooden** [I had an ex boss who always said, "Make sure to do your homework beforehand.]

*You should practise with a purpose. It's the quality of the time you spend practising that counts, not the length of time.* **Jimmy Connors** [Quit for the day when form starts to deteriorate.]

It is just human nature, but we all l have the tendency to practice the things that we already do pretty well. In truth, we should do just the opposite if we hope to improve. **Nancy LopezI** [Peter Mayer, great Canadian marathoner, said: do the thing that you hate to do.]

*If you don't invest very much, then defeat doesn't hurt very much, and winning isn't very exciting.* **Dick Vermeil**

*When I arrived at the gym Cassius Clay was always there, ready to go. When our training session was over he was the last to leave. There was always an extra minute on the speed bag, or the heavy bag. Boxing demands dedication, and invariably it pays off. Cassius Clay is proof of that.* **Angelo Dundee** [Cassius hated the workouts but he said suffer now and be a champion forever.]

# *19*

# MY INTERVIEWS

## CANADIAN RUNNING MAGAZINE INTERVIEW

## August 2015 except where noted

### Background Information:

Born in Elstow Saskatchewan, coincidentally the same tiny town where legendary Olga Kotelko was born and raised. Some believe the rugged climate in Saskatchewan is character building.

### Running History

I trained with the Red Devils Track Club under the famous coach Lloyd Percival in Toronto 60 years ago. I competed for Central Tech and the U of Toronto, in the 400m and 800m, loved to practice the hurdles, could run under 52 seconds in the 400m; and was on a lot of winning 4x400 relay teams. Due to an injury requiring an operation I took a 33 year layoff from running, but believed in in some exercise every day. I started running at age 56 with the North Your Track Club. Initially, I would just watch my two young sons Curtis and Tyler train. Then I started training with them at training camps in Florida. When they stopped running I continued on with the North York Club and a year later was able to tie an indoor 400m world record at age 57 in the 55-59 age group. I thought this is a good hobby. Due to successful aging and a reasonably active life in the previous three decades I adapted back to running very quickly. At about age 55 I was tested and declared in the top two percent of fit males in Canada. In addition to training with the North York Track Club I built up a lot of endurance by also training with the Credit Valley Marathon Club —frequent runs over an hour for many years.

## Some Running PB's

When I retired at age 62 after 34 years designing nuclear power reactors with the Atomic Energy Canada Ltd where I was one of the Canadian pioneers in this industry— I started running in the pool in the morning and on land later in the day. Now, due to a circulation problem in my left leg since about age 75 I stopped the cross country running in the fall and do negligible long aerobic running. Instead I do three days a week high intensity interval training on the track or soft even trials. In between running days, I do easier cross training (running in the pool and swimming,, elliptical machine, rowing, cycling and weight training). But still able to break world records since age 76 with this method.

At age 66 in the 65-69 age group after 10 years training I reached a peak in performance at the World Masters Championships in 1996 at Buffalo NY—breaking three world records: in the 800m in a fierce howling wind in 2:14.33 (my best race ever and still a standing record), in the 400m in 57.97—and also the 300m hurdles. This resulted in two drug tests immediately after my world records. What helped me tremendously at this meet was the strong foundation of training with the North York Track Club for 10 years, and also two years training with the Saugeen Track Club.

At age 69 I had one of my best 800m indoor specific age world record races running 2:17.05. (age graded 103 %).

At age 75 in the 75-79 age groups I broke 3 world indoor records at the Boston US National meet—the mile in 5:41.95,. the 800 in 2:32.48 and the 400m in 66.28 following just an hour after the mile race.

In 2005 at age 76 I received the prestigious Male Master of the World for 2005 award from the World Masters Athletics (WMA). This was to a large extent due to my two age group world outdoor records that year at the World Masters Athletic/championship in San Sebastian Spain in the 800m and 300m hurdles and a gold medal in the 400m. The previous year in a new age group I had five age group world records. This may have helped my selection and good fortune in 2005.

In 2014 at age 85 I had five world records in my new age group— indoor and outdoor 400m and 800m in Budapest World Masters (WMA)Indoor and in Canadian Masters Outdoor meets in Toronto and the 200m hurdles in Costa Rica. My 400m outdoor record in 77.12 was age graded 106.33% breaking the previous record by over 3 seconds.

At age 88, in 2017, overall, I had 14 WMA age group world records currently (previously I had over 20 WMA records at one time), 12 WMA age group records were lost to others, and I have 30 specific age records listed in the last edition 2006 of Masters Age Records—a total of 56 world records broken as of 2018, including relay records in 4X400m and 4X880m at age 80-89. And no double counting, i.e., only counting the best not those leading up to the best. My list of world records is based on indoor and outdoor events: long hurdles, 400m, 800m,1500m and mile events. It is notable that 10 of my world records were in different age groups in the 800m in 2015—no one has more 800m WMA age group records.. Since then two of my 800m outdoor world records were broken: In age group 75-79 a 2:30.59 by Jose Rioseco (ESP) in 2016— and in age group 80-84 a 3:06.69 by David Carr (AUS) in 2017. Two superb records which I predict will long withstand the winds of time. In this memoir I give away all my training secrets, It is rare.

## Questions answered:

### What kind of running wisdom can you pass on to younger runners or those approaching their master years?

Enjoy the journey (the training) to make better progress. Gradually go faster, longer and with shorter rest. Always train within your present capabilities. Ideally, join a running club, have a coach, and a running partner of comparable ability. Be knowledgeable about your sport to help avoid injury and to avoid mistakes that will hinder progress; See my book published in 2005 and 2007 in color: " The Complete Guide to Running," available on Amazon Books.

## Do you think more runners over 40+ should be running or being more active?

There are a lot of advantages. During my 33 years without running I still believed in some exercise every day. But after I started running training again at age 56 I got stronger with more muscle, more flexibility, and with more energy. Also being more seriously active automatically leads to a much better diet. This adds up to disease prevention and a longer higher quality life.

## What is it that keeps you running and challenging yourself?

I believe running, good diet and genes, have reduced my biological age to about 15 years or more younger than my birth age, and these will add many high quality years to my life. The comradery with my running friends worldwide have also enriched my life. After a short time running becomes a necessary habit which is self-motivating. I must admit the recognition as a world international champion is also motivating; for example my five Hall of Fame awards, the bench with plaque in our local park that my neighbours honoured me with last year; being on the cover of the last specific world record booklet, or being announced as the Great Earl many times over, or a simple compliment by a complete stranger watching me stretch," I want to be like you." All these are motivating but it is important thing is to stay humble "There is no greatness without humility."

# SELF INTERVIEW

## What are your thoughts on age graded percentage tables?

The age graded tables compares the athletes time with approximate world record time. Hence 100% equals the open world record. 90% is world class and above 80% is national class.

As we age performance declines due to loss of muscle, flexibility and endurance. I have examined the yearly % decline for master world record holders in running distance events and found the decline is 1% per year up to about 60 or 65, and from 60 to 70 about 1.5%/yr. and from 70-80 about 2%/yr, and from 80-90 about 3 to 4%/yr. Also, I found sprinters decline at a slower rate than distance runners since sprinters do more fast interval training which helps reduce decline in fast twitch muscles. The yearly decline for most athletes will be higher than for world record holder athletes and much higher for the sedentary coach potatoes.

The age graded percentage tables have been kind to Earl Fee. The Canadian masters for many years awarded big prizes for the Athlete of the Canadian Championship meets based on the highest age grade percentages. I was fortunate to win this award about 5 times including a trophy. he prizes went all to one person male of female. with the highest age graded percentage, and included for example: a watch, running shoes, clothes, airplane ticket sometimes, and memberships to fitness centers, etc. A world class athlete, Ruth Carrier, would normally obtain these prizes from various companies. I was embarrassed and guilty to win this so many time that the Canadian masters committee decided one year that I would not be eligible. I think it best that they stopped this generous practice..

I have also won $500 US twice at the Southeastern Masters meet in Raleigh NC for the highest age graded percentage of all athletes competing. This well run masters meet has been discontinued unfortunately.

In 2017 at the NCCWMA meet at York U in Toronto my 400m race in 1:24.30 was age graded at 108.3%, my highest ever. It showed that I am aging much slower than other master world record holders. All in all I say thank you to age graded tables, they have been very kind to me.

In February, 2018 at the Ontario Masters indoor championships I ran the 400m at age 88 in a time of 1:25.39. It was age graded at 107.05%. It was reported by the Ontario Masters as the highest age-graded for all masters male and female indoor 400m performances worldwide in 2018 and also the highest age graded in 2018 for all World male running indoor performances from 60m to 3000m. See the attached photo. In the summer I should be able to lower my time further, as I didn't think my training for the above race was complete. This latest development shows that I am aging much slower than the average athlete. It is highly likely the tips in my anti-aging book are working.

**Earl's 400m indoor age 88**

## What are some of your major diet habits?

I stopped at my local Chinese food market today (April 2018) for a few items —a pound of walnuts, 4 mangos, strawberries and a Fuji apple. " A lot of vitamin," commented the cashier in her Chinese accent. Actually my diet is predominately vegetables, and no rice or potatoes. Would you believe about 2/3 of a pound steamed vegetables of many varieties at dinner. I am convinced a vegetable diet provides an abundance of vitamins and minerals and fibre. But I believe: ideally protein is important at each meal and including mainly fish and also chicken during the week.

For protein I have fish (salmon or trout) three or four times a week, and at other times skinless chicken legs —for the healthier dark meat. Not large servings, about 120 grams. I try to get some protein at each meal. For breakfast: I usually have steelcut porridge with walnuts, sunflower seeds, maple syrup and a banana—and once or twice a week two eggs and a red potato microwaved. For lunch: I have a shake with mainly fruit or greens—or a fruit salad —or just soup and a cheese or salmon or tuna sandwich. For snacks: I eat a lot of peanuts, peanut butter, and sunflower seeds, or fruit but no fruit juice since I minimize sugar. I also love multi grain bread, a small glass of red wine at dinner, and Greek yogurt for desert a few times a week.

I also take the following supplements daily, a very comprehensive multi vitamin/ mineral (Ortho Core), vitamin E, vitamin K2, Q10coenzyme Ubiquinol, 80mg aspirin, and also a magnesium pill before bed. Magnesium is a super supplement with many benefits for the body. It is also important to get eight glasses of water daily, so I start with three glasses distilled water in the morning with a tablespoon of ground flax seed.

It is essential to get enough fibre (30 grams per day) for the healthy microbes in the intestines (the microbiome). The microbiome is the hot topic at present and will be in the future. Healthy microbes in the intestines have a major effect on the brain and its function, as well as for general health.

There are other important foods such as Omega 3 essential fatty acids which have to be obtained from the diet (fish or fish oil) as they are not manufactured in the body.

See my book "100 Years Young the Natural Way," in three parts Body, Mind and Spirit, for details on a healthy diet, how to fight major diseases and its effect on longevity, and 24 ways to increase longevity.

## What are some of you your favourite peeves?

Firstly: Donald Trump. The world would be a much happier place without this bull in a china shop, narcisstic false sayer. Then there are most restaurants that seem to hate vegetables and love only meat. This enables restaurants to charge more. The usual serving in too often 90% meat and 5% vegetable. but should be 85% vegetable and 15% protein. Then there are the auto dealers who charge over a hundred dollars an hour for a particular service that has a fixed exorbitant time to repair, hence a double whammy. On top of this is the usual statement that you need other repairs —most likely not essential. Unfortunately, we are stuck with auto dealers when a computerized check is necessary, to locate a problem. Then there is ordering articles through the internet.— three times I tried it and all a foul up or a disappointment, e.g., two articles instead of one, I didn't read the small print another time resulting in exorbitant charges, and the last time excessive customs tax and arriving after 5 weeks. However there are good and fast results with Amazon.

## What are some of your recurring dreams during sleep?

I don't dream too often. Many decades ago I would fly and soar like superman. My powerful mind would activate my body and I would be horizontal gliding effortlessly, the wind in my hair, peering down at the passing earth hundreds of feet below. A glorious experience. And no crash at the end. It didn't happen often enough. Unfortunately I am only dreaming.

I am somewhat of a perfectionist but used to have to have dreams or mild nightmares of failure. I was ill prepared and failed at an exam or some project. Or I was at work and doing nothing useful, working on some useless project. I put in some time walking through the mostly unoccupied office building. And I would up in a sweat.

Sometimes it is a dream with one of my sons or daughter when they were less than about 10 years old. Then sometimes I fall in love with a beautiful lady. Unfortunately, again I am only dreaming.

This morning (in 2017 with memoirs 75 % finished) at about my usual waking time someone was calling. "Hello,hello!" from downstairs, at my front door I supposed. I jumped out of bed to check, but there is no one there. It was my shortest dream ever.

Occasionally I have dreamt I am running fast and effortless with boundless energy —a great feeling.

But when I wake I definitely find it is the best time for inspiration. On awakening, I often think of a bright idea for a poem or for something to add in my memoirs, etc. It is a good idea to have paper and pencil at bedside to write down any clever thoughts as they can disappear shortly after.

## What are some of your most amazing happenings?

I have noticed in the past year or so a strange happening in my bedroom. I have two scatter rugs in my bedroom one is 3 feet by 5 feet and the other is 3 x 4 feet. They both are moving westward. The larger one moves about one foot in two months. The smaller one does not move as much, but definitely still westward, as I wal kover it on the way to the bathroom and it gets a few of my foot prints during the night. Sorry too much info. I suspect one possible explanation for these westward movements: may be the Earth's circular movements are involved here.

When I was working many decades ago I was just five minutes by car to work. One winter sunny day I took a different route on a side street My windshield was frosted and I did not use the scraper as I was a little late in leaving for work. As I drove slowly into the sun visibility was not good due to the frosted windshield. Suddenly, I had the urge to stop. When I stopped… there was a workman right in front in a manhole with just his upper body showing. Something made me stop as there was no shouting warning.

### Is there anything exciting or highly unusual in the past that happened to you which you can talk about?

Yes on May 1, 2018, a stroke of bad luck. I described this in a Facebook post: **Earl is Not Running**.

I will be brief. I had a setback in May 2018, actually my biggest personal disaster. First problem; a cataract operation gone wrong to put it mildly, basically: two dropped items (the old lens and a big piece of cataract into the bottom inside my eye—a very rare problem. Beforehand, many were telling me, "cataract operation no big deal, and just takes 15 minutes " but not in my case. An urgent second delicate operation just two days later to remedy the problem was essential. I spare you the gory details. I look on the bright side; for the 2nd operation I had the top eye surgeon, Dr. David Wong, at the large Saint Michaels Hospital in Toronto, on short notice. And the operation was done quickly as the items could not be left in the eye for more than a week. For over a week I was seeing a large golf sized gas bubble and blurriness, and the feeling of a large obstruction in my eye for nearly a month. But I was able to run slowly and swim after five weeks. The good news is my eyesight is much better out of the operated eye and the white colors are super white compared to the previous grey white.

The Canadian government has a too strict rule —"if you have cataracts and can't read a particular line on the chart you need the cataract operation or lose driver's license." Now at 89 I plan to run and drive for another 10 years. But there are very few who are fortunate and able to do this. But the charts say I have the right lifestyle, i.e., on the right track. So, there it was— a bump in the highway of life. I love operations —if you survive—you get to talk and brag about them for the rest of your life.

## What is one of your favourite sayings?

"Life is to short to drink cheap wine," (something I saw in a pub in Las Vegas 13 years ago.) Also, "There is price for everything," or, "There is no pleasure without pain." "Nothing comes easy until it does." My son Tyler says, "You only live once." meaning don't hold back. And, of particular current interest to me and fellow seniors, "You can't take it with you."

## What is the world's best invention?

Women!. Not surprising as God is a hard one to compete against.

## What is next best world's invention?

Next to electricity— red wine or coffee. Some might say the contraception pill.

## What is the best Canadian Invention?

It is not the snowmobile but the CANDU nuclear reactor to produce electric power. On the other hand, the best Swiss invention is the Cuckoo clock. Just kidding,I love the Swiss.

## What is your greatest fear?

Failure or wasting time.

## What is the greatest gift you've ever been given?

Two sons and a daughter.

## What are the traits you most admire?

Charity, humour, gratitude, empathy, positivity and trust.

## What are the best health tips in order of importance?

Eat plenty of vegetables and fish, moderate to intense exercise three times a week, reduce or eliminate sugar, reduce saturated fats, reduce trans fats (e.g., processed foods or anything in a box), don't overeat, drink alcohol in moderation, believe you can live longer than average, avoid stress and socialize. And remember you are only as old as your actions. And read my book, "*100 Years Young the Natural Way*," in three parts, body, mind and spirit which includes in the 1st chapter 24 ways to fight aging, and in other chapters how to reduce the probability of the major diseases, etc.

Most people are not concerned about longevity, but completely absorbed in their present enjoyment, or bad habits. For example, at my annual retirees Christmas banquet there is a draw for choice of prizes consisting mainly of alcoholic beverages, chocolates, cookies, and some female beauty products. Last year I donated one of my anti-aging books "100 Years Young the Natural Way". It is a 600 page book since it covers body, mind and spirit, the three essentials, and normally costs over $30 not counting shipping. Another possible advantage was it is written by a fellow employee. Information in the book could increase longevity by at least a year or even a decade. But my book was completely ignored until the very end after all the alcohol, chocolates and female products were selected. In other words alcohol and chocolates trumps longevity. The moral of this story is: it is easier and more enjoyable to treat the senses than to read, and learn to live longer. A big mistake in my biased opinion. Unfortunately, the general feeling appears to be—no pleasure or bad habit is worth giving up for the sake of two more years in the Happy Dreams retirement home.

## What is your recommendation to athletes to maintain performance with age?

As we age we age we lose flexibility and suppleness, oxygen uptake, balance and strength every year— and increasingly faster every year. For example, loss in performance for world record holder distance runners is 1%/year at age 60 or 65 and 4%/year at age 80. The smart senior is already working on frequent (weekly or daily) sessions of stretching, of aerobic capacity (VO2max), of balance, and weight training. It is essential to continue the above with increasing age—ideally one should increase some of these activities —such as weight training—rather than the usual decrease with age. Thus, the decrease with age can be decreased to a large extent. For example, Ed Whitlock successfully increased his frequent aerobic runs around his local cemetery from 3 hours to 4 hours in his latter years. It is a case of developing the right habits.

It is best to have targets, something to achieve in the future, and prepare well in advance. In my case I have been preparing for several years and now at 89 in March 2018 to be in the best possible shape when I turn 90 in my new age group. I can see myself breaking some records in this new age group—this is my incentive. And a long preparation is best.

## What are two of your best jokes?

Older women are very clever. For example, on checking out of a hotel for one night an elder lady was shocked to learn it was $300 a night. She spoke to the hotel manager. 'He said the $300 is reasonable, since we have a huge convention center, a beautiful swimming pool and fitness room, and free WFI service. The lady said, " But I didn't use any of these. He said, "Well you could have." The lady replied, "You owe me $300 for sleeping with my beautiful body last night." He replied, "But I didn't slept with your beautiful body." The lady replied, "No, but you could have. "

In the mid 1800's an American preacher enquired about purchasing a mule from a local farmer. The preacher learned the mule was blind but the farmer assured him it didn't matter. He explained all you had to do to get it moving forward was to say: "Praise the Lord," and to get it to stop say: "Whoa. " The farmer wanted only four chickens for the mule. The preacher was happy to buy a religious mule and besides the price was a bargain in those days. With the preacher on his back the mule started off at a very rapid pace as soon as the preacher shouted: "Praise the Lord." However the pace was way too fast and soon they were heading for a huge cliff. "Stop, Stop," yelled the preacher but without success. Just at the edge of the precipice he remembered to shout "Whoa." Feeling quite relieved to have escaped disaster he looked down to the bottom of the steep cliff, removed his hat, wiped his brow, raised his head to the heavens, and in appreciation shouted out: "Praise the Lord."

Remember to do your mental exercises to keep the memory and mind sharp or the consequences could be deadly.

## What were some of your worst paying jobs?

In my early teens selling my mother's donuts from door to door. As a delivery boy delivering groceries on my bike to pretty ladies, I had also the associated duty of drowning the rats caught in a trap during the night.

While at high school I had a part time job of separating food from paper garbage at a bakery. And as an engineering employee meeting some impossible schedules.

## What athletes do you most admire?

Mohammed Ali, the boxer/ poet, friend Ed Whitlock, multi world record holder/distance runner, Payton Jordan, sprinter and coach, Johnny Bower NHL Maple Leaf goalie, All gone but remain in my memory and others memory forever. See details for these legendary athletes in Chapter 16 for all but Mohammed Ali,

## What are your thoughts on breaking master's world records?

Breaking world records and striving for number one ranking or high world rankings and the resulting satisfaction, achieving your dream, and the resulting accolades are good motivators. On the latter Ed Whitlock and I agree. I must admit. But for me there is also the reality that the necessary training will prolong my life and result in extra years of healthy independence. (Whitlock said he was not doing it for health reasons.) The pursuit of these dreams results in the friendship of many like minded athletes. And I also enjoy the great satisfaction of the improvement in my body that comes from persistent correct practice.

On the subject of master's world records, I recall a multi world record holder telling he was proud of the fact that all world records he had broken were done at WMA world masters championships. It was Simon Hurler of Holland. What was alluded to was the fact that these championships are harder than local meets in one's own country since the World Masters Athletics (WMA) championships involve tiring travel, preliminary heats, different diet and sleeping, and more stress than a local meet. Also a small local meet can have a wide spread of young and older competitors in the same race; hence there is the possibility of arranged or inadvertent pacing by a younger faster runner. For example, in the 800m following closely another runner results in less wind resistance, less stress and and perhaps a perfect pace— and worth about 2 or 3 seconds from less wind resistance alone. Try following closely sometime—you will be more relaxed and with noticeable less effort. In open events a rabbit is legal and often used in world record long distance running attempts except for near the final lap, e.g., Bannister of

England had two rabbits to break the 4 minute mile in the 1950's. However, I believe pacing should not be allowed in masters events. And WMA world records should be allowed only at sanctioned meets.

## What is your favourite song?

The Dancing Queen by ABBA. I also like Eagle by ABBA.

## What is your latest poem?

Beautiful Sounds. I now have over 100 new poems. I would love to include appropriate professional photos in color my next poetry book but it makes the book expensive.

## What is the most beautiful sight you have seen recently?

And not talking about your recent monthly retirement cheque or any recent cheque from your Sun Life Insurance company for recent physiotherapy.

Seriously now, at night recently on January 1 2018 there was a dazzling new 'supemoon". Seeming much larger than most full moons since this day it's closest to Earth in orbit, and low on the horizon, also looking a creamy orange and surprisingly surrounded by an outer red blazing ring like the moon was on fire. It was an amazing sight better than a thousand fireworks. And foretelling a lively new year of happy promise —a great start to the new year for me and billions of others fortunate enough to see this celestial wonder. For a person like me that lives in a city where a single star or a blazing sunrise or sunset is a rarity or novelty—the above must suffice.

One summer morning in 2018 I emerged outside in the early morning invigorated by the bright sun, azure blue sky and the fresh damp air. Immediately, I was shocked and thrilled by a double rainbow filling the whole eastern sky....I had never seen such a beautiful double rainbow... It seemed so close— I felt I could nearly touch it. I rushed inside for my camera. But the ringing phone needed attention. When I emerged frantically just minutes later my glorious double rainbow had disappeared to another world leaving behind only a dense mist. Opportunity is fleeting. But the memory remains fortunately.

Always take time to smell the roses.

## What would you do different if you had it to do over?

My friend John Ward said he would change nothing. Someone said they wold part their hair in the middle. But here are my small improvements

- I would phone my mother every day.
- Be more spiritual in my youth, e.g., with gratitude, empathy positivity and helping others.
- More appreciative of Nature in youth.
- Take up Karaoke at an earlier age since it is good for the morale, and the mind.
- And most important: start the exploration of women at an earlier age since it is not practical to make up for lost time as a senior.
- And perhaps find a younger woman to look after me in my final decades? On 2nd thoughts, no, not practical. It is best to be doing more at my age rather than less.

# *20*

# GRATITUDE, RELIGION, LEGACY

## GRATITUDE

I HAVE LEARNED THAT A HABIT OF GRATITUDE HAS MANY ADVANTAGES. Be grateful at the end of the day especially for the small and big favourable happenings and those things that were avoided by chance or by your own actions— and even if all may not be good in your life. And If you have a bad experience be grateful for the lesson. With this constant grateful attitude, each day is a precious gift.

As one gets older the body and mind deteriorate, but spirituality can increase. And there is a feeling that time is running out, so each hour becomes more precious. By appreciating poetry your spirituality is awakened, sharpened and developed. Connect to your spirituality so it is a constant companion rather than an infrequent visitor. Rope it in. Don't let your senses get dull. Sharpen your sensory skills to increase your enjoyment of life. Awaken your awareness of all around you. Be aware of your sight, hearing, feeling and taste senses. Be aware of the subtle sounds and aromas. Tell yourself— today I am going to appreciate these more fully. Your aim should be to enjoy each precious hour to the fullest extent. Sadly many people are not smelling the roses—too busy rushing around in our concrete jungles, committed to mundane habits. With more appreciation of the beauty of Nature and gratitude for large and small mercies spirituality grows and soars. "*Open your eyes and see the good that you now have, and then keep alert and alive to recognize each new manifestation as it comes to you. Be thankful for all the good things of your life.*"" Paramahansa Yogananda

A year of greater appreciation and gratitude is worth more than many years of oblivion. With gratitude as your constant companion— kindness, empathy, contentment and happiness will also be at your side. And If you exhibit and plant kindness, spirituality and the soul blossoms. Just try it.

There are negative people who if you associate with will suck the vibrant energy out of you, i.e., those who do not have the habit of gratitude, usually due to some bad happenings in their life. And they have chosen the woe-is- me attitude on life, an attitude causing stress, bad health, and a shorter life. A change of attitude stressing the good things in their life such as their health and their loved ones would result in a magnificent transformation for the better.

We are all too often taking for granted our good fortune. There are many unrecognized things that deserve gratitude such as: our legs, our eyes, hearing. our heart, the universe and nature, singing birds in the morning, sunsets and sunrises, and the loves in our lives. Oh the wonder of it all! Below I mention some of the things in my life that I am grateful for. What is on your list?

## I recognize I have a lot to be grateful for:

Firstly I have a good pension that I worked and paid for from 35 working years in the nuclear industry. One day on the subject of money—I told my daughter, Melanie, "I am not interested in money, (meaning, it's a necessity, but there are more important things in life. She said. "You are not interested in money since you have money." I would rather be writing some poetry and doing running training rather than accumulating money and material goods. So I am grateful for my style of retirement living.

I am grateful for those who say I look much younger than my age. I realize my health is much better than average at age 88, and soon 89. As an athlete I am grateful for my healthy knees, hips and joints which afflict many seniors.

And grateful for a heart that has helped me break many world records in running and hurdling in spite of Tachycardia episodes (unexpected rapid heart beats even without coffee or stress and anxiety). Due to my intense exercise for many decades my resting heart beat is normally about 43 bpm on rising in the morning —this means my heart is enlarged. (Incidentally, how large may be revealed one day as I have donated my body to the U of Toronto medical faculty for research.)

I have reason to be grateful for an improvement in the blood circulation in my left calf. For many years I had a condition called Intermittent Claudication due to calcium deposits in my left calf—causing a lack of oxygen in the area So, it was at after about age 75 that I turned to high intensity interval training, HIIT. Fortunately I could do HIIT without a problem in this area. But after about age 87 I was able to run slow much longer than a few years previous before the left calf became too sore to continue. I believe this improvement resulted from several years of HIIT and leg movements during cross training which built further capillaries for blood flow.

I also have reason to be grateful for an improvement in my Tachycardia episodes (caused by an electric impulse in a heart valve. At age 88 the problem is subsiding in some ways for some reason, less rapid maximum heart beats, i.e., 100 bpm instead of 120 bpm previously. Alcohol causes it to be more frequent, so I have reduced from one 5oz glass of red wine per day. I have reduced frequency of episodes in the morning by taking cold or warm water instead of hot water first thing in the morning. And when I have an episode lately, I can usually quickly (in a few minutes) rid myself of this (i) while sitting with my feet raised above my head and putting my mind in a day dreaming state (I call it mindlessness) and/or (ii) by slow diaphragm breathing. Also dehydration, too much carbohydrates without protein, caffeine or stress causes a Tachycardia problem. I try to reduce or avoid these now as well. Where many my age have the major diseases (heart, diabetes, prostate or obesity) I have Tachycardia, the lessor of evils.

I am also grateful that I do not have a similar problem called Atrial Fibrillation (A fib). In Afib, the heart rate goes much higher than for Tachycardia, even as high as about 250 beats per minute. And the dangerous thing about Afib which does not occur with Tachycardia, is that the heart may go into a quivering state and a heart attack or stroke may occur. A good neighbour of mine died recently in his sleep from a form of Afib at an early age of 58.

In my neighbourhood there is plenty to be grateful for— five minutes away by car I have the U of Mississauga with its nine laps to the mile indoor running track, a huge eight lane 25m length swimming pool, sauna and whirlpool, and a large fitness center with many weight and exercising machines, and instructors if I wish— all at my disposal for a modest price since I am a past U of Toronto alumni graduate, in mechanical engineering in 1953—would you believe 65 years ago.. The 180m indoor track is soft and the huge pool is not usually busy. Just beyond the university is a good cinder running trail beside the wide Credit River which runs through beautiful Erindale Park. Also, the smooth Sawmill Creek earth trail. just minutes away from my house, runs through an oxygenated wooded area beside the creek with 13 man-made impressive waterfalls. And about 15 minutes by car a large Lifetime FItness Center on three floors has all the equipment and classes that an active person would ever hope for. In the summer on a sunny day you would likely catch me at the huge busy pool for adults and children outdoors in one of its hundreds of lounges— or doing some laps in the lanes. The scenery is good too if you catch what I mean.

I am also very happy and grateful for my neighbours on one side Shirley and Renzo, and Darlene and Phil on the other side—all of whom are frequently doing me some favours Like trimming my monster cedar bush once a year or looking after my grass on their side, fixing out mutual wooden fence frequently, etc. And my fine neighbours provide an immaculate garden on one side and a forest of pines on the other side to enjoy. Then across the quiet street there are more good friends Louise ( ex running partner) wife of the late Cameron, and Sabrina and Karl. So there are frequent parties (Italian, Octoberfest, and Christmas— wine and cheese with my running friends) to enjoy. Sadly… our chief party organizers Sabrina and Karl are leaving in mid 2018 to retire in Greece.

My house on secluded Sir John's Homestead I chose in 1979 from five models, and I selected the largest lot in the area I believe. Sir John's Homestead was just five minutes by car to my past fulltime engineering supervisor position designing Candu nuclear power plants, at AECL for 34 years. All the above are good reasons to be grateful.

And in the boulevard at front of my house I have beautiful tall Elm tree—it is rare and heathy unlike others in Mississauga with a potent worm disease. For example, 10 mature Elms nearby on my street had to be chopped down, but somehow mine survived. At entrance to my back yard beside the gate a maple tree has sprung up by itself providing a canopy at entrance —it is like entering an Alice and Wonderland Garden of many varieties including Roses of Sharon rose bushes, burning bushes and many green and colourful plants, See also in my expansive backyard two other mature maple trees (one a gift from my neighbour's Darlene and Phil)— two spruce trees, one will grow to over 30 feet in width in 10 years (I hope and expect I am here to see it) — and also a giant oak tree now 39 year sold. My oak tree towering over all the nearby homes—I admire it for it's strength and beauty and its uplifting branches as if in prayer to the Almighty. Also in my backyard I am blessed with frequent visits from a family of beautiful shimmering red cardinals, a fat contemplative rabbit who has made this his second home and playground, and also a fat robin who visits frequently my pink rock patio. And just recently after 39 years I noticed the soft pink siding on the upper level at the back of my house was a perfect coordination with my dark red brick on the lower level. I makes me realize there are many things to be grateful for that we don't always notice, but sometimes we do— too late.

In the glorious spring in early May we are blessed with 14 apple blossom trees in bloom down the hill from my house on Sir John's Homestead. And also at the bottom this hill is a beautiful parkette with a bench "*In honor of Earl Fee, long time resident, world record runner, and author.*"—a gift from my kind neighbours. This hill about 250 metres in length provides for excellent running training for myself and other ambitious runners.

And best of all I am grateful for my faithful friends and loving family. While I'm writing this it is Canada Day! 50th Year Celebration. This remands us of something we often take for granted. But the fact is our home Canada is one of the very best countries in the world. We have so much to be proud of, the natural beauty of Canada, our diversity, our comprehensive health system, our government, a sensible prime minister, etc. I could go on and on. When I returned to Canada after completing three years in England —two years on an Earl of Athlone Fellowship and one year working the English Electric Nuclear design department—I felt a great surge of pride as the boat docked in Montreal. I had managed to escape marriage in England. When

I travelled by back pack and hostels in Europe in the early 1950's I found how well Canadians were well received compared to Americans. My personal experience with Americans has been admirable. I am grateful and blessed to have many American fellow master athlete friends—and many friends in other countries met in my running travels.

So all in all, I have need to be very grateful, an essential goal for anyone hoping to be happy. It is a habit leading to happiness and contentment with many other advantages. I hope you will be with me on this. What is on your gratitude list? I hope some of the above examples will awaken some of your reasons to be grateful which you may have taken for granted.

# RELIGION

In short I believe in a God. And I believe our minds are too finite compared to God and the Universe, making it impossible to understand God's plan and purpose. I can believe there is a Heaven but find it impossible to believe as Pope Francis does that there is a Hell (a central tenet of Catholicism). Or perhaps the Pope is just using this to scare his followers

I realized recently there is one sure thing about religion—there will be no disappointment after our departure from Earth. You either realize you are in Heaven or there is no awareness of anything whatsoever.

I was about 12 years old when a female teacher at Essex Public School In Toronto convinced me there was a God. But my parents had my brothers and I saying our prayers every night, although there was no Sunday School attendance. I am a quiet believer with a Christian philosophy. I do not push religion in my books as most people shy away from bible thumpers. I feeI I am a stronger person with God on my side. When nervous before a race I sometimes ask for God's assistance. Since our minds are finite compared to the infinite universe and God it is not possible to understand and grasp God's plan, or for instance understand why good and evil exists together. Of course. if there was only good and no evil then this would be heaven.

I have always had a peaceful feeling attending church. For a few years when living in Toronto in my mid 30's around 1960 I attended the impressive Timothy Eaton Memorial Church (TEMC) on Saint Clair. And I was president of the young adult Trident club at TEMC with about 750 members.

We raised money for charities and enjoyed the company of other religious, kind helpful people.

The church these days has a big problem —losing attendance. The local churches are becoming more and more empty. Perhaps it's partly the miracles in the bible which I personally find hard to believe and fathom. People like me are leaving the church but not giving up God. And I have not forgotten the church in my will as they do a lot of good work.

We are so finite within this mind goggling universe that in reality our world is much less than a drop of water in the ocean or a speck of dust in comparison to the the100 billion galaxies and 100 billion stars within each galaxie, Our ever expanding universe is so huge it has no boundaries. How did you come to be, who created you and is still creating you? But for most there is not this wonderment— for most the universe is hidden by smog and concrete and oblivion. Most are not impressed by what they cannot see. And since they cannot see God they are non-believers. One memorable night I dreamt I was in a space ship travelling around the constellation Orono, the hunter, the brightest constellation in the winter sky. It would most likely take many light years to travel around and a light year is 186 million miles per sec The problem is our minds are finite, too tiny to understand a universe or God's mysterious ways.

Our sun has 12 planets, with Earth the only one with the right conditions for life. It is highly or extremely unlikely that there are not billions of other planets with various stages of life in our galaxie. Some would be further progressed or less progressed than the humans on Earth.

I can foresee a problem in Heaven. I can see some members going on strike. God will ask," What is the problem?" "I give you everything you can ask for?" In reply a spokesman, "Lord, there is too much happiness here." For example, on Earth a dozen roses every day to the wife is boring and goes unappreciated. Here in Heaven, for example it is all sunshine and no rain, no change at all is tiresome. The Lord says," Hmm, I see— too much perfection. I will think on it, and get back to you shortly, in a million years "

# LEGACY

Everyone should have a legacy. What do you want to leave behind when you depart, or do you care?

*"Do not go where the path may lead, go instead where there is no path and leave a trail."* **Ralph Waldo Emerson**

As for me I feel if I depart with many hopes and dreams unaccomplished I will be a disappointment to myself. You will regret more the things that you have not done rather than the things that you have done. Mark Twin said, "So *sail off from the safe harbour. Catch the trade winds in your sails—before it is too late."*

Here is my thinking on the above subject. My mother at age 60— who looked and acted 40 at the time—learned to swim. I am at age 89 taking dance lessons and it's all coming back to me. Dancing is a great mental and physical exercise—and besides you get to mingle with like-minded opposite sex. And you can't practice effectively with a broom. Here is the serious lesson. When your dreams are just dying embers and you stop doing the new or reviving the old—you have lost your mojo— and you are old brother or sister…*old.*

I would like to be a good role model for older people to live a longer high quality life by good mental and physical health habits and particularly healthy diet and frequent exercise, including stretching and weight training regularly. So I aim to do these things as a good example to other seniors— demonstrating what can be accomplished at an older age. To do this it is necessary to associate with like minded and positive people. I short, I want to be remembered after I am gone as someone who has accomplished something: leaving some footprints in the sands of time that are not easily blown away. So it is not hope in doing, but working at doing before I leave. And we should realize time is short. Read in my poem below how the soul and spirit can awaken and blossom with age.

## YOUTH WAS YESTERDAY BUT TODAY THE SOUL AWAKENS

### YOUTH

Yesterday when we were young
The sweet taste of youth was forever on the tongue
We laughed at life and thought we'd be forever young
Some climbing the ladder to success rung by rung

Others had dreams to find, pursue and fulfill or fail
Or lost years in revelry while chasing their own tail
Others were hormone driven chasing female or male
Leaving behind many shattered hearts on life's hectic trail,
But too soon youth was gone leaving but an echo of our song
Yesterday when we were young.

It was the spring of life testing the body and mind on life's fickle ocean
Each day fresh frivolity and adventure.
Seeming like a series of roller coaster rides
And dizzy merry- go- rounds —ah! the freedom decades
We tasted and relished life with hungry tongue all at rapid pace
Saw with eager eyes, heard and sensed rapture everywhere
Felt youth with glowing hearts
Tossed life about like a colorful balloon bouncing against body
and mind
Never realizing the true worth of youth or what a gift we had in
our hands
Never doubting it all would end one day.
All the while taking life and time for granted like the nose upon
our face.

## TRANSITION YEARS

Too soon the wonder of it all was gone with the play.
Then necessary work that seemed to last forever and a day
And marriage— got in the way.

## OLD AGE

Eventually Old Age comes a rapping at your door
At first you refuse to answer but reluctantly let it in
And soon it settles in and takes over everything.
At first there is bewilderment—where did the years all go?
For most, hopefully, it is like a retreat to some safe harbour
Happy just to drift along ——

But for the ill prepared it can be a jagged journey
Like a ride down a perilous rapid filled river.
In youth life was often fast and furious —a hyped up dog escaping the leash,
But now in old age for too many it is an elephant walk
For the mind and body — but it need not be.
It can be a time to be forever young —for you and me with the right attitude—
An awakening of the soul, a time for helping others, and daily gratitude,
But also longitude of life if forever active.
Now we trade youthful activity for solitude and quietude.
In youth there was excess time— but now there is no time to waste:
Many family and faithful friends all gone but new friends abound.
For the inactive it may be a mere contemplation of a bulging belly,
But for some it's a soul awakening time.
It can be for you and me— a soul revelry
Instead of the youthful mind and body revelry.
Now we see the neglect of soul in youth,
Now in this autumn of life is the time for greater awareness.
Where In youth there was:
Seeing but not discerning beneath the surface,
Hearing but not listening in earnest,
Sensing in the body and mind but not in the soul.
But now trading mind, body revelry in youth for spirit revelry.

In youth too often missing out by not noticing or appreciating, for example:
The millions of tiny stars in the snow blanket on a dazzling winter day;
The magic of colour everywhere: of a multi colored duck in a pond,
Or just the magic of a brilliant blue sky;
The music of birds singing welcoming you on a fresh new morn;
The cry of a lonely loon on a glassy lake;
The sight and sound of a V of honking geese in the heavens—
On a frosty autumn morn going nowhere in particular;
The feel of soft rain on the skin on a sunny summer day;

In spring, glorious spring the sight and scent of blazing
flowers everywhere;
Or to stir the soul, with the sight of the myriad diamond like stars
Glittering in the heavens above on a black night —
All more frequent than the sand on all the beaches in the world.
All these mostly lost on frivolous frantic youth.
Now in old age life can be more grand
With spirit and soul coming alive.
Now young in spirit but not in body
I pray you do not leave dances unswung and songs unsung
Or your golden dreams undone.

## End of the Trail

*Near the end of the trail*
*In the yawning years*
*When each sunrise and sunset*
*Appears more precious—*
*The Ultimate Race Director*
*Calls out our number.*
*Then with life collapsing—*
*Hopefully we recall*
*When we did fail or fall:*
*How we rose up again—*
*Hardened for the fray—*
*Unvanquished;*
*How we played the Game,*
*Slaying the beasts of Fear and Pain—*
*Giving all,*
*Befriending Confidence, Courage and Spirit,*
*And making the world a better place*
*In passing by.*

# APPENDIX

## MONTREAL MASTER ATHLETE STUDY

At age 83 in 2012 I was a participant in a McGill Montreal Masters Study of track and field athletes, age 75 and older and most with world records—compared to non-athletes of the same age The study results on my body are listed below followed by the **non-athlete group average of similar age in brackets.** (I have not listed some units which require a lot of explanation—and in any case the relative comparison of my results with the sedentary are of most interest. If you are also an athlete the comparison will indicate the advantages in your own body due to an active lifestyle.

### Body Composition

Body Mass Index. I am in the middle of the average weight group: 22.1 (26.2 lower end of overweight group)

Fat Mass Index (%). When I was 60 I was measured twice at 5% and 7%: now 14.6 %, (32.3%)

### Cardio Function

Average Daily Minutes of moderate to vigorous activity: 36, (6.3)

Peak Exercise Heart Rate during VO2max cycle test (beats per minute): 165, (126)

Peak Work Rate (watts)during VO2 max cycle test: 180, (91)

Forced Vital Capacity (litres), max. amount of air expelled from lungs after a max. inhalation: 5.7, (3.4)

Peak Rate of Oxygen Utilization (litres per min. : 2.52, (1.6)

Peak VO2max (ml/kg/min) my results higher than two Olympic cyclists 3 years younger: 36.8, (20.80)

Resting Heart Rate beats per min. This is not from the study but I know my own value :43, (68)

## Muscle Strength and Size

Leg Extension (quadriceps, kick out strength while sitting: 178.9, (144.4)

Motor Unit Number, measures neuromuscular activity: 78, (55.7)

Mean thigh cross sectional area, includes muscles of quadriceps and hamstrings (cm2): 63.0, (45.2)

## Functional Tasks

Mean Balance, standing on one foot and keeping balance (sec.): 60, (8.2)

Chair Stand Test, (sec.) time to stand and sit from a chair as fast as you can 10 times : 11.9, (28.6)

Normal Walking Gait Speed (m/sec):1,7. (1.2),

## Muscle Biopsy

Muscle Biopsy ( MRI results indicate very favourable quality of my muscles with minimum of fat in my case. Results below indicate I have more slow twitch than fast twitch fibers.

Average Fiber Size, (micro m), large fibers contributes to increase in muscle strength with age: 5614, (3595)

Slow twitch fibers ( %) for endurance events: 61.5, (41.4)

Fast Twitch fibers (%) for sprints/power events: 38.5, (41.5) Note: there seems to be a problem the non athlete numbers since total % should be 100%.

Mitochondrial Volume, energy production/gram of muscle (declines with age): 9.7, (4.8)

## Bone Density

Bone Mass Density, (BMD). Some parts of the skeleton decrease with age from age 20 and some decrease from age 50. My BMD is at the upper limit expected of an 83 year old or equivalent to the average 20 year old.

## Aging

In many cases the benefits of a heathy lifestyle diminish each year with age, e.g., bone density, cardio functions, muscle strength, balance, flexibility, stride length etc. so it pays to keep active to reduce the decline.

# RECOGNITIONS

Lincoln said: to be recognized by your fellow man is the greatest recognition. I for one admit that this is a definite boost to inspire further effort. Recognition can be a boost to the ego but it is important to realize there is no greatness without humility. I mention some of these morale boosting actions bestowed on me. Who would not appreciate these?

Hall of fame awards: Ontario Masters— Canadian Masters Athletic Assoc.— Mississauga Sports Council —and World Masters Athletics (WMA).

Earl Fee running photo on cover of Masters Age Records,, 2006 Edition (After 2006 there was no specific age world records kept so I had to stop sending in my results to Pete Mundle,).

Earl Fee honoured to carry the Canadian flag at the World Masters championships in Miyazaki. Japan, the best and largest (12, 000 competitors) masters championships ever.

Male World Masters Athletics master of the year 2005.

A bench in a local parkette in 2014 honouring me, from my Sir Johns Homestead, Mississauga neighbours. (Refurbished like new in 2018).

Being announced in the USA as the "Great Earl for many years.

Five large International Achievement Awards certificates, 1986 (the year I started back to running after a 33 year layoff), 1987, 1988, 1989,1990, and 1991 from the Province of Ontario "for distinguished performance in the field of amateur sport." These large certificates were presented at an annual lavish banquet, but discontinued after 1991.

**56 world records broken, since age 57 in 1986.** It took a lot of races and travel. The over 700 medals, trophies and plaques in my home, providing further inspiration, are a testament to the time and effort..

At age 88, in 2017, overall, I had 14 WMA age group world records currently (previously I had over 20 WMA records at one time), 12 WMA age group records were lost to others, and I have 30 specific age records listed in the last edition 2006 of Masters Age Records—a total of 56 world records including relay records in 4X400m and 4X880m at age 80-89. And no double counting, i.e., only counting the best time not those leading up to the best. My list of world records is based on indoor and outdoor events: long hurdles, 400m, 800m,1500m and mile events. It is notable that 10 of my world records were in different age groups in the 800m in 2015—no one has more 800m WMA age group records. Since then two of my 800m outdoor world records were broken: In age group 75-79 a 2:30.59 by Jose Rioseco (ESP) in 2016— and in age group 80-84 a 3:06.69 by David Carr (AUS) in 2017. Two superb records which I predict will long withstand the winds of time.

At age 90, my next age group I plan to increase my total to 60 world records broken, and am presently working towards that goal. It is a long way off but it is always best to have a long term goal.

# ABOUT THE AUTHOR

Earl Fee is a retired nuclear power consultant, author, poet, artist, champion runner, coach and motivational speaker. He graduated with a BASc and a MASc in mechanical engineering in 1953 and 1962 respectively. Earl has broken over 56 world records in master's running and hurdling in the past 32 years since age 57--indicating the correctness of his training methods and healthy lifestyle. In 2005 he was recognized by the World Masters Athletics as the Male Master Athlete of the World. For several decades he has been honoured in the USA and Canada with the name: "The Great Earl." He has had four books published: How to Be a Champion from 9 to 90, The Complete Guide to Running, 100 Years Young the Natural Way, and The Wonder Of It All (a poetry book). He is still going strong at age 89 in 2018--which adds to the credibility of his healthy anti-aging lifestyle.